CU00641007

Affluence, Mobility and Second Home Ownership

Despite the current recession, the frequency of second home ownership is still surprisingly high throughout the western world. While the UK and Ireland previously had lower occurrences of multiple dwellings compared to the rest of Europe, they are quickly catching up with a current surge in the ownership of second homes. The recent MP expenses scandal in the UK has also drawn attention to the prevalence of second homes (or more) within the middle classes, and the fact that the concept is becoming increasingly popular.

Chris Paris uses this text to address the reasons behind why second homes are becoming more popular, both within the usual domicile of the individuals, and in international locations. The socio-economic factors and historical contexts of homes in cultures across the world are fundamental to explaining the choices in transnational home ownership, and Paris' case studies and comparisons between additional homes in Europe, Australia, America and Asia expand upon the motivation for people to own a second home.

Affluence, Mobility and Second Home Ownership draws together debates on gentrification, globalisation, consumerism, environmental factors and investment to provide a balanced look at the pros, and cons, of second home ownership, and what implications it has for the future. An ideal text for students studying geography, urbanism and planning, this book is also of interest to individuals interested in the changing ways in which we make choices on our places of residence.

Chris Paris was Professor of Housing Studies at the University of Ulster until 2008. He has worked in universities and research institutes in the UK, Australia and Ireland, including the Australian National University and the Centre for Environmental Studies. He has wide international experience of scholarly and applied research and is author/co-author/editor of over 30 books, monographs and research reports on housing, planning and urban policy and over 100 journal publications.

Housing and society series

Edited by Ray Forrest
School for Policy Studies, University of Bristol

This series aims to situate housing within its wider social, political and economic context at both national and international level. In doing so it will draw on the full range of social science disciplines and on mainstream debate on the nature of contemporary social change. The books are intended to appeal to an international academic audience as well as to practitioners and policymakers – to be theoretically informed and policy relevant.

Affluence, Mobility and Second Home Ownership
Chris Paris

Housing, Markets and Policy
Peter Malpass and Rob Rowlands

Housing and Health in Europe
Edited by David Ormandy

The Hidden Millions
Graham Tipple and Suzanne Speak

Housing, Care and Inheritance
Misa Izuhara

Housing and Social Transition in Japan
Edited by Yosuke Hirayama and Richard Ronald

Housing Transformations
Shaping the space of 21st century living
Bridget Franklin

Housing and Social Policy
Contemporary themes and critical perspectives
Edited by Peter Somerville with Nigel Sprigings

Housing and Social Change
East–West perspectives
Edited by Ray Forrest and James Lee

Urban Poverty, Housing and Social Change in China
Ya Ping Wang

Gentrification in a Global Context
Edited by Rowland Atkinson and Gary Bridge

Affluence, Mobility and Second Home Ownership

Chris Paris

Routledge
Taylor & Francis Group

LONDON AND NEW YORK

First published 2011
by Routledge
2 Park Square, Milton Park, Abingdon, Oxon OX14 4RN

Simultaneously published in the USA and Canada
by Routledge
270 Madison Avenue, New York, NY 10016, USA

Routledge is an imprint of the Taylor & Francis Group, an informa business

Typeset in Times and Frutiger by
HWA Text and Data Management, London
Printed and bound in Great Britain by
TJ International Ltd, Padstow, Cornwall

British Library Cataloguing in Publication Data
A catalogue record for this book is available from the British Library

Library of Congress Cataloging-in-Publication Data
Affluence, mobility, and second home ownership / Chris Paris.
    p. cm. – (Housing and society series)
  Includes bibliographical references and index.
  1. Second homes – Social aspects. 2. Wealth. 3. Residential mobility. I. Title.
  HD7289.2.P37 2010
  333.33'8–dc22   2010004586

ISBN: 978-0-415-54891-5 (hbk)
ISBN: 978-0-415-54892-2 (pbk)
ISBN: 978-0-203-84650-6 (ebk)

Contents

Tables

Figures

Foreword

The Housing Executive, Northern Ireland's regional strategic housing authority, attaches great importance to research as a means to provide an evidence base for its strategic intervention in the housing market. The wide-ranging research programme combines in-house research, such as the regular House Condition Surveys, with a suite of research commissioned from universities and other external specialists. Professor Chris Paris has undertaken a range of very relevant and extremely useful research studies for the Housing Executive over a period of nearly 20 years, including most recently his work on *Second Homes in Northern Ireland: growth, impact and policy implications*. This case study of planning and housing issues surrounding the development of second homes in a number of rural areas in Northern Ireland has provided an invaluable evidence base for both government departments and the Housing Executive to develop more sensitive policies that benefit the whole community.

We are delighted that his applied study, undertaken in partnership with our Research Unit, has contributed to the production of this book about second home ownership in many countries. It is a wide-ranging work of international significance and is based on extensive scholarship and detailed knowledge of the topic in many countries, especially the UK, Ireland and Australia. We are pleased to support its publication in the certainty that it will be of great interest to anybody concerned about housing and planning issues in general and especially about the role of second homes in household investment and consumption decisions.

Paddy McIntyre
Chief Executive
Northern Ireland Housing Executive

Brian Rowntree
Chairman
Northern Irerland Housing Executive

Preface

Winter days are short in north-west Ireland. The sun barely gets above the horizon on those rare occasions when it manages to break through the clouds. Thanks to the warming currents of the Gulf Stream, however, such winter days are much milder than similar latitudes in eastern England or further east in Moscow. Visiting the coast of County Donegal in January 1993, I was struck by the harsh beauty of the jagged coastline with endless sandy bays and rocky headlands, set against the ancient Derryveigh Mountains. It was a ghostly landscape with few people but many ruined houses marking a former pattern of denser settlement. Most local hotels and pubs were shut, not to reopen until St Patrick's Day when visitors traditionally returned.

I had moved to Northern Ireland in September 1992 from the Australian capital Canberra. Sited in high mountainous country inland from the coast, Canberra winters are cold, especially at night, so it was pleasant to spend the odd weekend on the southern New South Wales coast, staying in a local motel or rental holiday home.

I looked towards Bloody Foreland, the last tip of the land before the Atlantic stretched to eternity and remarked to my companion, 'If this was southern New South Wales it would be wall-to-wall holiday homes. There's only a few here; it must be because of the miserable weather.' I was wrong about one thing: the relative absence of holiday homes was *not* due to the weather. Winter days are still short, mainly dark, and often wet, and there are few visitors, but much of this coastline *is* now wall-to-wall with holiday homes, though much of north Donegal still closes down during the winter, including the second homes!

These recollections take me back to a waypoint in my journey towards this book. I have studied housing one way or another for 40 years. My childhood interest in town planning led to degrees in geography and planning and research in Birmingham and London, mainly focusing on sociological and political aspects of housing and urban policy (Lambert *et al.*, 1978; Paris and Blackaby, 1979). I developed a more comparative perspective in Australia, at Flinders University in 1979 and later at the Australian National University and the University of Canberra (Paris, 1993). My move to the University of Ulster came with a brief to focus on housing in Northern Ireland, albeit within wider UK, Irish and European contexts (Paris, 2001).

0.1 'Wall-to-wall' second homes: Downings, Co. Donegal, 2005 (source: Gardiner Mitchell)

You cannot work in Northern Ireland as a social scientist without taking into account the unique local history and geography of social and political division. The region suffered before and during the Troubles, but the atmosphere changed during the 1990s. After a faltering start, the paramilitary ceasefires took hold and violence subsided. The border with the Republic, the most fortified in Western Europe after the fall of the Berlin Wall (O'Dowd *et al.*, 1995), was transformed almost overnight as armed checkpoints were removed and freedom of movement re-established between the two jurisdictions.

Northern Ireland was prospering, though not as dramatically as the booming 'Celtic Tiger' economy in the Republic, and border areas were changing rapidly. Economic growth generated housing booms in both jurisdictions (Paris, 2005a, 2005b, 2006) as more and bigger houses were symptomatic of growing affluence. House building output increased year upon year and house prices surged ahead of inflation. Together with Terry Robson, I explored the changing housing scene in the border counties, noting the remarkable growth of second homes, especially in Donegal in the Republic, and Fermanagh in Northern Ireland (Paris and Robson, 2001).

The Regional Development Strategy in Northern Ireland attracted much public comment and second homes development emerged strongly as a contentious issue especially on the Causeway Coast. Wider reading, however, highlighted similarities between local concerns about second homes and issues that had been debated in many other countries. The literature also revealed many differences between Britain, Northern Ireland and the Republic; even more variations became apparent when comparing diverse countries and cultures, so I wanted to avoid a narrowly British or Irish perspective on second homes to get a better understanding of how they related to different societies and cultures.

0.2 At the peak of the boom: estate agency sign, Creeslough, Co. Donegal, 2005 (source: Gardiner Mitchell)

My growing interest in second home ownership was taken further through work with the Northern Ireland Housing Executive (NIHE) on the impact of second homes on local housing markets and communities (Paris, 2007a, 2008b). The research included a literature review, case studies of second home 'hot spots', surveys of second home owners and other residents, plus analysis of other available data. During the same time, colleagues at University College Dublin conducted a similar study in the Republic (Norris and Winston, 2009) so we worked together to develop a comparative perspective on second homes across the island of Ireland (Norris *et al.*, 2008). I have also conducted collaborative research on second homes in Australia with colleagues at La Trobe University and the Department of Planning and Community Development in Victoria (McKenzie *et al.*, 2008; Paris *et al.*, 2009). Other elements of research have included monitoring newspaper reports on housing with a focus since 2001 on second homes, and searching widely on the internet. I have discussed and corresponded with dozens of individuals and organisations relating to second homes and other forms of leisure and retirement-related housing provision.

The property pages of newspapers increasingly carried advertisements and reports on overseas second homes. The trend towards increased overseas second home ownership was confirmed by the Survey of English Housing (SEH). My interest in comparative aspects of second home ownership developed further through collaboration with colleagues in many countries especially a workshop at the European Network for Housing Research (ENHR) conference at Ljubljana in 2006. My scholarly fascination with second homes also has justified field work in many interesting locations including southern France, Barcelona, Malaga, coastal resort areas in Asia and Australia and the Central Highlands of Tasmania.

Acknowledgements

I am grateful to Ray Forrest for encouraging me to submit this book to Routledge, and to the anonymous reviewers for their suggestions. I am especially grateful to Alex Hollingsworth, Catherine Lynn and Louise Fox at Routledge for helping me complete this project. I owe thanks to many organisations, especially: the NIHE for supporting much of my recent research; the University of Ulster for an academic base and research assistance; RMIT University, La Trobe University, Flinders University and the Australian National University for supporting my work on Australian second homes; the University of Hong Kong for a base to study second homes in Asia. I am grateful to many public officials, housing market specialists, politicians and community activists who agreed to be interviewed about this and related topics and to hundreds of people in Northern Ireland and Australia who responded to surveys.

I thank the many copyright holders of images and other material reproduced in this book for granting permission for use, especially: Gardiner Mitchell and Clive Forster for their original photographic images and other valued help and support; Sam Rule, of the Commission for Rural Communities, for the map of second homes in England. Some copyright clearance has been granted through 'commons' but in other cases copyright holders have given written agreement, including Coastal Partnership Ltd, the NIHE, Natural England, Savills, Solo Syndications, Muir Vidler, *Private Eye*, Worldmapper, and contributors of photographic images to Google Maps, Google Earth, Panoramio and other web sources. Crown Copyright material is reproduced under the terms of the Click-use Licence by permission of the Office of Public Sector Information (OPSI).

Many other individuals have helped me think about this topic, including Kathy Arthurson, Roland Atkinson, Roger Baker, Michael Barke, Bill Beck, Andrew Beer, Mike Berry, Ian Binnie, Terry Burke, Stephen Boyd, Patrice Carmichael, Rob Carter, Rebecca Chiu, Terry Clower, Tony Dalton, Joyce Farr, Terry Farr, Joe Flood, Kosta and Rosalie Flourentzou, Jean Forbes, Joe Frey, Brian and Ros Galligan, Pearl and Roy Graham, Alastair Greig, Yvonne Hamilton, Riaz Hassan, Frank Hicks, Peter

Acknowledgements

Hills, Keith Jacobs, Brad Jorgensen, Jack Laidlaw, Elma Lynn, Fiona McKenzie, John Martin, Alaric Maude, Andy Meenagh, Michelle Norris, John Palmer, Mary Rainey, Jeremy Reynolds, Chris Richards, Terry Robson, Susan Smith, Pat Troy, John Warhurst, Steve Wilcox, Peter Williams, Nessa Winston and Ian Winter.

I am most grateful of all to Maeve Paris for putting up with my bizarre work patterns, frequent absences and occasional grumpiness.

As ever, I remain responsible for views, arguments and evidence presented here.

Abbreviations

ABC	Australian Broadcasting Corporation
ABS	Australian Bureau of Statistics
AHURI	Australian Housing and Urban Research Institute
AONB	Areas of Outstanding Natural Beauty
AR	additional residence (in AuSSA survey)
ARHC	Affordable Rural Housing Commission
AuSSA	Australian Survey of Social Attitudes
BTL	buy-to-let (investors *or* types of mortgages)
CGT	capital gains tax
CLNC	Coleraine/Limavady/North Coast
CPRE	Campaign to Protect Rural England
DCLG	Department of Communities and Local Government (Britain)
ENHR	European Network for Housing Research
EU	European Union
GDP	gross domestic product
HMRC	Her Majesty's Revenue and Customs (UK tax authority)
HVS	Helford Village Society
ICT	information and communications technology
LAT	living apart together (relationships)
LGA	Local Government Area
LME	Lower Mill Estate
MMSH	Malaysia My Second Home (Malaysian government programme)
NAMA	National Asset Management Agency
NIHE	Northern Ireland Housing Executive
NISRA	Northern Ireland Statistics and Research Agency
NSW	New South Wales
ODPM	Office of the Deputy Prime Minister (became DCLG in May 2006)
OECD	Organisation of Economic Co-operation and Development
ONS	Office of National Statistics

List of abbreviations

OPSI	Office of Public Sector Information
PIIGS	Portugal, Italy, Ireland, Greece and Spain
PIPWE	Department of Primary Industries, Parks, Water and Environment (Tasmania)
RICS	Royal Institute of Chartered Surveyors
RRS	rural renewal scheme
RV	recreational vehicle
SEH	Survey of English Housing
SRS	seaside resorts scheme
SUV	sports utility vehicle

1 Introduction
Affluence, mobility and second homes

What greater source of injustice could there be, that while some people have no home, others have two? Yet the vampire trade in second homes keeps growing … uninhibited by government or by the conscience of the buyers… The real problem is that almost every MP with a constituency outside London has two homes or more, and there is scarcely a senior journalist who is not sucking the life out of a village somewhere, or a paper which does not depend on advertising by estate agents. Two weeks ago the *Sunday Times* revealed that the Labour MP Barbara Follett, who owns a £2m house in her constituency (in Stevenage), a flat in Soho and homes in Antigua and Cape Town, has claimed £76,357 in Commons expenses over the past four years for her London pad. Perhaps it isn't hard to see why MPs aren't clamouring for something to be done.

(Monbiot, 2006)

Introduction

Second homes were headline news in the UK during 2009 when the *Daily Telegraph* ran a series of exposés about MPs' expenses, especially how the 'second homes allowance' was used to maximise expenses payments and avoid paying capital gains tax (CGT). Second homes allowances had been introduced to enable MPs who live outside London to afford a base in the capital. Such allowances are common in many countries, though in some cases elected representatives are allocated accommodation on a rent-free basis. In 2009 in the UK, however, it became clear that many MPs maximised allowances payments despite already owning second homes in London. The public was shocked to learn about 'flipping', whereby MPs changed the status of their residences between 'principal residence' and 'second' homes to boost their expenses payments.

The Chancellor of the Exchequer, Alistair Darling, was described as a 'serial flipper' who switched his 'designated second home three times in four years'

(Webster, 2009). Many MPs justified these practices on the grounds that they were 'within the rules'. In some cases there was evidence of deceit although most culprits claimed to have 'made a mistake'. Some MPs and even Cabinet Ministers were brought down by these exposures and subsequent public and party opprobrium. Among other factors, the issue of MPs' allowances for second homes resulted in calls for reform of the system of parliamentary expenses and allowances.

A junior Treasury Minister resigned from the government after revelations that she had 'temporarily changed the designation of her main home for tax purposes' thus avoiding paying capital gains tax by 'flipping' the status of her 'principal residence' and 'second home':

> Telegraph.co.uk can disclose that Miss Ussher told the tax authorities that her Burnley home was her 'principal residence' for a single month in 2007, enabling her to avoid capital gains tax. According to a letter from her accountants, Miss Ussher had previously told HM Revenue & Customs that a house in south London was her principal residence.
>
> (Winnett & Beckford, 2009)

Members of the House of Lords were also criticised. It was alleged that Labour peer Baroness Uddin claimed a second homes allowance by registering as her main home an unoccupied two bedroom apartment in Maidstone (40 miles from the House of Lords) despite living in social housing in Wapping, just four miles from Westminster (Savage, 2009).

Second home ownership had figured prominently in media reports for many years before the spring of 2009 with widespread evidence of social and economic conflicts, mainly regarding its impacts on communities and places. It was argued that the purchase of second homes in attractive coastal and countryside areas had priced lower income residents out of many areas in England. One particularly trenchant social commentator, George Monbiot, claimed (2006) that the owners of second homes 'are among the most selfish people in Britain'. Such concerns were explored in two reports in 2006 by the Affordable Rural Housing Commission (ARHC) and a House of Commons Committee (House of Commons ODPM Housing, Planning, Local Government and the Regions Committee, 2006). Both concluded that the growth of second home ownership contributed to growing problems of housing affordability facing low income households in high amenity areas.

The growth and impacts of second homes have been noticeable in the UK and Ireland since the early 1990s. Both countries previously had much lower levels of second home ownership than most other western European countries (Hall and Müller, 2004a; Gallent *et al.*, 2005). The rapid growth in second home ownership and wider public debates provide the first reason for this book. Why did second home ownership grow so much in these countries and how different were their experiences from those of other countries? Recent research on second homes in

Ireland highlights differences between Northern Ireland, Great Britain and the Republic of Ireland. The international literature also highlights the distinctive nature of second homes development in Britain, especially how the restrictive land-use planning regime has resulted in widespread gentrification in high amenity areas (Gallent *et al.*, 2005).

A core argument of this book is that the diversity of second home experiences between places and at different times requires a comparative sociological and historical perspective: there is no single set of reasons why people have second homes and the concerns that are raised vary enormously between cultures and over time. Comparisons and contrasts are explored in Chapter 3 through a review of different histories and types of second homes, with examples from the UK, Ireland and Australia. My perspective is 'the social relations of housing provision' (Paris, 1993), which combines insights from a range of academic disciplines: economists' concerns for market relations and housing production; a historical perspective on change over time; a socio-legal dimension; and a housing systems approach that examines actors and relationships between households and institutions. My approach combines awareness of structural features within which individuals and households make choices, but also conceptualises individuals as knowing agents. This approach owes much to social theorists, particularly Giddens (1987, 1991, 1998) who has explored changing relations between individuals and societies, especially the tensions between globalisation of production and socio-economic relations and changing individual perceptions of their places in a changing world. There is no significant conceptual difference between my perspective and what Clapham (2005) called a 'pathways approach' to housing.

Housing scholars, with some notable exceptions (Perkins and Thorns, 2006), have paid very little attention to the topic of second homes, though there is extensive scholarly coverage in other academic areas. The second core argument here is that the study of second homes should be located more firmly within *housing* studies. Most of the literature on second homes derives from geography, sociology and planning, or cross-disciplinary research and scholarly areas including leisure and tourism studies and rural studies. This literature examining second homes rarely overlaps with the housing studies literature, for example on the home, housing provision or housing policy.

Many housing scholars have argued that 'the home' has special significance, regardless of its tenure (for example, Somerville, 1997) and that home ownership provides a special form of ontological security and basis for family life (Saunders, 1990). Such arguments typically assume that households have a single 'home', but an increasing proportion of households own more than one home for their own use; so what are the implications of this for the meaning of the home? This is explored further in Chapter 2, which provides an overview of the international literature on second homes and examines the ownership of more than one home within household investment and consumption strategies. Chapter 2 also examines a range of theoretical issues relating to the growth of second homes, including debates about gentrification and the post-productivist countryside.

The media contains extensive advertising in the property pages of newspapers and many websites aimed at prospective purchasers of second homes. Much of the commentary and many advertisements reflect the growth in second home ownership overseas by British and Irish households, from small mobile homes to huge luxurious properties. The in-flight magazines of budget airlines regularly contain features on the benefits of overseas second home ownership and many advertisements from estate agents, removal companies and specialists in financial services. The property pages of daily and Sunday newspapers also report growing ownership of mansions in London and south-east England by non-UK residents, with diverse implications for housing markets in that region and across the UK.

The third core argument of this book is that the growth of second home ownership was driven by growing affluence and mobility during the decade-long economic boom in Britain and Ireland from the mid-1990s. Although prominent second homes scholars have suggested that there had been little change in the level of second home ownership after 1995 (Gallent *et al.*, 2005), the Survey of English Housing (SEH) shows that there was significant growth, by English households at least, between 1995 and 2005. Table 1.1, based on data from the Department of Communities and Local Government (DCLG), shows continuous growth between 1996/97 and 2006/07 in the number of English households with second homes (DCLG, 2008): from around 338,000 second homes in 1996/97 to 525,000 in 2006/07.[1] Table 1.1 also shows that much growth of English second home ownership after 2001/02 was outside Britain, fuelled by a long period during which the pound had strong purchasing power against the euro. Spain and France were the main European destinations, accounting for 33 and 24 per cent respectively overseas; about 4 per cent of second homes were in the USA and another 18 per cent of second homes were in non-European countries. The main reasons given by SEH respondents for having second homes were 'long-term investment' (47 per cent) and 'holiday home' (31 per cent).[2]

Table 1.1 English households with a second home

	Households with a second home			
	Location of second homes (%)			Total[1]
Year	England	Other GB	Outside GB	(000)
1996/97	59	7	34	338
2001/02	56	8	35	403
2006/07	46	7	47	525

Source: DCLG Live Tables, S366.
1. Three-year moving averages are used because annual survey figures fluctuate considerably

Recent research in Northern Ireland and the Republic of Ireland has highlighted rapid growth in second home ownership, associated with strong economic growth and growing affluence, especially in the Republic of Ireland (Norris and Winston, 2009; Paris, 2008b). Savills (2007) estimated that second homes account for between one and two per cent of the English housing stock and that, combined with overseas second home ownership, around 765,000 second homes were owned by UK residents in 2006 with a net total value around £125 billion.

Surging growth in affluence has been checked since 2007 in the UK and Ireland as well as many other countries, during the most widespread recession since the 1930s. But this does not alter the fact that second home ownership grew strongly in the UK and Ireland between the early 1990s and 2006 and that the substantial increase in second home ownership was due largely to increasing wealth and assets, especially domestic residential property. However, it remains necessary to ask whether we are a tipping point in terms of the future expansion, or possible contraction, of second home ownership. The recession of 2007–2009 has had major impacts on financial markets especially relating to residential property ownership and investment. These developments may have consequences for second home ownership across society as a whole, and not just with respect to MPs' second homes allowance.

Affluence

Most commentators on income and wealth focus more on inequalities than overall growth in assets and incomes. Irvin (2008) provided a trenchant critique of growing inequality in Britain and the USA and argued that differentials have increased considerably since the deregulatory surges of Thatcher and Reagan. He showed that by 2000 the UK was the most unequal in the European Union (EU) among states with comparable incomes, with continuing inequality by 2007 despite 10 years of Labour governments. In terms of inequalities, the UK resembled the USA much more than other EU countries, and Irvin argued (2008: 91) that 'growing inequality is above all a *political* phenomenon, attributable to the policies followed by specific right-wing government, rather than an inevitable attribute of globalization' (emphasis added).

There are many dimensions to affluence and inequality, including the gap between the merely affluent and the super-rich. In the UK and the USA, '[t]he gap between the "rich" and the "super-rich" has become as great as that between rich and poor' (Irvin, 2008: 91) and 'inequality among the superrich is the same as the inequality among the simply rich' (Taleb, 2008: 234). Many super-rich UK residents, or part-time residents, are foreign nationals, as 'Britain's relatively lax tax residency law, coupled with the absence of direct taxation of land or financial assets and low rates of tax on income, helped make the country a leading tax haven' (Irvin, 2008: 11) thus 54 billionaires in Britain, with total assets of £126 billion, between them paid just £14 million tax a year.

A recent study by Dorling *et al.* (2007) examined the changing geography of poverty and wealth in Britain. The main focus was on inequalities and growing social and spatial polarisation, with asset-based wealth growing most in London and south-east England and falling in relative terms in northern England and Scotland. The growth of dual high earning income households during a period of very low real interest rates contributed significantly to growing inequalities. Dorling *et al.* (2007: 84) concluded that 'wealthier households have become wealthier still' and that 'as breadline poverty has increased, so too has the share of wealth held by the wealthiest, but the proportion of households that are asset wealthy has actually fallen'. This echoed Irvin's conclusion that the middle classes had fallen behind the rich in relative terms since the early 1990s.

But there can be growing inequality during a period of buoyant overall growth in real incomes and assets. Such inequality, moreover, can be a driver of increased second home ownership because better-off households are more easily able to out-bid other possible purchasers of dwellings that they wish to use as holiday homes. Thus we need to focus on changes in overall income and wealth as well as just measuring inequality. The annual official publication *Social Trends* provides one of the best sources of data on wealth and income as well as distinguishing between them:

> Although the terms 'wealthy' and 'high income' are often used interchangeably, in fact they relate to quite distinct concepts. 'Income' represents a flow of resources over a period, received either in cash or in kind. 'Wealth' on the other hand describes the ownership of assets valued at a particular point in time.
>
> (ONS, 2002)

Assets may or may not generate income and some can only generate income when they are sold. Some assets cannot be sold at all; *Social Trends 31* (ONS, 2002) gave the example of an individual's stake in an occupational pension fund, which does not allow the possibility of 'cashing it in'. A house that is owned by one person and let to another generates an income stream, but the asset value of the house can only be realised when it is sold. Hence we distinguish between 'marketable wealth' that can be sold and 'non-marketable wealth'. *Social Trends 31* (p. 94) remarked on strong growth in net household assets in the UK since the early 1970s: 'household disposable income per head, adjusted for inflation, *doubled* between 1971 and 1999' (emphasis added). More recently, *Social Trends 38* (ONS, 2008) showed that 'household net wealth in the UK more than doubled in real terms between 1987 and 2006'. Compared to other G7[3] economies, moreover, gross domestic product (GDP) per head in the UK rose from last place in 1991 to third place in 2005 (with the USA remaining firmly in top spot). GDP continued to grow to mid-2007 in the UK, but subsequently fell sharply (see http://www.statistics.gov.uk/cci/nugget.asp?id=192).

Housing wealth and affluence

Increasing house values constituted a major factor in asset growth. The 2008 *Housing Finance Review* recorded spectacular growth in gross assets since the mid-1990s (Wilcox, 2008: 80). Table 1.2, based on Wilcox's data, shows gross assets more than doubling between 2000 and 2007. Wilcox (personal correspondence, 2009) argued that this asset growth provided a large equity cushion for anyone who had bought before 2000 though there was a risk of increased negative equity[4] for post-2004 purchasers. Table 1.2 also shows that there had not been a large increase in the ratio of loans to assets between 1990 and 2007, when borrowing had been at historically low interest levels. Thus the asset growth was not simply due to greater borrowing: it was real, at least so long as house prices remained at 2007 levels. In practice, of course, house prices have fallen, but they would have to fall by over 50 per cent from 2007 levels to return to 2000 real values. That has not happened yet and is extremely unlikely to happen in the next few years; interest rates, moreover, fell to even lower levels.

There was even more spectacular growth in household wealth in the Republic of Ireland, where most affluent households were first-generational rich, rather than having inherited large assets like many of the UK's most affluent families. Leading Irish banks chronicled the extraordinary growth in incomes and assets resulting from the economic boom between the early 1990s and 2007:

> Household wealth has doubled in a little over five years, and by the start of 2008 aggregate household wealth in Ireland will surpass €1 trillion for the first time.
> (O'Toole and Callan, 2008: 6)

> Last year was another year of very strong economic growth in Ireland with real GDP growing by 6%... We estimate that the net wealth ... of domestic households increased by 19% or €126 billion in 2006 to stand at €804 billion.

Table 1.2 Personal housing wealth, borrowing and net equity in the UK (£ billion)

	1970	1980	1990	2000	2007
Net equity	36.5	258.3	850.3	1,431.5	2,951.4
+ House loans	11.5	52.6	294.7	536.4	1,187.1
= Gross assets	48.0	310.9	1,145.0	1,967.9	4,138.5
Index of real growth in gross assets	62.8	100.0	217.8	356.7	651.1
Ratio of loans/gross assets (%)	24%	17%	26%	27%	29%

Source: Wilcox, 2008, Table 6, p. 80.

> Irish household wealth per capita increased from €168,000 to €196,000 at the end of last year. Based on the 2005 number, Ireland still ranks second in terms of wealth in a survey of eight leading OECD countries.
>
> (O'Sullivan, 2007: 2)

As in the UK, much Irish wealth took the form of residential property, though there was a higher level of debt per capita in Ireland, partly because so much of this wealth was first-generational. O'Toole and Callan (2008: 10) argued that the emergence of wealth in Ireland 'is *not* an illusion of the property market, but is reflected in our now substantial holdings of financial assets' (emphasis added). O'Sullivan (2007: 1) was bullish about prospects, predicting 'strong growth in wealth over the remainder of this decade. O'Toole and Callan (2008: 3) saw Ireland 'entering a new period of economic development'. Recent events have shown O'Sullivan's prediction to have been wildly optimistic as growth has halted and house prices have been sliding downwards since early 2007, thus reducing net wealth. The 'new period of economic development', however, was not as envisaged by O'Toole and Callan, rather it comprised contraction, recession and serious fiscal problems for the Irish state. Again, though, the enormous growth in household assets from 1995 to 2006 had left a substantial legacy of real wealth in property.

Despite significant falls in house prices, Irish households who purchased before 2004 are unlikely to suffer significant negative consequences from falling prices, though more recent purchasers have faced problems of asset depreciation and negative equity. *The Independent* reported in May 2009 that over 12,000 Bank of Ireland mortgage borrowers were in negative equity having lost on average almost €30,000; the bank's previous 'worst case scenario' of writing off up to €6 billion in bad loans over three years had become its main forecast (http://www.independent. ie/national-news/over-12000-boi-customers-in-negative-equity-1744560.html). Whilst this is bad news for the households concerned, it also this means that more affluent households may have to pay less to acquire investment properties or even 'trophy' second homes. The bigger issue for second homes in Ireland, during 2009, concerned the large number of unsold recently built dwellings aimed at the second homes market.

Many affluent countries experienced similar surges in wealth after the mid-1990s, and growing inequality. In some cases, this was a roller-coaster ride from rapid growth in wealth to sharp declines. *The Age* newspaper in Melbourne reported research showing that household wealth in Australia increased by more than 50 per cent between 2002 and 2006 with the average net worth of households increasing by Aus$207,000 in four years to Aus$608,000 (Cooke and Schneiders, 2008). A few months later, however, the same newspaper reported a change of fortune, literally, citing an Australian Bureau of Statistics (ABS) 'conservative' estimate that Australian households 'lost a quarter of their wealth since the global financial crisis began late last year' (Martin, 2008). Unlike the UK and Ireland, however, the... ... been a large a fall in Australian house prices. In all these countries, moreover, overall house price growth between 1997 and 2008 was sufficiently robust to leave most homeowners with considerable real asset growth.

The importance of outright home ownership

The level of outright home ownership varies between countries, but may be a crucial indicator of the capacity of households to acquire a second or subsequent home. Households owning their homes outright have more disposable income and borrowing capacity, other things being equal, than households repaying a housing loan or mortgage. Growth in the numbers and proportions of outright homeowners increases the pool of prospective second home buyers, especially if property is considered a relatively attractive investment. But growing outright home ownership has gone largely unnoticed by UK housing scholars who have focused much more on issues of affordability for first home buyers and homelessness.

Table 1.3 shows strong growth between 1991 and 2001 in the number of households in the UK that owned their homes outright. In England alone, the number of households owning their own homes increased by 1.5 million between 1991 and 2001: a *huge* growth in the number of potential second home purchasers. Growth in number of outright homeowners was strongest in Scotland, although the proportion remained below the UK average. One objection to this argument may be that most people who own their homes outright are elderly, thus unlikely to acquire additional homes. This is true but irrelevant because growth in outright ownership in the 1990s was highest among younger homeowners (Paris, 2008b). An apparent contradiction between growing problems for first time buyers, on the one hand, and surging second home ownership, on the other, is thus resolved in terms of growing differentials in terms of income and housing-related wealth.

By 2009, moreover, there was no evidence that growth in outright home ownership had slowed down significantly. *Housing Statistics 2008*[5] showed continuous growth in the number of households in England that owned their homes outright: from 5.9 million in 2001 to 6.5 million in 2007. This in turn indicates considerable scope for further growth in second home ownership.

Table 1.3 Households owning their homes outright, 1991–2001

	1991	2001	Intercensal change	
	(000)	(000)	(000)	(%)
England & Wales	4,849	6,381	1,532	32
Scotland	332	514	182	55
Northern Ireland	138	184	46	33

Source: Special census tables commissioned by the NIHE for Paris (2008b).

9

Introduction

As more and more households own their homes outright, there has also been enormous growth in the value of domestic residential property, including investment properties and second homes:

> Sustained price appreciation across almost a decade has turned housing into a major store of wealth, particularly in the 'home ownership' societies of the English speaking world... This has attracted attention because, of all personal wealth holdings, housing is the most salient driver of consumption ... especially in settings like the UK where mortgage markets are most complete.
>
> (Smith, 2007: 16)

Smith (2005: 9) argued that housing wealth 'is no longer a fixed asset' but 'is mobile in all kinds of ways'. She suggested that low interest rates and the low cost of secured loans combined to make borrowing against the primary residence an easy and highly cost-effective way of funding spending. The available funds, moreover, appear to be massive, with 'estimates of unmortgaged housing equity now standing at £2.2 trillion' (loc. cit.) and equity withdrawal may be routinely utilised in households' financial planning and investment; her research, however, showed few signs that households were using equity in their homes to purchase second homes (personal correspondence). She also emphasised the risks involved in maximising investment in the family home and noted high levels of house price volatility, especially in some countries (S. Smith, 2006). Her work, with others who assess the significance of personal wealth in housing, highlights the major role of investment in housing in many societies. Susan Smith (2006) argued that most households have few other investment options though other scholars have noted how financial institutions in the UK stimulated increased investment in private rental property through 'buy-to-let' (BTL) mortgages (Sprigings, 2008; Kemp, 2009). The number of BTL mortgages increased rapidly between 1999 and 2006, from 44,000 to 330,000, representing just 4 per cent of all mortgages in 1999 but 29 per cent in 2006 (Sprigings, 2008). This was a major driver of speculative house and land price inflation in a volatile deregulated housing finance sector.

But all booms come to an end. A review of global house prices in *The Economist* in March 2009 noted a sharp increase in the number of countries that experienced house price falls and suggested that the days of house price booms were over, raising the possibility that 'house prices may overshoot on the way down' (Unattributed, 2009). Table 1.4, based on data in *The Economist* report, shows that house price growth had been much stronger in the UK, Ireland and Australia than in the USA, in stunning contrast to massive real falls in Hong Kong and Japan over the 10-year period. This underlines the significant role of housing wealth in the UK, Ireland and Australia in terms of households' capacity to purchase second homes.

Table 1.4 House price indicators, March 2009

	Percentage change in house prices	
	Latest on one year earlier	1997–2008
Ireland	−9.8	193
UK[1]	−17.6	150
Australia	−3.3	163
USA	−18.2	66
Japan	−1.8	−33
Hong Kong	−14.0	−35

Source: Unattributed (2009) article in *The Economist*
1. The original stated 'Britain'.

Global wealth and inequalities

At a global scale, wealth and inequality increased strongly after 1990, with some of the highest levels of inequality in the three countries of most focus in this book: the UK, Ireland and Australia. Irvin (2008) showed that overall income inequality was lower in Europe than in the USA, with the Nordic countries being the most equal and the UK nearest to the USA. The least equal European countries were some of the (then) least-developed, Greece and Portugal. Irvin also considered inequality as measured by the ratio of the 90th to 10th percentiles of incomes. On this basis, the Nordic countries again were the most equal, the USA extremely unequal, closely followed by the UK, Australia and Ireland.

Davies *et al.* (2008) attempted to estimate and compare wealth at a global scale. They noted a general trend during the twentieth century towards reduced income inequality in richer countries, but that this reversed during the 1970s, with growing inequality in most of those countries especially the USA. Inequality has not increased since the 1970s at a global level, mainly due to relatively strong income growth, albeit from very low initial levels, in China and other emerging economies. Even so, Davies *et al.* (2008: 1) identified a 'very high disparity of living standards amongst the world's citizens' with massive inequalities between countries.

> About 34 per cent of the world's wealth was held in the USA and Canada in the year 2000, 30 per cent was held in Europe, and 24 per cent was in the rich Asia–Pacific group of countries. Africa, Central and South America, China, India, and other Asia–Pacific countries shared the remaining 12 per cent.
> (Davies *et al.*, 2008: 26–27)

There is a greater concentration of wealth at the very top of the affluence scale, with 39 per cent of the top global 1 per cent of wealth holders living in North

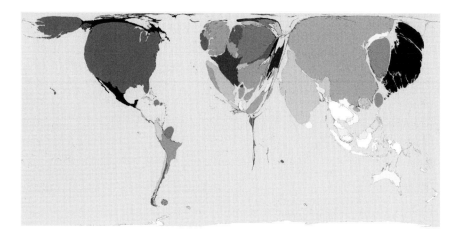

1.1 Wealth growth cartogram (Source: Worldmapper © Copyright 2009 SASI Group (University of Sheffield))

America, with just 6 per cent of the world's population (Davies *et al.*, 2008: 27). Such disparities are at the very core of the capacity of affluent citizens in richer countries to view the world as their playground for second home ownership. These differences are shown in brilliant graphic form by the Sheffield University Worldmapper team in their 'cartograms' – maps within which the size of countries are adjusted for differentials between countries. Figure 1.1 shows the relative shares of wealth growth in the world between 1975 and 2002 compared to the population of different countries, whereas their base map in Figure 1.2 shows the spatial distribution of the countries' populations. This graphic illustration combines the relatively strong performance of China and India with the absolute strengths of dominant national economies, especially the USA and major EU economies.

Worldmapper also shows house price variations across the globe. Figure 1.3 shows relative housing prices on the basis of what can be purchased for US$1, with European housing standing out as the most expensive per person. The commentary beside the cartogram on the Worldmapper website notes that housing is an important investment item in Europe and, despite much higher average housing prices, average household size is much lower than in countries with lower house prices (http://www.worldmapper.org/display.php?selected=194 accessed 10 March 2009). Growing affluence in already affluent countries during the last 30 years is partly a function of the spread of home ownership and house price increases, with the home being the main asset for most households in many countries. Indeed, it is precisely the growth in housing assets in affluent countries that has driven much of the growth of transnational second home ownership (Forrest, 2008) (see Chapter 4).

Investment in housing retains a prime role in households' investment strategies, especially in the UK and Ireland. Media and other commentators often suggest that

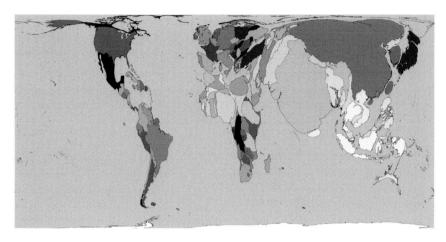

1.2 Population cartogram (source: Worldmapper © Copyright 2009 SASI Group (University of Sheffield))

there is a growing preference for investment in property (buy-to-let private rental housing, holiday homes to let and second homes) rather than pensions or the stock market (e.g. Francis, 2006b). Even more critical analysts, including Smith (2005) and Irvin (2008) identify property investment as a crucial element of households' financial planning especially in the UK and Ireland, including purchase of second homes.

> As privately funded occupational pensions become riskier and their benefits unpredictable, so the young are turning increasingly to the property market where asset appreciation has enabled so many ageing baby boomers to retire in comfort. The new generation's eagerness to get a foot on the ladder before it's too late is one of the factors driving what has until recently been the apparently limitless upward trend in house prices.
>
> (Irvin, 2008: 99–100)

Growing affluence was accompanied in the USA, the UK, Ireland and Australia by widening inequalities, but poverty remained relative and the base from which it is measured has continued to rise. Housing, moreover, remains a positional good and more affluent households have chosen to occupy ever-larger homes and to acquire more residential property, whether to use for private purposes, to let to tenants, or even to leave empty in anticipation of a future capital gain on resale. Will the period of rapid wealth growth and widening inequalities in the UK and Ireland between 1996 and 2006, due partly to low interest rates, be seen as a 'one-off' that cannot be sustained? Possibly so, but only if the 2007–2009 recession has led to a major shift in social and economic behaviour. In any case, there is no reason to suppose that further growth in affluence will have any different *relative* effects.

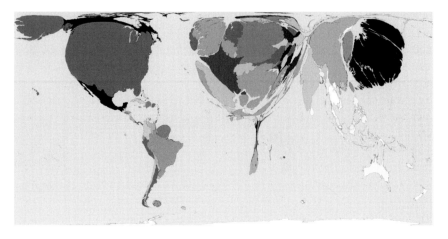

1.3 Housing prices cartogram (source: Worldmapper © Copyright 2009 SASI Group (University of Sheffield))

Mobility

In addition to being an era of growing affluence and home ownership, there were also dramatic transformations in mobility during the twentieth century. The word 'mobility' has many meanings, including changes in social status. The term 'social mobility' refers to people from lowly origins achieving higher status and/or wealth or others, starting from more privileged positions, descending the social ladder through misfortune, foolish behaviour or reckless habits. The term mobility is also used to refer to migration, as some people relocate, whether temporarily or permanently, over shorter or longer distances. The term is also used to refer to other types of movement, from blood circulation within the body through moving our bodies from one room to another, to the many mechanically enabled capacities to travel by car, boat or plane (Cresswell, 2006; Urry, 2007).

Cresswell (2006) showed that mobility as travel or relocation over large distances was a 'luxury item' in feudal Europe and even in the nineteenth century 'people regarded as "foreign" those from the next province every bit as much as those who came from other "countries"' (p. 13). But this has changed and mobility 'now seems central to Western modernity' (Cresswell, 2006: 15). Urry (2007) argued that the growth and diversification of mobility requires a new perspective on society: the 'mobilities paradigm', which conceptualises social relations as being 'beyond societies'. He advocated the development of 'appropriate metaphors' for 'a sociology which focuses on movement, mobility and contingent ordering, rather than upon stasis, structure and social order' (Urry, 2007: 9).

How much travelling do we actually do? The simple answer is that we have been doing more and more. *Social Trends 38* reviewed travel patterns and trends in Britain, both internally and overseas, showing people moving around more than ever and in increasingly complicated ways. In 2006 British people travelled over 800 billion passenger kilometres by road, rail and air – almost twice as much as in 1971 (p. 164). Travel by private transport increased considerably but travel by bus and coach fell between 1971 and 2006. Nearly two thirds of all trips in 2006 were by private car, mainly for commuting and leisure purposes, reflecting the massive increase in car ownership, especially the growth of households with more than one car increasing from 7 per cent to over 30 per cent between 1971 and 2006 (p. 168). The growth in domestic air travel was even more spectacular: a five-fold increase in domestic passenger kilometres between 1971 and 2006, to 10 billion passenger kilometres in 2006. International travel has also grown enormously, mainly through increased use of aviation. The number of trips abroad by UK residents increased by more than 300 per cent from 1982 to 2006, with air travel growing from 58 per cent of all trips in 1982 to 80 per cent in 2006. Such travel is obviously not confined to the UK: Urry has emphasised the enormous volumes of international travel, citing a prediction that there will be at least one billion legal international arrivals each year around 2010 compared with 25 million in 1950 (Urry, 2007: 3).

The growth of second home ownership is strongly associated with growing mobility, using the term in the sense of capacity to travel, because the ownership and use of more than one home necessarily involves travel between two or more homes. Most travel to second homes is by private car, though growth in overseas second home ownership is associated with increased air travel and the growth of 'budget' airlines. Just as railways and the London underground facilitated the expansion of commuter suburbs in the 1930s, so budget airlines have expanded the scope for overseas second home ownership from the early 1990s. *Social Trends* (ONS, 2008:150) explored the growth of second home ownership in general and attributed the rapidly increasing share of second homes abroad to 'the increasing affordability and accessibility of foreign property markets' (ONS, 2008: 15). Will extensive international travel remain easily available and affordable? And what costs does such travel impose on travellers themselves as well as other people, especially when associated with the development of transnational second homes? These questions are explored in Chapter 4.

There is a growing literature on changing patterns of residence, mobility, social organisation, and orientation to places, largely in sociology and tourism studies, relating directly and indirectly to second home ownership. Many authors have emphasised growing mobility and enhanced capacities for consumption in affluent societies, the changing nature of tourism as a vital element of enhanced mobility, and the many ways in which places are created, changed and 'consumed' by tourists and other leisure users (Urry, 1995, 2000, 2004; Sheller and Urry, 2004; Hall, 2005). Hall argued that time–space structures have changed enormously over the last 25 years and that 'advances in transportation and communication technology' have meant that 'for a substantial proportion of the population in developed countries or for elites in developing countries being able to travel long distances to engage in leisure behaviour … is now a part of their *routine* activities' (Hall, 2005: 24; emphasis added). The revolution in information and communications technology (ICT) has blurred distinctions between leisure and business travel so even whilst travelling we are almost constantly connected to others anywhere in the world by mobile telephone and through the internet. This has enabled the development of 'transnational communities in which movement is the norm' and 'dense sets of social, cultural and economic networks stretching between the two ends of the mobility spectrum from daily leisure mobility through to migration' (Hall, 2005: 25).

Greater levels of mobility, both of people and of financial assets, have resulted in massive expansion of leisure and lifestyle related investment and consumption (Barnett, 2007; Forrest, 2008). Globalised mobility and affluence mean that 'the summer cottage is increasingly available for short, intermittent stays' and 'advances in communications technology blur what remains of the distinction between work places and vacation space' (Williams and Van Patten, 2006). Growing affluence and mobility have facilitated growing second home ownership and travel between primary and second homes, blurring distinctions between 'residents' and 'visitors' and changing patterns of personal and family ties to places:

> The result has been an evolution in the types of people with strong ties to this place to include local residents who live and work full-time in the area, tourists who visit the area for limited periods yet develop lasting relationships through repeat visitations, and second home owners whose ties to the region exhibit characteristics of both residents and tourists.
>
> (Williams and Van Patten, 2006: 35)

Citizens of different countries have hugely different capacities to be mobile, both in terms of the financial costs of mobility and differential rights to mobility (relating to national jurisdictions etc). In some countries it may be easier for non-nationals to buy a second home, to come and go more freely than nationals and to be regulated by different rules and legislation (legal access to alcohol, tax free shopping opportunities etc). Some governments actively seek transnational investment by second home purchasers, for example Malaysia and Dubai, but others, most notably Australia before 2009, have imposed barriers to second home ownership by non-citizens.

Growing affluence and mobility since the 1970s have been accompanied by other socio-economic and demographic changes resulting in more 'flexible' lifestyles and lifestyle choices and emphasis on individualism, especially for wealthy individuals and households (Bauman, 1995). Lifestyle choices include ever-greater consumption and expenditure on luxuries, new models of cars, houses or jet planes, described as 'luxury fever' by Frank (1999, 2007). The growth of specialised interests and social fragmentation increasingly renders one residential space less suitable for all actions and identities. Lipovetsky (2005) uses the term 'hypermodernity' to refer to those social milieu typified by hedonistic affluence and consumption, where fashion reigns supreme but individuals are torn by doubts, anxieties and uncertainties.

> Anxieties about the future are replacing the mystique of progress. The present is assuming an increasing importance as an effect of the development of financial markets, the electronic techniques of information, individualistic lifestyles and free time. Everywhere the speed of operations and exchanges is accelerating; time is short and becomes a problem looming at the heart of new social conflicts. The ability to choose your time, flexitime, leisure time, the time of youth, the time of the elderly and the very old: *hypermodernity has multiplied divergent temporalities*.
>
> (Lipovetsky, 2005: 35; emphasis added).

Commenting on Lipovetsky's work, Charles (2005:11) suggested that contemporary societies contain signs of hyper-consumption transcending even the narcissistic individualism of the 1980s. Charles defines hyper-consumption as 'a consumption which absorbs and integrates greater and greater portions of social life', driven by 'an emotional and hedonistic logic which makes everyone consume first and foremost for their own pleasure rather than out of rivalry with others'. Other commentators on wealth and affluence have emphasised the growth of mass 'luxury' consumption (Brooks, 2005). One implication of these arguments is that in addition to being investment items, second homes can be objects of desired consumption purely for the sake of consumption by the individuals and households consuming them.

Second home ownership

Having argued that affluence and mobility have been key drivers of the growth of second home ownership, what do we mean by the term 'second home'? National censuses typically distinguish between a 'usual place of residence' and 'second homes'. The UK census definition of 'second residences' includes 'company flats, holiday houses, weekend cottages … in permanent buildings which were known to be the second residences of people who had a more permanent address'. Most definitions of second homes distinguish between permanent and non-permanent structures, often only including the former, and excluding tents, caravans, boats or other mobile structures, though mobile homes or caravans on site are counted as primary and/or second homes in some countries. Part-time second home ownership, as in timeshares, may not be identified in second homes statistics and can be complicated by different forms of tenure. Tenure categories, as well as legal systems and practices, also vary significantly between countries.

The SEH definition of second homes excludes dwellings that are the 'primary residence' of another household:

> Second properties are properties owned or rented by a household member, which are not the household's main residence. However, properties which are the main residence of someone else, or which the owner intends to sell because they have moved are not counted as second homes.
>
> (DCLG, 2008: 174)

Although a small proportion of second homes are rented, most commentators on second homes focus on second home ownership and the rest of this book is no exception. SEH data on the growth of second home ownership has the merit of having used a consistent definition of second homes. Thus changes over time are likely to be real rather than the result of changing definitions. The SEH definition allows the inclusion of dwellings that are occasionally let to other people but other commentators distinguish between (a) second homes used by family and friends solely for leisure or other occasional use and (b) 'holiday lets', which are mainly or solely let on a short-term basis to other leisure users (Coppock, 1977b).

Most commentators on second homes accept Coppock's (1977b) argument that they are not 'a discrete type' of dwelling, because 'the dynamic character of the second home, in particular the changing relationship between the first and second home ... makes identification and measurement difficult'. Such fluidity in definition is a recurring theme within the literature because the term 'second home' refers to how dwellings are used rather than to fixed and enduring characteristics of dwellings. Thus British MPs criticised for 'flipping' the designation of their 'principal residences' and 'second homes' were changing how dwellings were defined for the purposes of claiming allowances whereas the actual dwellings did not change.

There is no official definition or even concept of 'second homes' for UK tax purposes (Paris, 2008b). Rather, Her Majesty's Revenue and Customs (HMRC) distinguishes between the 'only or main residence', on the one hand, and any other dwellings that may be owned and subsequently sold (HMRC, 2005). Owners who sell their main residence do not have to pay CGT but are required to do so when any other dwellings are sold at a profit. In the case of rented properties where an owner or owners have claimed tax relief against costs associated with purchasing and maintaining the dwelling, HMRC will have records of ownership. If owners sell such dwellings without advising HMRC then they could be traced and tax levied retrospectively, or other measures taken. Dwellings used as second homes, where owners have never made any claims for tax relief, however, would not have been recorded for tax purposes. HMRC does not seek actively to identify such sales, so it would be up to such owners to notify HMRC on disposal of their properties in order to pay CGT. This is unlikely to occur very often, if at all. Thus one implication of the tax treatment of second homes is that they constitute a very attractive form of investment for affluent households, combining free leisure or other use with the possibility of untaxed capital gains. The opportunity to organise and reorganise residential circumstances on and after retirement, moreover, means that such investments may become especially attractive towards the end of a working life as a legitimate way of minimising tax liabilities. And, as we have seen, some MPs 'flipped' the definitions of their main and second homes to avoid CGT.

The question 'when is a dwelling a "second home"?' further undermines attempts to fix categorical definitions. Some are used often for leisure purposes and solely by their owners, including weekends and holidays, but others are used much less often or sometimes let out on commercial basis. Seasonal variations in type of use compound problems of trying to define or count dwellings as 'primary' or 'second' homes. For example, some second homes are let to holidaymakers at peak time and others may be let to students for part of the year. In any case, no census or survey could be held at peak time for *both* ski and seaside holiday seasonal use! Such diversity has been reviewed by numerous commentators who generally accept that the key factor in identifying 'second' homes is that they are used for leisure by their owners, family and friends; as well, many second residences are owned for use during the working week and for other family-related purposes. The flexibility of the use of dwellings makes it impossible to obtain precise meaningful counts.

Second homes are often conceptualised as an aspect of tourism by scholars working in leisure studies (Hall and Müller, 2004b; Hall, 2005) where the use of second homes is sometimes conceptualised as 'multiple dwelling'. The term 'second home' has different meanings in different societies and cultural contexts. In Australia the term 'holiday home' is used to describe second homes used by households for their own leisure and other non-commercial purposes; the term 'holiday rental' is used for what would be called a 'holiday home' in the UK. The distinction between 'primary residences' and 'second homes' is stretched beyond breaking point when we consider that a growing number of affluent households own more than one 'second home'. It then becomes preferable to think in terms of 'multiple homes' (Paris, 2008b) as in Chapter 2.

Variations between countries in terms of official definitions of second homes (if they are defined and identified), and legal systems render it extremely difficult to develop meaningful comparative data (Gallent *et al.* 2005; McIntyre *et al.*, 2006; Oxley *et al.*, 2008). One recurrent complication is that many surveys and censuses record the ownership of 'second residences' without distinguishing between (a) properties that are used primarily as second homes and (b) properties that are let to tenants. The most reliable source of data about second home ownership within the UK, the SEH, does make this distinction; but there are no equivalent sources for other UK jurisdictions or in many other countries. Data on second home ownership is routinely collected in some European countries, for example Sweden. The decennial census in the USA defines second homes as dwellings that are not 'primary residences' but are maintained for 'seasonal, recreational or occasional use' (Shellito, 2006). On that basis it was estimated that second homes accounted for around 3 per cent of the housing stock in 2000, with high concentrations in Florida, California, New York and Michigan.

There are other barriers to accurate counting of the numbers of second homes. One problem arises from official statistics on dwellings that are not occupied on the night of national censuses as it is difficult to determine whether they are vacant on a long-term basis or are empty on census night but regularly used as a second homes. Researchers in many countries have identified a consistent tendency to undercount the number of second homes and record many as 'vacant' in national censuses (Frost, 2003; Wallace *et al.*, 2005; Paris, 2008b; Norris and Winston, 2009). Another barrier to identifying the number and location of second homes relates to owners' motivations for defining their properties as 'primary' or 'second' residences. In some cases tax or other advantages have accrued to one or other definition (Gallent *et al.*, 2005), thus couple households that own two homes may define one dwelling as the 'primary residence' of one member and the other as the 'primary residence' of the other. Thus whichever one should be sold is the 'main' residence and so CGT would not apply. Different analysts may interpret the same phenomenon in different ways. Birch (2006) complained that official statistics underestimated the number of second homes because couples owning two dwellings each claimed one as their main residence to avail of single person's rate of local tax in each dwelling; he noted other 'scams' including classifying second homes as small businesses to pay lower local taxes. Referring to the same issues, in contrast, a journalist in the *Sunday Times* Money section wrote positively about 'tax perks' (Francis, 2006a).

Conclusions

Affluence and mobility have been the key drivers of the growth in second home ownership. Household wealth has increased considerably in the UK, Ireland, Australia and many other developed countries since the 1970s, especially in the form of domestic residential property and with an increasing number of households owning their homes outright. Affluence, combined with a preference for investment in property and expanded mobility, drives growing second home ownership. This chapter has also raised questions about the concept of 'second homes'; debates about the nature and diversity of second homes, as well as their impacts on communities and localities, are explored in the next two chapters. Chapter 3 also explores different traditions and histories within countries, with country-specific case studies. Chapter 4 examines the growing transnational dimension and the rapid growth in the ownership of second homes overseas and Chapter 5 reviews public policy issues relating to second home ownership. Chapter 6 provides an overview and considers some possible future scenarios.

One reviewer of my initial book proposal asked, 'what portion of affluence is "paper wealth" in the ranks of upper-middle income households and how has this impacted hyper-consumption?' also 'what is the role of banking regulation and lending practices on the growth of affluence that has fuelled portions of the second home market?' These questions require a balanced response. Much affluence *was* 'paper wealth' as many fortunes have been reduced during the global financial crisis and some of the excesses of development aimed at second home buyers have resulted in bankruptcies and left a legacy of unsold properties and unfinished developments. However, the recession was not 'unexpected' and many commentators had predicted the likely demise of the sub-prime housing sector (especially Harrison, 2007; also Mandelbrot and Hudson, 2005), especially in the USA, so many affluent households had reorganised their asset and investment portfolios to avoid the worst impacts of recession. The extent of the repercussions may have been impossible to predict, though perfect prediction is logically impossible anyway, as shown clearly by Taleb (2008) who also suggested that people overestimate the length and depth of any misfortune. Even Krugman (2008: 181), who famously predicted the credit crunch and is seen by many economists as a doomsayer, argued that '[t]he world economy is not in depression; it probably won't fall into depression, despite the magnitude of the current crisis'.

We have looked at the overall growth in wealth rather than just focusing on inequalities, but relativities do remain important. Although many affluent people have suffered a reversal of their fortunes, in most cases they still have fortunes. The ownership of second homes remains a minority pursuit even in affluent societies, thus overall falls in house prices mean that affluent households are able to take advantage of lower prices. We may be witnessing a repeat of previous housing cycles. Coppock (1977b) attributed an apparent fall in the level of second home ownership due to recession in the early 1970s and Gallent *et al.* (2005) argued that falling UK house prices in the early 1990s dampened the growth of second home ownership. But growth of second home ownership quickly resumed after both recessions and took off dramatically in Ireland in the 1990s. We show in Chapter 3, moreover, that there was no evidence by 2009 of any fall in the level of second home ownership in the UK during the latest recession.

Most commentators in the USA and UK believed that the worst of the recession was over by the end of 2009. *The Times* reported an upturn in sales of new houses as a positive sign whilst also noting remaining risks: unemployment was still rising and mortgage finance remained tight (Hosking, 2009). The *Homes Overseas* newsletter of 15 June 2009 claimed that 'the overriding view of finance ministers was positive' at the recent G8 meeting in Italy and there were signs of growing consumer confidence, greater availability of mortgage finance and a rising level of mortgage approvals. The same issue of *Homes Overseas* had as its 'property of the week' a nine-acre estate on the Aeolian island of Lipari, famously the home of 'legendary Music Maestro Sergiu Celibidache', with 'price on application'. And so it goes on.

2 Homes, second homes and *many* homes

The concept of 'home' is closely bound up with the creation and sustaining of self-identity. Home is a source of selfhood, a visible demonstration of chosen identities and the place where people (normally) find security from the risks and challenges of the world beyond the front door, a place where they can 'be themselves'.

(Lowe, 2004: 67)

… the potential for individuals to develop close relationships with multiple localities either through migration, second homes or employment not only spawns temporary movement that is inherently culturally influenced and predicated by previous mobility and the path of the life course, but also interrogates the notion of a 'singular' home.

(Hall, 2005: 95–6)

Introduction

The first chapter argued that growing affluence and mobility had generated explosive growth in the ownership of 'second' and more 'homes' with an increasingly transnational dimension. But housing scholars have paid little attention to second homes apart from the 'problems' associated with second home ownership: research studies and commentaries have examined unequal competition between second home owners and 'locals' in attractive high amenity coastal or countryside areas, especially National Parks, and issues relating to the sustainability of 'rural' communities (Satsangi and Dunmore, 2003; Wallace *et al.*, 2005). Housing policy and practice textbooks barely mention second homes; for example, five recent overviews of UK housing policy and provision said virtually nothing about the topic (Bramley *et al.*, 2004; Lowe, 2004; Malpass, 2005; Lund, 2006; Mullins and Murie, 2006). This lack of interest may reflect concerns about equity and social justice, with housing scholars seeing second homes as luxury goods, the preserve of affluent households and property developers, thus of limited interest.

The *Daily Telegraph* reported that a new 'luxury housing development' in the seaside village of Worth Matravers, Dorset, 'was daubed with graffiti reading "No More 2nd Homes" and "Go Away"' (Prince, 2009). The village was 'known locally as "Ghost Town", because nearly 60 per cent of its properties are holiday homes and locals complained that they could not afford the £465,000 price tag of the new development' (Prince, 2009). This may seem just another example of local problems in rural or coastal areas of little interest to housing scholars. But second homes probably account for at least 3–4 per cent of the housing stock in the USA, UK, and Australia and they are a significant element of housing markets, especially in 'hot spot' areas where they may constitute 25 per cent or more of the local housing stock.

Timothy (2004) estimated there were over 3.5 million 'seasonal/second homes in the USA with concentrations in the Southeast, West, Midwest and Northeast regions'. They account for much higher proportions of the housing stock in many European countries: between 10 and 20 per cent in many cases (Gallent *et al.*, 2005). There has also been rapid growth in the number of second homes in many countries and this will increase as 'baby boomers' swell the ranks of second home purchasers, especially in the USA (Engelhardt, 2006). The high concentration of second homes in some places means that local housing markets are disproportionately affected by changes in demand for second homes. They are very big business in some areas, including many inner cities and high amenity countryside, coastal and mountain zones where both local and international estate agencies actively buy and sell them. Developers and builders identify second home buyers as valued potential customers and target new developments to attract their interest.

Despite the disinterest of housing scholars, there is an enormous literature on second homes. Following Coppock (1977a) much scholarly interest derives from leisure and tourism studies, planning, rural studies, geography, sociology and cultural studies (Gallent and Tewdwr-Jones, 2001; Hall and Müller, 2004a; Gallent *et al.*, 2005; Hall, 2005; Hettinger, 2005; McIntyre *et al.*, 2006). Recently, however, some housing scholars have connected housing debates and the wider second homes literature (Perkins and Thorns, 2006) and begun to assess the impact of second home ownership on housing markets (Belsky, Zhu and McCue, 2006).

Some scholarly work on second homes is heavily theorised but other work is more empirically oriented, often involving detailed local case studies. Other studies develop national perspectives or international comparative analyses. The diversity of scholarly and analytical literature on second homes, including material in disciplinary and interdisciplinary journals, renders it impossible to derive a single theoretical perspective on this topic. It is possible, however, to present this material in a way that is consistent with established perspectives in housing studies in terms of the social relations of housing and housing pathways.

My focus, the social relations of housing, is consistent with the housing pathways perspective developed and elaborated by Clapham (2002, 2005). Clapham (2005: 27) defined a housing pathway of a household as 'the continually changing set of relationships and interactions that it experiences over time in its consumption of housing'. He emphasised the importance of social practices and individual choice, conceptualised households as changing 'containers' of people, and rejected any assumptions 'that households have a universal set of preferences and act rationally in their attempts to meet them' (op. cit.: 29). Following Giddens, he suggested that '[h]ouseholds undertake life planning in a search for identity and self-fulfilment' albeit within changing contexts and the possibility that individuals may have multiple identities. This approach recognises that the circumstances of individuals and households change over time, through both individual life cycles and household formation and deformation processes. Clapham's argument that 'buying a house is part of lifestyle choice' (2005: 33) applies especially well to the purchase of second homes. Clapham discussed mobility only in terms of relocation and moving between dwellings rather than movement between two or more dwellings that were owned simultaneously, but he did use striking time–space mobility metaphors:

> Households will travel along a particular housing pathway over time. Sometimes the pathway will be a motorway and they will be travelling with many others. However, there will be junctions at which choices have to be made… Nor does the journey necessarily lead to the same or even any predetermined destination. Travellers can travel in hope or enjoy the journey for its own sake… Journeys can be straight or vary in any direction.
>
> (Clapham, 2005: 34)

Changing household composition, together with changing lifestyle choices and preferences are important elements of the 'housing pathways' approach *and* of a nuanced analysis of the growth, meaning and significance of second home ownership. Individuals and households knowingly make choices about how they invest in and consume housing, whether 'primary residences' or second homes. Clapham's emphasis on household preferences and lifestyle choices, within market-driven processes of change, relates directly to a first theme from the wider second homes literature: the role of second homes in life course investment and consumption strategies. But different households have dissimilar capacities to buy and use housing, and the outcomes of one set of household choices can affect other people's opportunities and choices. Thus the second theme in the literature concerns the impacts of second home ownership on people, places and communities. As more households own more than one 'second home', it may be more useful to think in terms of 'multiple homes' rather than simply distinguishing between 'primary' and 'second' homes.

'The home' or many homes?

Although housing scholars largely overlook second homes, many have discussed the concept of 'the home', despite Kemeny's (1992: 9) concern that this focus 'unnecessarily limits the scope of housing research'. Lowe (2004) provided a clear review of issues and debates relating to housing, the home and society but in common with most housing specialists he never discussed the possibility that households have more than one 'home'. Easthope (2004) reviewed different ways in which the concept of home has been understood: as a socio-spatial entity, as a psycho-social entity, as an emotive space or as a combination of all three perspectives. She suggested that these perspectives all conceptualised homes 'as places that hold considerable social, psychological and emotive meaning for individuals and groups' rather than simply as a physical structure or region (Easthope, 2004: 135). She concluded that '[o]ne's home, then, can be understood as a particularly significant type of place with which, and within which, we experience strong social, psychological and emotive attachments', (Easthope, 2004: 135–6). She argued that this perspective transcends the simplistic dichotomy between a dwelling 'as a physical structure and home as a social, cultural and emotive construct' (loc. cit.) but she still shared the implicit assumption that there is one such place for every household. The widespread existence of second homes, however, questions whether people only have *one* 'special' place; indeed, scholars in cultural and leisure studies have suggested that 'second' homes may be more valued by individuals that their main residences (e.g. Quinn, 2004).

Perkins and Thorns (2006) sought to connect two largely separate literatures about the 'home', deriving from unconnected 'housing' and 'leisure' perspectives, in a discussion of second home ownership. They suggested that the 'leisure' literature raised questions about the primacy of the 'main' residence for family life because it showed that second homes were often valued precisely because they are retreats from normal stresses, contexts for enduring attachment to places and sites for multigenerational familial interaction. They argued that the distinction between 'primary' and 'second' homes in terms of family life was increasingly problematic 'as the remoteness and separations of work, leisure and routine patterns of life become rather disturbed by wider structural changes' (Perkins and Thorns, 2006: 80) and, even in second homes, 'much of life is shaped by gender, work, family, security and concerns about wealth accumulation'.

With many households owning more than one home for their own use, often attaching great meaning to their second homes, how can 'the' home be a special place of sanctuary and haven from the world? Rather, for many people 'homes' are conceived simply as investment items and dwelling spaces to be used as convenient at various times during any year; or as investment items as well as possessing other characteristics their owners may value. However, one correspondent with much experience of owning two or more properties at the same a time, argues that we can *only* have one 'home': Roger Baker's thoughts are set out in Figure 2.1.

The main problem with owning a second home, 'in the country' or 'at the seaside', is that it becomes a bit of a tie. After a while you feel you have to go there even if you'd rather go some place else, especially if the purchase is linked to recreation or a longer-term goal, such as retirement. It is difficult to justify the cost of going some place else when you have a second dwelling sitting empty. To justify it you have to use it. The landscape quickly shrinks and becomes increasingly familiar.

Clouds that floated above a city's grimy culverts were my childhood mountains and streams. On one ambitious attempt to reach out for them, I lived Monday to Friday in a north London flat, driving to a few acres and a pile of dilapidated stone farm buildings with a home in the delightful Dartmoor National Park, at weekends. Three hundred miles each way (before carbon footprint), ploughing my earnings into high interest rates and fuel, but a not so illusionary version of my future. Two dwellings one home, after seven years I didn't so much get off the merry-go-round, as fall off.

The difference between a house and a home is that the latter has got your stuff in it. Your heart drops and later you become angry when you discover that the party of four who stayed in your cottage last week was actually a cheapskate touring cricket team. Imagine eleven fit lively blokes after winning, or more so after losing a game. You may find that the nicest people to arrive leave the darkest stains on your financial decision to share. Real despondency comes when the recreational resource that attracted you in the first place disappears. Total, abject failure by the Common Fisheries Policy, could have been the first clue that all was not well behind the Cornish bank's closed doors. If every fisherman in Cornwall emptied his pockets there wouldn't be enough to buy a single modern trawler.

I sold the Cornish cottage for £120k, realising what I'd put into it except my own labour, exchanging the capital for US$170k, the purchase price of a nice, adequate property in the Florida Keys suitable for spending decent chunks of time, seasonal monthly letting to pay overheads, and maybe even retirement. The value of the property in Florida stood still for most of the time I owned it. The value of the sold Cornish property almost quadrupled in the meantime! But after a while the Florida Keys seemed increasingly like an anorexic city, 180 miles long by 200 yards wide, whose residents are either migrated consumer product specialists or issue-ridden fundamentalists Prices in southern Ireland were still compatible with the Keys and there were still bargains that no one wanted, because the Celtic tiger wanted only new. I bought in southern Ireland with my partner and we sold up in England and the Keys. We moved 'for the long haul', as the locals put it, and we brought

(*continued overleaf*)

plenty to the party. Enthusiastically, we started two small businesses and invested, as obedient citizens, in government-lead, bank-infested national savings schemes. The dollar dipped sharply and the exchange to euros was postponed. The old property in Florida quadrupled in the highest seller's market ever, while the dollar fell further against the euro. The capital has been trapped in dollars for nearly seven years, waiting for improvements in its euro value for as long as possible. At one point the value of the dollar retirement nest egg equated to approximately 20% of the Cornish property value from which it was realised originally. It is too cruel on others to call it good news, but we could now buy back the old Florida property with the same dollars, but our hearts are no longer in it.

In Advaita philosophy, the literal Sanskrit translation of 'home' means, 'not two'.

2.1 'Bringing it all back home' by Roger Baker

Second homes in life course and family investment and consumption strategies

Second home ownership had been the preserve of the rich in most countries before the twentieth century and some very rich people still inherit many properties and much land. The 'Official Residence' of Queen Elizabeth II is Buckingham Palace but she has numerous other homes: she inherited Sandringham House in Norfolk as well as Balmoral Castle and estate in Aberdeenshire; she also has use of Windsor Castle and other royal residences. In humbler cases, ordinary people who inherit property may choose to use it as a second home, like the Queen. Somebody who inherits a house on a small block of land by the coast could use it as a second home or pursue other options such as selling it, renting it to holidaymakers or to longer-term tenants, or simply leaving it empty whilst deciding what to do with it. In all such cases people make *choices* as they evaluate their options, whether they do so consciously or intuitively.

The ownership of 'country' and 'city' homes has been widespread among the British aristocracy for hundreds of years. Many of the richest families in Britain derive their wealth from the ownership of vast amounts of land, including the highest-ranked British-born person in the *Sunday Times* 'Rich List' in 2008, the Duke of Westminster. He inherited landed assets but he also has expanded his wealth considerably by property development and through other business interests. He 'owns vast estates in Lancashire and Cheshire, great swathes of Mayfair and Belgravia in central London, and tracts of land in Canada and Australia' and another '200 acres of Belgravia are held in family trusts worth about £4 billion' (Coxon, 2008: 16).

Growing home ownership during the twentieth century resulted in widespread asset accumulation involving life course investment and consumption decisions.

Home ownership was the dominant tenure in English-speaking countries by the 1950s, especially the USA, Australia, Canada and Ireland. Just as there were generational shifts in attitudes towards, and capacities to achieve, home ownership during the twentieth century, Hall and Müller (2004b) suggested that *second* home ownership ceased to be the preserve of elites during the twentieth century and became much more common and widespread.

The growth of home ownership was examined in the 1990s in a book on housing and family wealth, exploring aspects of reciprocity, intergenerational cooperation and transfers of wealth through inheritance (Forrest and Murie, 1995a). Most chapters examined the topic in relation to primary residences, though some considered second home ownership and others left open the possibility that their analysis could be extended to second homes. Forrest and Murie (1995b) suggested that some studies showed housing investment and consumption as collective family projects rather than being limited to atomistic households. Forrest and Murie (1995c) also highlighted growth in the real value of accumulated and inherited housing assets in Britain and that inheritance often leads to multiple house ownership.

Growing home ownership and the accumulation of family assets have resulted in more widespread inheritance of dwellings, providing beneficiaries with second homes for leisure use or assets that may be liquidated in order to acquire second homes. Inheritance is an important factor in the growth of second home ownership in many European countries (Gallent *et al.*, 2005), Britain and Ireland. Some studies of housing and family wealth have explored the role of second homes in family investment and consumption strategies. Bonavalet (1995) argued that many French families rent in cities but own second homes in provincial areas. Class differentials in second home ownership were explored in Greece (Emmanuel, 1995) and Japan (Hirayama and Hayakawa, 1995): much higher levels of second home ownership were reported among wealthier families in both countries, with more variable levels of second home ownership among middle class families. Kemeny (1995) suggested that the high level of second home ownership in Sweden was related to strong family links with rural areas. In Hungary, Ladányi (1995) suggested that many families had bought second homes as big as or larger than their main residences; he considered this as a rational response to an irrational (pre-1989) society!

Many other studies have shown that second home ownership has figured strongly within conscious short-term and longer-term elements of household and family investment and consumption strategies (Coppock, 1977b; Hall and Müller, 2004a; Gallent *et al.*, 2005). Coppock (1977b: 3) noted that second homes were often purchased for leisure use in the shorter term but with a longer-term view to eventual retirement, possibly with an interim phase of semi-retirement, 'until the second home becomes unambiguously the first'. Thus what had been a 'second home' would cease to be an item of *leisure* consumption and become the 'primary' home facilitating the utilisation of assets accumulated in the previous 'main' residence.

The idea that owning a second home is an *investment* recurs strongly across the literature, although this is typically seen in terms of potential capital gain or asset accumulation rather than as an investment to generate income. One of the main reasons given for purchasing second homes in the SEH has been as an investment. Other studies in the UK (Paris, 2008b), Australia (Paris *et al.*, 2009) and the USA (Engelhardt, 2006) have shown that they were considered good long-term investments. Most studies show that second home owners are already home owners, often owning their principal residences outright, typically aged between 45 and 60 and with household assets and incomes well above national averages. While the purchase of second homes may not always be the main investment apart from the primary residence, especially in America (Engelhardt, 2006) it is clearly something that is undertaken mainly by affluent middle-aged to older households as part of conscious strategies of property investment.

One distinguishing feature of second homes as investment items is that they are also an attractive and distinctive form of leisure consumption. The value of most leisure consumption goods almost invariably depreciates, including 'semi-mobile' and 'mobile' second homes such as caravans ('trailers' in the USA), mobile homes, recreational vehicles (RVs), motor homes and tents (Hall and Müller, 2004b). The value of houses and apartments, however, usually appreciates at least in line with inflation, albeit largely as a function of increased land values. In a perceptive conference paper first presented 40 years ago, Dower (1977: 160) argued that second homes 'are at the point of overlap between housing and tourism – neither squarely one or the other, but having the nature and implications of both'.

It is impossible both practically and logically to identify meaningful barriers between 'housing' and 'leisure' markets, though they may have different tax or regulatory requirements and contractual arrangements (most of which may be routinely ignored). It is therefore a matter of personal choice, partly influenced by legal and regulatory conditions, whether and when a particular dwelling is used as a second home for personal consumption, and/or let on a commercial basis to other leisure users ('on holiday') or private tenants as an investment. Any appreciation in value depends on overall market trends, not whether the dwelling is conceptualised as a second home for personal consumption or as an investment for financial gain. Many 'boosters' of second homes claim that they increase in value well above the rate of inflation, though such claims may be based more on wishful thinking or hype than sound business planning. The extent to which second home ownership is a good investment, therefore, will almost always in practice be an empirical question.

Second homes and lifestyle choices

Much of the literature on second homes explores their roles in lifestyle choices. Gallent *et al.* (2005) and Hall and Müller (2004b) have reviewed diverse scholarly sources to identify a range of reasons why people buy second homes. These are summarised in items 1 to 6 in Figure 2.2, which also lists some additional factors. These factors are not mutually exclusive and may be combined in different ways in different instances and over time, but this list covers most of the possible reasons for acquiring a second home.

Gallent *et al.* (2005) focused primarily on why people have second homes in 'rural' areas, including coastal areas, but the factors equally apply to second (or more) homes acquired in *any* areas; for example, some people wish to escape from working in the country to enjoy the pleasures of urban life. Their emphasis on rural second homes, perhaps, led them to a strong interest in aspects of nostalgia for an idealised rural past. Taking a wider international perspective, Hall and Müller (2004b) related second homes to a desire to step back to nature, often in countries with countrysides very different from Britain.

Urban–rural differences have changed in terms of house price differentials in England, thus the first factor no longer applies there. A Halifax House Price Index press release in 2006 reported that average rural house prices were 19 per cent *above* average urban house prices. Thus there had been a supply of cheaper rundown housing in British country areas, but that supply had run out, partly because of the growth of second home ownership 'leading to direct competition – and accompanying tensions – in some local markets' (Gallent *et al.*, 2005: 21). The very exclusivity of housing in high amenity areas encourages further purchase by second home owners, confident that the planning system will prohibit substantial additional development and protect their investment. Hence factor 5 in Figure 2.2: buying into an area to demonstrate achieved status. In many other countries, however, there are no such restrictions or tensions because there is an abundant supply of cheap older housing with relatively little demand from 'locals' or second home buyers: for example, in many small towns in outback Australia that have experienced long-term population decline.

A preference for owning a second home in the countryside is widely recorded in England, though many people buy into an idealised chocolate-box cover version of the countryside, with little or no understanding of the history of the countryside. There also has been extensive purchase of dwellings in coastal areas of England, often in places that were working ports or fishing villages but where local industrial activity has switched from primary production to pampering the tourists and second home owners. Thus the 'countryside' consumed by tourists and second home owners is itself the product of processes of cultural production. The literature on leisure and mobility has many examples of the ways in which places are created, changed and 'consumed' by tourists and other leisure users (Urry, 1995, 2000, 2004; Sheller and Urry, 2004; Hall, 2005). One of Urry's themes is how distinctive kinds of 'places' were created as locales for consumption through 'cultural production' involving tourism and tourism-related industries and actors. He showed how the image of the English Lake District was transformed from being considered unpleasant, uncivilised and hostile, and reconceived as an area of

1   Urban–rural differences: cheaper rural house prices, rising urban incomes and mobility and a 'cult of nostalgia' for the countryside attract second home owners to buy into the rural experience (Gallent *et al.*); step back to nature (Hall and Müller).

2   To escape from everyday pressures: escape the pressures of urban living (Gallent *et al.*); removal from everyday life (Hall and Müller).

3   Access to particular activities or resources: requiring access to rural resources (Gallent *et al.*); diverse other lifestyle or cultural activities, e.g. skiing, sunbathing.

4   Desire to retain links with a (rural) area that owners or relatives originated from (Gallent *et al.*; Hall and Müller).

5   Search for identity or status: buying into an area to demonstrate achieved status (Gallent *et al.*); expression of globalisation or changing regional identities (Hall and Müller).

6   Household and family investment strategy, including inheritance and possible future retirement and/or migration (Gallent *et al.*; Hall and Müller); also associated with opportunities to reduce, evade or avoid tax.

7   To achieve anonymity that is not possible in 'main' residential location or country

8   Other household and work-related factors: to use as a residential base during the working week; base for children living away from home during tertiary education; LAT and other relationships.

References in are to Gallent *et al.* (2005) or Hall and Müller (2004a)

2.2 Factors inclining people to buy second homes

'natural' beauty that is highly valued by a wide cross section of society (Urry, 1995). He argued that ideas of 'nature' and 'leisure' were themselves cultural products that became combined in aesthetic approaches to 'landscape' and typically presented in romanticised pastoral forms (Urry, 2005: 211–14). This critique is consistent with established bodies of writing on the countryside and landscapes of Britain and Ireland by historians, geographers and sociologists. Few parts of British or Irish countrysides are wholly 'natural', apart from the wildest moorlands, mountains and estuaries, because virtually every part has been affected by many centuries of human use and occupation (Hoskins, 1955; Rackham, 1986; Aalen *et al.*, 1997).

In many other countries, however, people have second homes in entirely different countrysides with different histories and with many much more natural wilderness areas. There has been a long history of 'cottages' in forested or lakeside areas in Canada where there never was any European-style agriculture or settlement (Selwood, 2006). In Australia, vast swathes of 'bush' were barely touched by white invasion and settlement,[1] though there are some completely abandoned ghost towns and rundown remnants of denser nineteenth century settlement. But Australians have increasingly sought their second (and first!) homes on the coast, sometimes in places that once contained primary or secondary industrial functions – a few still do – but in many cases much of the development has been driven by construction aimed at complex and overlapping 'markets' for second homes, downsizing, home-working, long-distance commuting and retirement. Many contemporary second homes in Ireland are along the Atlantic seaboard in areas that were characterised by high emigration during and after the famine; there is more bitterness than nostalgia for that rural past, but many Irish second home owners also are reconstructing associations with areas that their families came from.

Timothy (2004: 134) suggested that affluent settlers on the east coast of the USA 'found favour in country and mountain havens'. He described a long history of second home ownership among affluent Americans, with many originally escaping the booming cities of the East and Midwest. As second home ownership spread, a wider socio-economic range of households participated in long-range seasonal migrations to second home developments that often 'took on the properties of suburbia' (Timothy, 2004: 136). He also noted that tax breaks enhanced the investment attraction of second home purchase.

Second home ownership as a way of retaining links with traditional areas is discussed widely in the literature relating to many European countries (factor 4 in Figure 2.2). Kemeny (1995: 297) noted that many urban-dwelling Swedes 'inherit the family country house or cottage and use it as a second home' and that others acquire second homes near their areas of origin to retain and sustain family and kinship networks. There is also growing ownership of second homes in countries of origin by people who themselves, or whose parents, migrated elsewhere, typically as economic migrants. For example, many British people of Afro-Caribbean descent buy homes on Caribbean islands, often with a view of eventually retiring there. In most studies of second home ownership in the new world, however, there is no reference to any desire to retain links with traditional areas or a rural past.

Place attachment does not only arise from particular historical and/or familial associations, but also develops from a search for identity or preference for a particular lifestyle associated with certain places. The decision to acquire a second home often reflects a developed preference for chosen localities rather than deriving from other associations. People may attach importance to *many* locations rather than a single 'home', and high attachment to tourist destinations may be a key factor in decisions to purchase a second home (Perkins and Thorns, 2006; Tuulentie, 2006). Quinn (2004: 129) suggested that second home ownership was 'part of an adaptation to dwelling in modernity that relies on *multiple belongings* between two, or possibly more, places of residence' (loc. cit., emphasis added). Second home owners in her Wexford study used their properties often and were more relaxed in their second homes than their 'primary' homes. She questioned 'the historically accepted notion that the practice of holidaying and the location of the holiday destination are clearly distinguishable from the rhythms, practices and places associated with home life' (loc. cit.). Stedman's (2006a, 2006b) research in high amenity areas in Wisconsin challenged the view that 'permanent' residents have greater place attachment than seasonal or occasional users of second homes. He also argued that many studies of rural change that started from assumptions about how 'real' communities may be affected by 'outsiders' tended to privilege the accounts and claims of permanent residents. These studies and arguments reinforce the possibility that there is nothing special about 'the home' that may not be equally or even more special in people's *second* homes.

A desire to escape from everyday pressures is not limited to people who live mainly in cities. Some people who live in lowly populated areas acquire a second home for other reasons: for example, many second home owners in Australia are country folk who have a second home on the coast to escape the pressures of farming or simply to have somewhere cooler to relax and unwind. Many people want to participate in particular activities requiring access to specific resources: English fox hunters may choose to have a second home near the hunt of their choice. Other rural pastimes and recreations also have contributed to second home developments: many 'shacks' in the Central Highlands of Tasmania were developed primarily by trout anglers and their families. But there are also signs of growing ownership of second homes for leisure use in cities. Many people acquire second homes to gain access to activities and cultural resources that are only available in metropolitan areas. Cities also provide more opportunities to remain anonymous and thus play out roles that may not be possible in a rural area. Direct Line Insurance (2005: 6) identified key factors as 'affordability, accessibility, economic growth' as well as the beauty of a city's hinterland and its proximity to London. Other commentators have identified growth in coastal cities such as Brighton, England, or buoyant continental locations, especially Barcelona, Spain. The purchase of second homes in other jurisdictions, typically overseas, may also be driven by a desire to achieve a different residential status in order to reduce, evade or, in some cases, avoid taxation obligations altogether.

The purchase of second homes in cities reinforces the point that leisure second home 'markets' overlap seamlessly with 'housing' markets. Metropolitan second homes may be perceived to offer potential for capital gains as well as flexible future options including future retirement, sale to owner–occupiers or investors, or retaining as an investment and letting privately, including letting to students or as 'holiday' lets. Other aspects of factor 6, household and family investment strategies, were discussed in the previous section. The growth in the ownership of second homes in other countries was conceptualised by Hall and Müller (2004b) as an expression of globalisation or changing regional identities: the growing phenomenon of households from affluent countries purchasing dwellings in many other countries is explored further in Chapter 4.

Many other reasons for owning or renting second homes relate to household, family and other relationships. Widespread demographic changes in terms of household formation and the mix of household types, together with more frequent breaking and blending of households, require the abandonment of linear models of standard 'life cycles' and 'housing careers'. For example, in Britain 'the most rapidly growing family type is the stepfamily, created when a new partnership is formed by a mother and/or father who already had dependent children' (Ferri, 2004: 22). The growth of 'living apart together' (LAT) relationships, where partners work in different cities during the week but come together at weekends, requires ownership and/or rental of at least two dwellings at the same time. As with the purchase of dwellings for use by children during their university studies, other forms of more fluid household arrangements are also resulting in a tendency for households to own more than one dwelling, often in cities rather than the coast or countryside. Hence Reuschke (2006: 5) emphasised the need to understand 'different types of living arrangements' with 'complex spatial arrangement, marital status and the status of residences of the partners'.

How 'dwelling' is conceptualised, finally, differs within recent sociological literature from the usage by most writers within housing studies who tend to view dwellings as physical objects. Following Heidegger, Urry (2000) used the word 'dwelling' as a verb rather than a noun. He conceptualised 'dwellings' as social practices not as physical objects; thus 'dwelling' is what people *do* rather than particular physical structures. This conceptualisation of 'dwelling' emphasises fluidity and change in contemporary social uses of physical structures and associations that are attached to them. Gallent (2007: 103) also explored Heidegger's conception of 'dwelling' as a process, as using buildings, and argued that 'the nature of being, of doing and of dwelling is changing' with second homes representing a component of those changes. Gallent (2007) argued that many critics of second homes have a narrow public policy perspective that ignores private choices and use of dwellings. These perspectives on 'dwelling', again, are consistent with the 'pathways' perspective on housing and are developed in the typology of dwelling use, below.

The message of this literature is the need to conceptualise the use of dwellings as fluid, changing and often transient. The past experiences of second home ownership, especially artisanal self-build during an era of low mass mobility, bears little resemblance to emerging forms including large commercial developments and more diverse individualistic developments, whether by the super-rich or by more 'bohemian' seekers of 'alternative' lifestyles (Brooks, 2001). These analyses by specialists from outside housing studies fit perfectly into Clapham's 'pathways' approach to housing, with its emphasis on the meanings that actors attach to their housing actions, and seeing households 'as creative agents acting upon, negotiating and developing their own housing experience through life planning and lifestyle choice' (Clapham, 2002: 67). Second homes may be acquired for a host of reasons, but especially as part of household and family life growth course planning, combining investment and consumption strategies. They are acquired for leisure/pleasure and business-related residential use. People may use their city bolt-hole during the working week but relax and unwind with their family at weekends in their country home. New types of relationships, characterised by multiple mobilities, especially LATs, require the use of more than one dwelling by people involved in ongoing relationships that do not fit the conventional census definitions of a household. All of these uses of second homes may vary seasonally and over time, so we need to think in terms of fluidity not permanent fixed categories, but not lose sight of the enduring dimension of market relations involved in second home ownership.

The impacts of second homes on communities and places

Critics of second home ownership often focus on conflicts between second home owners and 'locals' as well as growing social polarisation in high amenity areas as affluent outsiders push up land and house prices beyond the reach of most local working residents. Social polarisation and seasonality of use, it is argued, result in affluent enclaves and 'ghost towns' that remain barely inhabited for large parts of the year (Figure 2.3). As well, much development has taken place in areas of high ecological sensitivity and there are many reports of environmental damage. High proportions of non-permanent residential use is related to housing market distortions, including price volatility and overproduction; this has been particularly noticeable since 2007 in many coastal areas of Spain.

Concerns about the impact of second homes in the UK and Ireland often are expressed in terms of conflicting interests of 'locals' and 'outsiders' (Monbiot, 2006), with second home owners being particularly resented:

> In areas where the inflation of house prices has made it impossible for many local people to obtain their own homes, the sight of outsiders purchasing houses when they already have one elsewhere can be an affront to local dignity… The locals must leave, while houses in their village remain locked and empty for months at a time.
>
> (Newby, 1979: 176–7)

Whilst emphasising positive aspects of second home ownership in creating work for local permanent residents, (Robinson, 1990) argued that 'the very presence of second home owners alters existing situations' as new residents compete for property with 'local first-time buyers or renters' (Robinson, 1990: 123). Gallent *et al.* (2005), however, suggest that second home owners are often singled out to blame for changes in country and coastal areas, but growth in the number of second homes is hardly ever the *only* factor affecting a locality.

2.3 Dale Village (reproduced by kind permission of *Private Eye* magazine / J Hunter)

Rather, a range of other changes in many different combinations have affected countryside and coastal areas since the 1950s (Butler, 1998; Ilbery, 1998). Rural economic restructuring comprised mechanisation of agricultural production and job-shedding, farm consolidation, farm diversification and growth of new country economic activities. English villages were transformed from occupational communities to residential areas, dominated by middle class commuters, retirees and second home owners, though Newby (1979: 175) saw the 'middle-class exodus from the towns to the countryside' as a symptom of change rather than the cause of change. Many coastal areas have also undergone systematic transformations as artisanal fishing industries have declined in parallel with the decline of working class seaside resorts. New tourism-related developments have included resorts and marinas and the widespread use of existing dwellings as second homes or as 'holiday lets' to tourists. Many former working class resorts, exemplified by Margate in Kent, are typified as seedy and down at heel, increasingly home to welfare recipients and asylum seekers. The cumulative effects of these changes led to the situation in the first decade of the twenty-first century where many remote parts of the British countryside and coasts are home both to some households with very high incomes and others with very low incomes.

Halifax Estate Agents (2005b) claimed that first time buyers were 'priced out of the countryside', with North Cornwall being the least affordable rural local authority in England with average house prices nearly 14 times average local earnings. The Bishop of Truro complained 'it is virtually impossible for many people who have been born and bred in Cornwall to live and bring up their children in the communities which have formed them' (quoted in Morris, 2006). House price growth in Britain after the mid-1990s also included a strong east–west differential associated with high demand for second homes in picturesque western coastal villages and adjoining areas (Halifax Estate Agents, 2005a; Kendall, 2006).

These processes of change can be conceptualised as a form of gentrification in the 'post-productivist' countryside. The term gentrification was introduced by Glass (1964) with reference to inner London; it has been developed internationally mainly with reference to neighbourhood change in inner metropolitan areas across the developed world (Atkinson and Bridge, 2004). Although sociologists were aware in the 1960s that non-metropolitan places were being changed by processes of 'invasion and succession', none used the term 'gentrification' in that context. Pahl (1965) described the impact of middle class commuters moving into villages across south-east England as 'urbs in rure' to highlight the bringing of 'urban' people and incomes into what had been 'rural' settlements. Village gentrification 'has gone unchallenged for many years' with the effect that 'median wage earners are being locked out of some local markets, and the lack of affordable housing has become a principal engine for social change in rural England' (Gallent, 2008: 124). Thus attractive 'villages' within commuting distance of British cities have been transformed into exclusive residential enclaves dominated by commuters, retirees and second home owners.

Geographers have examined 'rural gentrification' as a process of 'class colonisation' (Phillips, 1993, 2005; Smith and Phillips, 2001; Smith, 2002). Identifying a number of differences between 'urban' and 'rural' gentrification, they have focused primarily on permanent movement into the countryside, suburbanisation and 'counter urbanisation', rather than second homes. Smith (2002) suggested that 'retirement hotspots' such as coastal resorts could be considered as cases of gentrification. The value of this perspective is threefold. Firstly, it relates the growth of second home ownership to displacement activities that previously had been studied with regard to 'primary' homes. Secondly, it reminds us that growing second home ownership is rarely separate from other processes of change, including counter-urbanisation, retirement migration and use of dwellings for holiday lettings. Thirdly, a focus on second homes as a form of gentrification adds to the gentrification literature. A recent issue of *Environment and Planning A* examined developments in gentrification theory and research; most contributors focused on metropolitan areas though the editors noted 'overlaps between gentrification and themes such as globalisation, gated communities, suburbanisation, higher education, edge cities and the changing role of the countryside' (Smith and Butler, 2007: 2).

Until the early years of the twentieth century most people living in the countryside were involved directly or indirectly in primary production, especially farming, fishing and forestry, and/or related local services and industrial production. Farming became much more intensive during and after the Second World War and by the 1950s country and coastal areas were depopulating through labour shedding and agricultural restructuring. The concept of the 'post-productivist' countryside refers to the ways in which rural restructuring has affected the use of space in the countryside, with much no longer being primarily the locale of primary production. The dualistic distinction between a 'productivist' period of agriculture and its transition to the 'post-productivist' period remains a contentious issue within rural studies (Halfacree, 1997; Evans *et al.*, 2002; Mather *et al.*, 2006). In order to avoid simplistic dualisms, the terms 'productivist' and 'post-productivist' are used here as *ideal types* to capture different circumstances that both may exist in actual cases.

These ideas are relevant to housing because changes in the countryside have resulted in out-migration of some people, often with associated abandonment or underuse of dwellings, and in-movement of quite different people. New demand for rural living from the 1960s, on permanent and part-time bases, was generated by greater mobility, wider use of cars, long distance commuting and counter-urbanisation so that an increasing proportion of residents have no relation to traditional 'rural' economies, despite the growth of new (or expanded) rural industries including industries associated with country leisure pursuits including horse riding, hunting or even anti-blood sports activism (see Figure 2.4), walking, fishing and shooting (Butler, 1998). The post-productivist conception of the countryside is less as a place for active production of crops, fish or forestry products and more as a residential and leisure setting, often just as scenery. And post-productivist countryside residents can defend that scenery – and their property

'We used to be called the Fox and Hounds, but that was considered too controversial'

2.4 Changing rural cultures? (reproduced with permission of Solo Syndications; cartoon by Heath/*Mail on Sunday*)

investment – by using the planning system to oppose further development, arguing that it is in everyone's interest to 'protect' rural areas.

By bringing together ideas about gentrification and post-productivism we conceptualise an ideal-type 'life course' of second home development in a hypothetical area, starting with 'pioneer' renovators of dwellings that were abandoned as a result of rural restructuring, continuing through revitalisation of areas and purchase of existing homes from former owners, whether landlords or lower-income owners, through to fully commercial involvement.

Many commentators on second homes have cautioned against using a simple dichotomy between 'locals' and 'outsiders' with its implications that 'locals' all share the same interests and priorities. 'Locals' rarely, if ever, constitute a homogenous group in social, economic or demographic terms: there may be as many, if not more, differences *within* any specified local community as between 'locals' and second home owners (Hall and Müller, 2004a; Gallent *et al.*, 2005; Gustafson 2006; McIntyre *et al.*, 2006). Some local residents are much richer than others; some are employers but others are employees or unemployed. Some own splendid homes whereas others are tenants and some may be homeless. Some local people benefit by selling land at enhanced value for housing development, whether for second homes or permanent residences. Other locals are builders, solicitors, surveyors and estate agents. Some sell goods and other services to second home users as well as to commuters and retirees. Some 'locals' may have moved into an area relatively recently, especially retirement migrants, whereas others have roots going back many generations. Some second home owners may be the children or grandchildren of 'locals' who left many years ago; second, third or subsequent generations may have emotional attachments to areas and perceive strong 'local' connections transcending distances in space and time.

Hall and Müller (2004b) cited many studies showing benefits accruing to local economies as a result of growing second home ownership, especially as an antidote to declining primary sector employment and depopulation of remote areas. Second home owners may contribute significantly to local tax revenues, consume few municipal services and constitute a significant element of demand for tourism and leisure services such as restaurants and bars, shopping streets and centres, golf courses, gambling, eco-tourism and more. They are valued customers of local businesses providing such goods and services. In some cases, though, second home owners and affluent newcomers to country areas bring different expenditure patterns and views on amenity and environmental considerations Thus new conflicts can emerge, for example where newcomers campaign against logging but locals gain valued employment in forestry industries such as timber-felling (McIntyre and Pavlovich, 2006). Some 'locals', including those who move to an area on retirement, may resent the growth of other leisure activities and markets (Paris, 2007b).

International comparisons highlight many differences between countries and over time and show that the British case is by no means the norm. Gallent *et al.*

(2005: 128) distinguished between housing markets in Britain, on the one hand, and most other European countries, on the other. Other national experiences explored in Chapter 3 offer strong contrasts with the British case. Indeed the relationships between second homes and other elements of housing provision in Britain may be the least typical of all affluent countries. In many other countries, second home ownership has been much more widespread and less contentious, mainly due to different attitudes to development of new housing and the nature of regulatory planning regimes.

Many criticisms of the growth of second homes are based on the argument that they are adversely changing places. In other cases, however, second homes were an element in making 'places', often in previously unsettled coastal areas. In Australia, for example, 'pioneer' self-built second homes in unsettled coastal zones were often followed by subsequent consolidation and growth into distinctive settlements (Selwood and Tonts, 2006). The case of coastal settlements discussed by Selwood and Tonts also highlights the significance of serial acquisition of second homes by family members or friends who met more regularly in second homes than in their primary residences.

Large, fully commodified second home developments, often including rental holiday homes and retirement accommodation, have become widespread in many countries. Such developments often take the form of gated 'communities', for example in attractive waterside areas in the Cotswolds (England) where former gravel pits are transformed into designer lakes for sailing or fishing and golf courses come as part of the deal (see Chapter 3). Elsewhere changes have created new kinds of 'place'; much of the local economy of the American state of Montana has been transformed:

> ... hunting and fishing have shifted from a subsistence activity to a recreation; the fur trade is extinct; and mines, logging and agriculture are declining in importance ... the sectors of the economy that are growing nowadays are tourism, recreation, retirement living and health care.
>
> (Diamond, 2005: 34)

For example, a former stock farm of 26,000 acres was developed as second homes for rich people from other states 'who wanted a second (or third or fourth) home in the beautiful valley to visit for fishing, hunting, horseback riding, and golfing a couple of times each year' (loc. cit.). Land prices escalated and locals were replaced by 'immigrants' whose externally generated incomes kept them immune to the economic difficulties experienced by local working people (Diamond, 2005: 60). Many immigrants were 'half-retirees' or had retired early 'supporting themselves by real estate equity from their out-of-state homes that they sold, and often also by income that they continue to earn from their out-of-state or Internet businesses' (loc. cit.). Meanwhile local schoolteachers' salaries are too low for them to buy homes in the area and locally born children must leave 'because many of them aspire to non-Montana lifestyles, and because those who do aspire to Montana lifestyles can't find jobs within the state' (Diamond, 2005).

The most intense problems associated with second homes in Britain and elsewhere are often the result of a change in scale, increasing overall demand and regulatory land-use planning, as Coppock pointed out over 30 years ago. 'As the supply of more accessible properties diminishes, prices rise and prospective purchasers look further afield' and 'what may have been tolerated on a small scale becomes intolerable when numbers increase sharply, especially when there is a greater awareness of the environmental consequences of such developments' (Coppock, 1977b: 11). Questions relating to planning control are double-edged because 'even tight planning control cannot avoid the social frictions which acquisitions of existing properties create (the more so as the market for first and second homes cannot easily be separated)' (loc. cit.). As planning control becomes tighter, ironically, it also becomes harder for lower income 'locals' to find a place to live. In other countries, however, planning regimes are less restrictive and some even encourage the development of second homes (see Chapter 3). Again, it appears that the British case is unusual among free-market economies, at one end of a spectrum from intense planning regulation to a free-for-all.

Two other possible impacts of the growth of second homes can be considered briefly. Firstly, it has been suggested that regions with high levels of second home ownership may be subject to distinctive housing market dilemmas, especially during any economic downturn. The 2005 annual Royal Institute of Chartered Surveyors (RICS) review of European housing markets argued (Ball 2005: 14) that local markets with high proportions of second homes may be much more volatile than 'primary' housing markets and warned (p. 35) that 'the longer the second homes markets boom, the greater is the chance that shocks will lead to serious short-term declines'. Secondly, there have been many criticisms of the growth of second homes on aesthetic and environmental grounds. Many criticisms of overdevelopment and environmental devastation may be justified and some developers may perceive strong demand for second homes in locations that are environmentally sensitive, and seek to overcome or ignore environmental problems. But there is nothing intrinsic to *second* homes that render them more or less likely than primary residences to be constructed in environmentally damaging or enhancing ways.

Overall, the impacts of second homes on places and 'locals' are contested, diverse and changing over time. There is no universal or systematic set of conflicts between 'locals' and second home owners, as relationships vary enormously between places and over time, with diverse patterns of cause and effect. Nor can second homes be considered as the only factor contributing to social polarisation or gentrification. In their case studies of local housing markets in England and Wales, Gallent *et al.* (2005: 77) showed that many factors were at work, as 'market activity comprised a mix of local movement, second home purchasing, buy-to-let investment, retirement, teleworking and commuting'. In combination with other factors, therefore, competition from second home buyers in high amenity areas in Britain has added to problems of affordability for lower-income households and first time buyers, but not been the only causal factor. The relations between second home owners, other 'local' residents and places with high incidence of second homes should be conceptualised as webs or networks of interaction, frequently changing over time, rather than in terms of simple and unchanging binary opposites. Whether or not differences of interest exist, and whose interests prevail, will be empirical questions to be assessed separately in different contexts and situations.

Diverse uses of dwellings: typology of dwelling use

The difficulties involved in attempts to define and count second homes in various countries, introduced in Chapter 1, include problems due to different descriptive terms used in various countries, varying official and statutory definitions, diverse legal, taxation and tenure systems, and absence of interest in some jurisdictions. It is impossible to give precise numbers of dwellings used as second homes because the use of dwellings often changes; for example, a pied-à-terre in London may be let to visitors during the Wimbledon fortnight or the forthcoming 2012 Olympic Games.

Multiple homes

Another problem with the term 'second' home is that a growing minority of highly mobile households in affluent countries own three or more 'homes' for household or family use, for leisure, including leisure-related investment, work-related purposes or other family activities. Thus frequent short-term moves 'between home and one or more destinations for work or pleasure are a fact of life for a significant minority of people today' (McIntyre *et al.*, 2006: 6). It is impossible in many cases to specify which dwelling is the 'primary residence' because different household members spend varying amounts of time in numerous dwellings, so that the term 'multiple homes' is proposed for instances of the ownership of two or more additional dwellings purely for private use.

The difficulties involved in attempting to count second homes are compounded in the case of multiple homes because these are often spread across different countries with diverse systems of recording ownership. Ownership status may be masked by corporate arrangements designed to take advantage of taxation and other benefits. In practice, ownership and use categories may be blurred, perhaps deliberately for tax avoidance, for example where parents buy a dwelling for their student children but charge rent to other occupants even though they do not declare the rental income to the tax authorities.

It is not proposed that the terms primary residence and second homes should be abandoned, because the great majority of household only have one 'home' and most owners of second homes only own one such dwelling. The term 'multiple homes', however, captures the extent to which affluent households own and use domestic residential properties. Crucially, the terms 'second home' and 'multiple homes' refer to how dwellings are *used* by their occupants and not to physical characteristics or dwelling types as specified in house condition surveys (e.g. detached houses, apartments etc). Dwellings that are physically identical, for example adjacent apartments or terraced (row) houses, can vary both in tenure and use. One apartment may be occupied by private tenants whereas an adjacent dwelling is owned by a household that uses it only occasionally for holidays.

It is helpful to employ a typology of dwelling use with the following types: primary residences; second homes; multiple homes; pieds-à-terre; other non-commercial family uses; and investment properties. This typology was developed for practical policy-related application in order to capture all possible dwelling uses for purposes of public policy development and implementation (Paris, 2008b); it attempts to cover all ways in which dwellings are used and identifies different forms of investment in dwellings (in the physical use of the term 'dwellings'). One practical lesson to be drawn from this typology is how difficult it can be for any attempt to specify dwelling use for the objectives of planning, taxation or other public policy purposes (see Chapter 5).

The typology of dwelling use can include caravans, mobile homes and RVs, holiday lodges, houseboats and cruisers, or many other physical dwelling types. Caravans and mobile homes are not included within counts of 'permanent dwellings' in many national official definitions, but they can be the only residence of households even in affluent societies. Many are also used periodically by owners of second and multiple homes; thus caravans, holiday lodges, mobile homes and other forms of semi-mobile or mobile dwellings can and do fit one or more of the types of dwelling use listed below. However, in the great majority of cases these do not enjoy freehold title of land, typically being either leasehold or with a defined contractual right to be based on site under specified circumstances. Some people own the land on which or their semi-mobile or mobile dwellings are situated; in these instances they may benefit from increased land values even if the dwelling itself depreciates in value.

The examples of different types of use in Figure 2.5 are chosen to highlight how identical physical dwelling types next door to each other can fit into different types of use. Some types and subtypes overlap and owners and occupants may often change how they use the dwellings. But that is the point of using a typology: it helps to distinguish similarities, differences, regularities and variations in the frequently fluid use of dwellings. There is also much blurring of categories due to many variations in legal and taxation arrangements across the globe; for example, timeshare ownership and use of apartments mean quite different things in different contexts. This typology shows how 'leisure' and 'housing' markets overlap seamlessly so that analyses of one may often include large elements of the other; for example, average house prices within a country or region include the prices paid for second and other multiple homes, including those purchased by non-resident citizens of other countries. Regional variations in house prices reflect such factors but this is rarely if ever taken into account by studies of affordability. Developers and house builders may have an idea of who are likely to buy new houses or apartments, but they are usually indifferent to the use of dwellings once they have been sold. Thus new housing production in some areas may have prospered through strong 'outside' interest from second home owners and investors, despite limited 'local' demand.

The typology of dwelling use

The typology of dwelling use in Figure 2.5 attempts to differentiate between types of dwelling use through identification of a range of types of use by households that usually have at least one permanent residence available to them. It is not a classification, so there are no rigid boundaries and in practice there are overlaps between the types, because the ways in which people use dwellings is fluid and changing. It does not include homeless people, or those who are usually resident in a 'communal establishment' (defined by the UK census as 'an establishment providing managed residential accommodation').

The typology starts from the most basic building block, retaining the term 'primary residence' because most households only have one place of usual residence and remain there most of the time, though different family members may spend varying amounts of time elsewhere on holiday or business-related travel. In other cases, the occupants may own second or multiple homes. In most cases in affluent English-speaking countries households' primary residences are owned, but some will be rented, more so in Scandinavian countries. It is also irrelevant within this typology whether or not such users of primary residences own other properties that may be let to tenants or holidaymakers. Thus the examples of primary residences in Figure 2.5 include a house that is owned outright by people with no other property investments, a rented apartment in Portstewart (a small seaside town in Northern Ireland) that is occupied by a couple who own a rental property in Dublin, and the home of the tenants living in that rental property.

Within this typology the term 'second home' is defined as a single additional dwelling used by the household, other family members and/or friends purely for leisure use, typically at weekends and for holidays. This definition is designed to differentiate between leisure second homes and other family-related uses. The first example here is a house in North Belfast that is owned by a medical practitioner whose primary residence is in a small country town 60 miles away; he bought the house as a base for weekends and holidays in the relative anonymity of a city where he can get away from his patients. This house is virtually identical to the permanent residence of the family in 1a. The second example is another apartment in

1 Primary residence: occupied by a household all or most of the time.
   a A house in North Belfast owned outright and occupied all year by a household that has no other property investments.
   b A rented apartment in Portstewart (a small coastal town) occupied by a retired couple who own a house in Dublin that is let to tenants.
   c The Dublin house rented by the tenants of the retired couple in 1b.
2 Second homes: a single additional dwelling for leisure or other family use.
   a A house in North Belfast, adjacent to the residence of the family in 1a above, owned by a doctor whose primary residence is in a rural community.
   b An apartment in Portstewart, next to the retired couple in 1b above, owned by a family from South Belfast and used at weekends.
3 Multiple homes: more than one other home in addition to primary residence.
   a A household with a 'primary' residence in London, an apartment in a Swiss ski resort and a condominium in Florida.
   b A household that owns and routinely moves between a Los Angeles apartment, a townhouse in London, a chateau in Bordeaux and a ski lodge in South Island, New Zealand; none of these are 'primary'.
4 Pied-à-terre': a dwelling used as a base away from home during the working week.
   a A house in Canberra, the national capital, used by an Australian Senator from Queensland.
   b An apartment owned by a fishing boat captain in Chesapeake Bay, Maryland.
5 Other non-commercial family uses.
   a A house purchased by parents for their children's use while they attend college.
   b The two apartments of a LAT couple during the week and their primary residence in the country where they meet at weekends.
6 Investment properties: dwellings let commercially and not occupied by the owners.
   a A house in North Belfast let to tenants on a six-monthly contract.
   b An apartment in Queensland's Gold Coast let on a weekly basis by an estate agent (realtor) to holiday makers.

Source: Paris 2008b

2.5 The typology of dwelling use

Portstewart, next door to the rented apartment in 1b, but this one is owned outright by a couple from South Belfast who use it at weekends and holidays.

The term 'multiple homes' refers to the ownership of more than one second home. It could be used as an umbrella term to include 'second homes' as in 2a but it is designed to specify the growing number of cases where affluent households own numerous dwellings in different places, including different countries, none of which is used to generate rental income. In the first example, a family spends most of the year in their primary residence but also spends periods of time in their Swiss apartment and their condominium in Florida. In the second example, family members travel frequently, but at different times, between their apartment in Los Angeles, the London townhouse, the chateau in Bordeaux and their ski lodge in New Zealand; but no family member usually spends more than a couple of months in any of them at any one time. Thus none of their homes is obviously a 'primary' residence.

The type of dwelling use described as 'pied-à-terre' refers to dwellings that are owned (or rented) in addition to primary residences, and used mainly as a base for work distant in space or time from primary residences. The SEH regularly shows a concentration of 'second homes' in London and these are generally assumed to be owned (or rented) by people whose 'primary residence' is outside the metropolitan area but who require a city base for use during the working week. Examples include dwellings used by political representatives when their parliament or assembly is in session; and bank executives' penthouses in the City of London or Manhattan, where they stay during the working week before heading to their country homes for the weekend. Although pieds-à-terre are typically in cities, a different example could be an apartment in Chesapeake Bay, Maryland, used by a sea fishing charter captain whose primary residence is in a city. He needs a base by his boat for peak season and weekends but returns to stay with the rest of his family at their 'primary residence' at other times.

The typology differentiates between pieds-à-terre and 'other non-commercial family use'. This refers to dwellings that are used by family members for a variety of reasons other than as a regular base during the working week. Such dwellings may be those used by family/household members for a variety of durations and reasons during temporary absences (though in practice some such absences may become extended over long periods). One example is an apartment in London that is purchased by parents for the use of their student child during university study (though if rent were paid by the family member student and/or co-occupants, then this would be considered an 'investment property' as below). Another example relates to LAT relationships, where two spouses or partners work in spatially distant places; such households may have two dwellings for use during periods of separation, typically during the working week. In some cases such households may have other dwellings for leisure and family use; this subtype overlaps with 'multiple homes'.

The final type of use of dwellings is as an investment, thus the term 'investment properties' refers to dwellings that are owned, but not occupied at all by the owners/ purchasers. The dwellings are used by other people, usually as primary residences or by holidaymakers (with a minority being used as multiple homes by tenants). These are usually houses or apartments that are rented to tenants: 'the private rental sector'. The legal and taxation contexts vary greatly between countries, but dwellings typically are let to tenants, or leased to licensees. The dwellings are thus the primary residences of the tenants but they represent investments by their owners who seek rental income and, they would usually hope, a longer-term capital gain. In most countries the landlords of such dwellings receive tax relief against the cost of acquisition and/or running the investment. One example of an investment property is a terraced house in North Belfast let to tenants on a 6-monthly tenancy; this property is identical to and set between the dwellings in 1a and 2a (Figure 2.5), and is used as the primary residence of the tenants. The second example is an apartment on the Gold Coast in Queensland that is let on a weekly or other short-term basis to holidaymakers. Such investment properties are usually described as 'holiday homes' in the UK and Ireland but as 'vacation rentals' in the USA or 'holiday rentals' in Australia (where the term 'holiday home' may be used interchangeably with the term 'second home'). These dwellings are let on a short-term holiday/leisure basis to other users, often using an estate agent or management company. Thousands of cottages across the UK and Ireland are routinely let for short terms to visitors on holiday. Timeshare accommodation and other forms of partial ownership and use of dwellings may fall into different types of use, though it can also be considered that such 'ownership' may constitute a form of leasehold tenure.

Conclusions

This chapter has argued that housing scholars have much been much more interested in 'the home' than second homes and attached greater significance to 'the' home than it merits. An interest in social and cultural dimensions of the home should not divert attention from the other dimension of homes: as physical structures embedded in market relations. Whatever their social or cultural meaning, dwellings in home-owning societies are seen by their owners as investments and it may be precisely the investment potential of housing that attracts people towards the ownership of more than one dwelling for their own use.

People have acquired second homes for diverse reasons, including inheritance, but investment is a major factor, especially because second homes combine pleasurable leisure/family consumption and potential for longer-term strategic options (retirement or sale) and untaxed capital gains (or as part of an estate to leave to heirs). Most second home owners are affluent 40–65-year-old homeowners and owning second homes has been an element of life course consumption and investment strategies. The ways in which owners use their homes, especially when they own three or more for personal consumption, also varies substantially as the typology in this chapter has illustrated. Growth in the number of second homes is rarely the only factor causing changes or conflicts in localities, but can be a significant driver of change – these are empirical questions that work out in different ways in different places and at different times. Thus we move on to explore some of these variations between places and over time in the next chapter.

3 Variations on a theme

Second home ownership in many countries

People rarely live in these ugly new developments all year-round … Instead, owners pour down in droves at the weekends, crowding out the local restaurants with their designer clad kids and crass urban jabber, or lie half-asleep in their smug SUVs, staring at the sea as if it owes them money.

(Price, 2008)

There are approximately 461,000 summer cottages in Finland today … every fourth household owns a cottage and more have access to one, since cottages are increasingly used by extended families. Consequently, owning a summer cottage in Finland today lacks the elitist connotations sometimes associated with owning a second home.

(Periäinen, 2006: 103)

Introduction

British and Irish commentators often represent second home ownership as a problem for local communities, as in Greystones in the Republic of Ireland, where Price scorned second home owners with their 'smug' sports utility vehicles (SUVs). In many other European countries, as Periäinen noted, widespread second home ownership has been a non-problematic fact of life for many years. Over 10 per cent of households in many European countries have second homes (including France, Italy, Spain and Norway) and over 20 per cent in some others (Greece, Finland and Sweden). Allen *et al.* (2004) noted that second home ownership was low in the UK compared to very high levels of second homes in southern European countries, averaging around 17 per cent in 1996. They also argued that official statistics typically have undercounted second homes and mis-recorded them as vacant.

Twentieth-century histories of second home ownership varied considerably between countries and continents. The international literature mainly dates from the 1960s, describing traditions of regional homes in European countries. Nordic 'summer houses' are typically located by sea or lakes (Bjerke *et al.*, 2006; Periäinen, 2006); 'country' homes in Southern Europe, tend to be located in higher and cooler countryside around cities, often on land inherited from family (Coppock, 1977a; Hall and Müller, 2004a; Gallent *et al.*, 2005). Leal (2006) reported rapid increase in second home ownership in Spain, estimating over 40 per cent of total growth in the housing stock between 1981 and 1991 to be second homes or vacant dwellings. Increasing second home ownership was associated with middle class affluence, a preference for investment in property and lifestyle preferences, including low density accommodation away from hot Southern European cities in summer, access to beaches and/or proximity to mountains and winter sports. Leal (2006: 8) argued that interest in winter sports has generated heavy development of second homes around Madrid and the repopulation of formerly abandoned villages. Much of the growth of second home ownership in Spain before the 1990s was by Spanish families, distinctively different from more recent developer-led transformation of the Spanish Costas aimed largely at overseas-based purchasers.

Second home ownership is widespread across the globe, especially and often associated with tourism development and the use of other dwellings as holiday homes or holiday rentals. But second home ownership is not just a feature of leisure and tourism; it is also an integral part of the routine operation of housing markets in many countries and regions (Barke, 2008). Whereas second home ownership was the preserve of small elites in the nineteenth century, this changed during the twentieth century as growing numbers and proportions of households in many countries acquired second homes (Hall and Müller, 2004b). This growth was associated in many European countries with a desire to retain links with rural origins by households who had relocated to cities during rapid twentieth-century urbanisation (Kemeny, 1995; Gallent *et al.*, 2005; Periäinen, 2006; Barke, 2008).

Müller (2004) described the growth of second home ownership as a 'marker' of changes within regions, using Sweden as his case study. In 'disappearing regions' with a surplus of housing due to rural depopulation 'the economic impact of second home tourism can be small; but still it means that at least some money is spent that can contribute to sustain local shops and services' (Müller, 2004: 247). Most Swedish 'disappearing regions' were in inland northern areas with low property values and many 'second homes' were rarely used by their owners. In contrast to these regions, growing second home ownership was more controversial in 'hot spots': attractive areas where demand for second homes exceeds supply, driving up house prices and squeezing out lower income residents, leaving such areas deserted for much of the year. He suggested that hot spots have increasing property values and turnover, with 'in-migrants and second home owners coming from rather affluent groups within society' (Müller, 2004: 248). Swedish hot spots were mainly in southern forest and coastal areas, partly stimulated by the 'internationalisation of Southern Sweden' as the number of German second home owners trebled between 1991 and 1996.

Müller's analytical distinction is useful for differentiating types of regional impacts of second home ownership, and it applies to stages in a historical process of change within regions: from rural depopulation to 'hot spot' status. This chapter focuses mainly on differences between countries whereas the next chapter looks at international dimensions of growing second home ownership. Some of the differences between countries have reduced with the globalisation of growing second home ownership, which constitutes a dynamic element of changing national and regional housing markets.

Second homes, known as 'dachas', were scattered across the countryside of Soviet Russia. At an elite level, Joseph Stalin used Massandra Palace, formerly a residence of Tsar Alexander III, as his dacha. Many city dwellers had much smaller places in the country. Struyk and Angelici (1996) drew on household surveys to estimate that about one in four urban households in Russia had country dachas, often little more than shacks on modest allotments, without power or running water, and only used in the summer; about 20 per cent were estimated to be more substantial and prestigious 'country house dachas'. There have been relatively permissive planning approaches to second homes in Nordic and Mediterranean countries as well as former Spanish and Portuguese colonies in South America. In the great majority of these cases there does not appear to have been significant displacement or competition with 'locals'.

Second home ownership also became widespread in English-speaking new world countries (USA, Canada, Australia and New Zealand) often initially through self-provision. Their planning regimes generally allowed new housing development in rural and coastal areas, often requiring conformity with local developmental regulations and building codes. Most were single storey detached houses, but some countries had distinctive vernacular traditions: Canadian 'cottages' were often by lakes (Selwood, 2006), New Zealanders had 'bachs' (Perkins and Thorns, 2006) and Australians had 'shacks' (below). Growing affluence during the post-war boom, especially in the USA, led to widespread second home ownership. Early vacation properties tended to be utilitarian structures in isolated areas; these were followed from the 1950s by a wave of prefabricated dwellings in 'second home neighbourhoods' and more recently by rapid growth in the ownership of RVs. RVs 'combine transportation and temporary living quarters for travel, recreation and camping'; almost 10 per cent of vehicle-owning American households owned one or more in 2001 with a total of nearly 7 million (Timothy, 2004: 143). Timothy also reported significant growth in ownership of second homes abroad: as the US dollar strengthened during the 1990s a growing number of Americans crossed borders to buy beach houses in Mexico or summer cottages in Canada, or even flew across the Atlantic to buy in the UK or other European countries (op. cit.).

3.1 New housing in Malaysia in a popular tourist area of Penang (source: Maeve Paris)

There has been widespread development of second homes targeted at cross-border or overseas purchasers in many countries. Much second home development in Asia has been linked with tourist development, for example in Thailand and Malaysia. The government of Malaysia even has a programme designed to attract overseas purchasers of second homes: 'Malaysia My Second Home' (MMSH). Other countries have initiated massive tourist and second home developments on previously unoccupied sites, most notably in Dubai.

Differences in politics, society, economy and geography run through local histories of second home ownership and must be taken into account in any international comparisons. Variations in terms of planning and regulatory systems are key variables, with the development of second homes in Britain and The Netherlands having been distinctively constrained by restrictive planning, especially in rural areas, compared to most other countries (Gallent *et al.*, 2005). The sharpest conflicts occur where a restrictive planning or regulatory system imposes strong constraints on additional development and thus any growth of second home ownership can only occur through the purchase of existing dwellings.

The self-provision of second homes seems to be increasingly less the norm, especially in cross-border developments, where large developers typically lead second home and resort projects, often combined with other leisure and commercial developments: shopping centres, golf courses and marinas (Gustafson, 2006; Paris, 2008c). In many cases, recent literature on second homes in the USA, Canada and Australia reveals new conflicts between 'locals', sometimes themselves retirees, and developers and further incoming second home owners. The relatively informal and vernacular origins of much second home development in Australia have been increasingly challenged by state governments through tighter planning and environmental controls.

Private sector housing industries, rather than individual households, are increasingly the key agents promoting the growth of second home ownership, including land development, house building, materials production, large property developers, finance and property professionals (estate agents, legal practitioners). There are also incessant promotional activities by estate agents, with extensive advertising in the property sections of newspapers. Many British TV programmes cover aspects of house purchase and property investment and development in the UK and overseas, often covering second homes. There seem to be almost innumerable series with ever more desperate combinations of key words: 'Property snakes and ladders', 'Location, location, location', 'A place in the sun – home or away', 'A place in the sun – home or USA', 'Relocation, relocation', 'Grand Designs' and even 'How clean is your home?' Channel 4 specialises in property programmes, with a dedicated website (http://www.channel4.com/4homes) where you can access 'All Your Favourite Homes TV'. The presenters are usually enthusiastic and knowledgeable 'property professionals', though it is often hard to differentiate between some of the characters' diverse roles as TV presenters, celebrities and/or publicity-seeking real estate agents.

Second homes in the UK and Ireland

Second home ownership expanded more recently in the UK and Republic of Ireland than in most other European countries. There was slow growth in the UK up to the 1980s, and then it boomed within both countries from the early 1990s, with rapid growth of second home ownership overseas. Differences between the planning regimes in Britain and Ireland have had crucial impacts on the ways in which the second homes booms have unfolded within each country: the tight regulatory approach in Britain contrasting with the permissive planning regime in Ireland. The case of Northern Ireland is also distinctive as the planning regime was very similar to the Republic of Ireland up to the late 1990s, but has become more like other parts of the UK since 1998.

Changing housing systems in the UK and Ireland

Housing systems in the UK and the Republic of Ireland have evolved within different social, economic and political contexts since partition in 1921 (Foster,

1988; Bardon, 1992). Northern Ireland remained a part of the UK but the Republic of Ireland[1] became a separate sovereign state. There were dramatic contrasts in the demographic and economic histories of Britain and Ireland (Bradley, 1999; Coleman 1999). The British population grew strongly during the nineteenth and early twentieth centuries, from 21 million in 1850 to 49 million in 1951 and then at a slower rate throughout the century. In Ireland, however, the population fell from the 1840s, due to deaths in the famine and out-migration for the rest of the nineteenth century. Population decline was strongest in the contemporary Republic of Ireland, from 6.5 million in 1841 to 2.8 million in the early 1960s.

Belfast was the major industrial city on the island in the nineteenth century and the Republic had a largely agricultural economy after partition with little urbanisation until the 1990s. Northern Ireland's economy contracted severely in the 1930s and failed to benefit from post-war growth, unlike the British economy, which grew strongly during the 1950s and 1960s. Despite economic growth in the 1960s and 1970s, the Republic of Ireland was in recession in the late 1980s and out-migration surged. Thus there were many economic and demographic similarities between Northern Ireland and the Republic in 1990: high unemployment, slow economic growth and net out-migration. Northern Ireland was the poorest UK region, with the highest unemployment and continuing internal conflict over constitutional and sectarian divisions. The Northern Ireland Parliament established after partition in 1921 had many devolved powers, but was abolished in the early 1970s leading to 25 years of 'direct rule' from Westminster. The movement towards peace in the 1990s led to the establishment of a power-sharing devolved government in 1998, but the Northern Ireland Assembly was suspended more often than not over the next 10 years.

Housing issues and policies in Britain after 1945 were related to distributional concerns during 30 years of economic and population growth, with priority given to new housing construction and replacement of slum housing (see, for example, Murie *et al.*, 1976; Mullins and Murie, 2006). Local authorities played major roles in housing provision after 1945, through widespread urban renewal and the development of council housing that accommodated around one in three UK households by the mid-1970s. In both parts of Ireland, however, low housing demand and abandonment of rural housing meant less pressure to replace slums; new building rates were low and house prices stagnant. Social housing in the Republic was provided by councils, more as a mechanism to facilitate home ownership than as a tenancy for life (Power, 1993). Housing conditions in Northern Ireland lagged behind the rest of the UK in the 1960s but improved after the creation of a non-departmental body, the Northern Ireland Housing Executive (NIHE), to undertake major programmes of slum clearance and house building (Paris, 2008a).

The public housing sector grew rapidly in Northern Ireland in the 1970s as a result of NIHE house building, to nearly 40 per cent of households in 1981. Councils in the Republic in the 1960s played a much smaller role, never housing more than 20 per cent of households; council housing waiting lists fell from 29,000 in 1981 to 18,000 in 1988 and new private housing output fell to around 16,000 (Paris, 2001). House prices were much lower in both jurisdictions than in Britain. Northern Ireland was also distinctive for sharp ethno-religious residential segregation, especially in public housing estates, which tended to be occupied almost totally either by Catholics or Protestants. Bizarrely named 'peace walls' separating Catholic and Protestant areas in Belfast remained in place 10 years after the introduction of devolved government (Murtagh, 2001, 2002; Shirlow and Murtagh, 2004).

Housing provision in Britain changed significantly after the 1970s, with privatisation through the sales of council housing, reduced public sector construction and deregulation of mortgage finance. Rapid growth of home ownership was boosted after 1980 when council housing tenants were given the 'right to buy' their homes (Malpass and Rowlands, 2009). Public sector urban renewal and housing construction ceased and new social housing was provided only by housing associations. House prices boomed in Britain to peak in 1989 before falling sharply to 1993, with an associated wave of mortgage failures, negative equity and repossessions.

Throughout all of the changes in housing policy, one thing remained constant: the long-term commitment to contain the growth of cities and 'protect' the countryside, chronicled in detail by Hall *et al.* (1973), which still remained dominant 25 years later (Bramley, 2009). Some of the housing policy changes also occurred in Northern Ireland, though public sector house building continued into the 1990s. Housing demand remained lower in Northern Ireland and the Republic of Ireland than in Britain into the early 1990s. There was no housing boom on the island of Ireland in the 1980s, nor was there any post-boom house price slump. Public policies favoured home ownership in all jurisdictions, especially in the Republic, where around 80 per cent of households were owner–occupiers compared to 70 per cent in Northern Ireland, England and Wales. The public sector was smaller in the Republic, with fewer than 10 per cent of households.

Land-use planning systems of Northern Ireland and the Republic of Ireland were in theory both based on British law and practice, but they differed significantly in operation. Low demand and the absence of lobby groups campaigning to 'protect' the countryside resulted in less regulation of development than in Britain and more easy-going attitudes to one-off housing in the countryside. The planning regime in Northern Ireland was permissive rather than restrictive: the 1993 *Planning Strategy for Rural Northern Ireland* included an assumption in favour of granting permission for one-off housing development outside specifically protected areas (Department of the Environment for Northern Ireland, 1993). Planning in Northern Ireland began to change in the late 1990s with a new Regional Development Strategy advocating a shift towards 'brownfield' development, reusing sites that previously had been developed, rather than 'greenfield' development on previously undeveloped land (Paris *et al.*, 2003). This strategic shift went further in 2004 with a new policy proposing stricter control of housing development in the countryside (Murray, 2005). These developments were introduced by British Secretaries of State when the Northern Ireland Executive and Assembly were suspended: the policy shift occurred despite, not because of, devolution after the Good Friday Agreement.

Economic circumstances had changed dramatically in the Republic of Ireland during the 1990s, boosted by low corporation tax rates with strong inward investment into manufacturing in the booming 'Celtic Tiger' economy (Mac Sharry and White, 2000; Clinch *et al.*, 2002). Economic growth averaged over 6 per cent per annum during the 1990s and per capita income overtook the UK. Critics argued that the boom was based on a 'branch plant' economic policy and brought greater inequalities (O'Hearn, 1998; Drudy and Punch, 2005). Growth was heavily concentrated in the greater Dublin region, with strong job creation in manufacturing and the buoyant services sector. Unemployment fell rapidly to be replaced by emerging labour shortages but a dramatic switch in migration patterns resulted in a growing inflow of migrants, both returning Irish-born citizens and immigrants from other EU countries and across the globe (Paris, 2005b). The Northern Ireland economy also picked up in the 1990s and unemployment fell strongly, though the economy remained heavily dependent on public sector employment.

Housing demand grew strongly due to a rapid increase in households in the 1990s, especially in the Republic of Ireland – by a staggering 26 per cent (Paris, 2006). Surging economic and demographic growth resulted in a boom in the Republic as house building increased year-on-year to peak at over 90,000 dwellings in 2006. House prices also surged, doubling from 1994 to 1998 and doubling again by 2003. Urban and rural landscapes were transformed by private redevelopment schemes with high density apartments, extensive suburban growth and widespread construction of single dwellings in the countryside (Gkartzios and Scott, 2005). Growth was strongest in the Dublin region and an 'edge city' formed around the new outer motorway box (MacLaren, 2005). Northern Ireland also experienced a housing boom with widespread counter-urbanisation and suburbanisation, population loss from Belfast and extensive development of one-off homes in the countryside (Paris, 2006). Land and house prices spiralled wildly between 2004 and 2007. New house building was much higher across Ireland than in Britain or most other EU countries: over twice the EU average in 2001 (Norris and Shiels, 2007), rising in the Republic to 19.6 housing completions per 1,000 inhabitants in 2005–2006, and 10.1 in Northern Ireland, compared to just 3.4 per cent in Britain (Norris *et al.*, 2008).

Development patterns across the island of Ireland contrasted sharply with Britain, where counter-urbanisation was not accompanied by one-off development of housing in the countryside (Champion *et al.*, 2005) and house price growth was not accompanied by an increase in house building. There had been a noted increase in the size of new dwellings in Britain in the 1990s but this was followed by a shift to inner city apartment construction after 2001. The economist Kate Barker (2004) was commissioned by the British government to assess why house price increases had not been matched by increased supply. She concluded that the planning system comprised a major brake on expanding supply, as many other housing economists had been arguing for over 30 years, most recently by Bramley (2009) and most passionately in Evans' (1988) review of the impact of planning on British land and house prices *No Room! No Room!*

This brief overview of similarities and differences between Britain, Northern Ireland and the Republic of Ireland in terms of housing provision and policy sets the scene for the following review of second homes in Britain, Northern Ireland and the Republic. In particular, it highlights:

- similarities and differences in socio-demographic, economic and political contexts;
- changes in housing provision in the different jurisdictions; and
- the influence of contrasting planning regimes on patterns of housing development.

We can now contrast the development of second homeownership in these three contexts. The first focus is on overall patterns of second home ownership, especially in England where we have the best data, which shows that second homes play a significant role within urban housing markets. The second focus is on second home ownership in rural and coastal areas, because these have tended to be the sites of most reported conflicts of interest between 'locals' and second home owners, and where the obvious contrasts are greatest between Britain, Northern Ireland and the Republic of Ireland.

Britain: gentrification and diversification

Some of the largest numbers of second homes are in urban areas of England, especially London. Most would count as pieds-à-terre in the typology in Chapter 2,[2] but their owners also have another dwelling purely for their own use, many of which are in rural areas. Many define their city home as the 'second' home to obtain council tax discounts there because tax levels are higher in cities and the discount is worth more than in country areas.

Table 3.1 shows the 20 local authorities with most second homes in 2006/07, based on DCLG council tax[3] data identifying households that applied for council tax discounts for second homes. Five of the top 20 were in London, with a collective total around 25,000 second homes, mainly in expensive areas including Westminster, Kensington and Chelsea, and Tower Hamlets with the regenerated London Docklands and extensive gentrified areas. Birmingham and Leeds also made the list with over 9,000 second homes between them. Many other top 20 councils are in towns in or near high amenity areas, especially Scarborough, Chichester and Great Yarmouth. These data cannot show all second and multiple

Table 3.1 English local authorities with the largest numbers of second homes in 2006/07

Local authority	Region	Number of reported second homes
Westminster	London	8,300
Birmingham	West Midlands	7,000
Kensington and Chelsea	London	6,400
North Norfolk	East	4,700
Tower Hamlets	London	4,200
South Hams (Devon)	South West	4,100
North Cornwall	South West	3,900
South Lakeland	North West	3,700
Scarborough	Yorkshire and the Humber	3,400
Bournemouth	South East	3,400
Isle of Wight	South East	3,400
Camden	London	3,200
King's Lynn and West Norfolk	East	2,900
Barnet	London	2,900
Chichester	South East	2,800
Great Yarmouth	East	2,700
Penwith	South West	2,600
Suffolk Coastal	East	2,500
Leeds	Yorkshire and the Humber	2,400
West Dorset	South West	2,400

Source: SEH, 2006/07, analysis of council tax returns to local authorities.

homes in England as they only include properties where the council tax discount was claimed. Many owners of second or multiple dwellings do not claim such discounts and overseas-based owners of second and multiple homes would not get council tax discount because these count as their 'primary' residences in the UK. Overall, these data confirm that urban second home ownership is widespread and substantial, with half of declared English second homes within districts that were classified as 'predominantly urban'.

An international real estate agency, Savills (2007a), used DCLG data to list districts with the highest concentration of second homes. Most of the top 20 were coastal and country areas, but three of the top 10 were in London; the City of

London (Figure 3.2) was clear first with 26 per cent of all dwellings being second homes. The concentration in central west London is shown in Figure 3.4. Savills' report affirmed the significance of second homes in household investment and consumption strategies and in urban housing markets and linked the growth of part-time work-related bases in cities to the growth of buy-to-let investments: 'the speculative purchase of newly built property in Britain's cities may also have led to an increase in the numbers being declared as secondary residences' (Savills, 2007a: 2). A report by Direct Line Insurance confidently predicted strong growth in the 'work based' sector of the second homes market especially in Newcastle-upon-Tyne, Liverpool, Glasgow and central London (Direct Line Insurance, 2005). As well, many parents purchase houses and apartments for the use of their children while they are living away from home attending university. The Halifax House Price Index has shown very strong price growth in university towns in Britain over the last 15 years and a Halifax economist suggested that many parents saw buying a property rather than paying rent as a very good investment (Unattributed, 2008). As student fees add to the cost of tertiary education, then this is an increasingly attractive option for many parents.

Table 3.2 shows the SEH estimates of the regional distribution of second homes in England in 2006. They were strongly concentrated in the South West, East and South East regions (see Figure 3.3). The South West stood out with 21 per cent of recorded second homes in England but only 11 per cent of all households. At the other extreme, the North West and North East regions between them contained

3.2 Across the Thames to Canary Wharf and the Isle of Dogs: city second homes? (source: Natural England)

Table 3.2 Estimates of the regional distribution of second homes in England

	SEH 2006/07 Share of second homes (%)	SEH regional distribution of all households
North East and North West	12	19
Yorkshire and the Humber	8	10
East Midlands and West Midlands	13	19
East	15	11
London	14	14
South East	19	16
South West	21	11
Total	100	100

Source: SEH, 2006/07

12 per cent of second homes but 19 per cent of households, despite the high concentration of second homes in and around the Lake District. The SEH data indicated that London contained about 14 per cent of all second homes and the same proportion of households.

The Savills Director of Research suggested that house price growth may result in growing second home ownership, and 'the investment motive is boosted by expectations of high capital value growth which results in higher levels of second home buying as well as buying to let' (Savills, 2007a: 3). This 'insider' view of links between investment in second homes and other residential property is consistent with Chapters 1 and 2 on household investment and consumption strategies, though Smith's research (2005, 2006, 2007) had not found evidence of equity transfer from 'primary' to second homes. Circumstances have changed since 2007 as the recession has resulted in falling house values across the UK and Ireland, and severe restrictions on credit availability have made it harder for people to trade down or borrow against the value of their homes. It is more difficult for people to sell their second homes, many of which now have negative equity, especially for those who have purchased overseas in areas where prices have fallen considerably.

Second homes in changing British countrysides and coasts

There was very little building in the British countryside from the late 1930s to the establishment of the post-war planning system. The 1947 Town and Country Planning Act and the statutory planning system stopped vernacular second home building in the countryside, and regulated development more generally. The 1949 National Parks and Access to the Countryside Act formed the basis for further

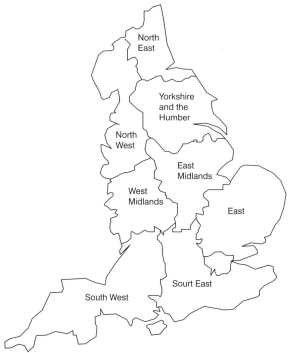

3.3 Government Office regions of England (source: www.search.com/reference/Regions_of_England)

restriction of development in high amenity areas. National Parks covered over 5,000 square miles in England and Wales by 2009, mainly in mountainous and coastal areas, plus two Scottish national parks established under the National Parks (Scotland) Act 2000. There is ongoing debate within Northern Ireland about a proposed national park in the Mourne Mountains. Other parts of the British countrysides are designated as Areas of Outstanding Natural Beauty[4] (AONB) where planning regulations seek to limit development, though some lobby groups, especially the Campaign to Protect Rural England (CPRE), argue that there is already too much development. Figure 3.5 shows that around 30 per cent of the land area in England and Wales lies within designated national parks and AONBs, such as the Cotswolds (Figure 3.6), with a higher proportion in Northern Ireland but much less in Scotland. Figure 3.4 shows that the relative distribution of second homes in England has a similar spatial distribution, skewed towards high amenity coastal and mountain areas, especially in Devon and Cornwall, North Norfolk and the Lake District (Figure 3.5).

The CPRE has been a major player in planning and environmental debates for over 80 years since its formation. It is a registered charity based in London with support across England. Queen Elizabeth II is its patron, the current president is

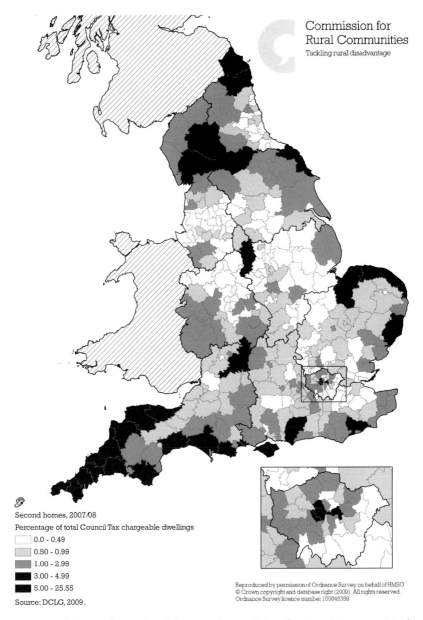

Commission for
Rural Communities
Tackling rural disadvantage

Second homes, 2007/08
Percentage of total Council Tax chargeable dwellings

- 0.0 - 0.49
- 0.50 - 0.99
- 1.00 - 2.99
- 3.00 - 4.99
- 5.00 - 25.55

Source: DCLG, 2009.

3.4 Second homes in England (source: Commission for Rural Communities)

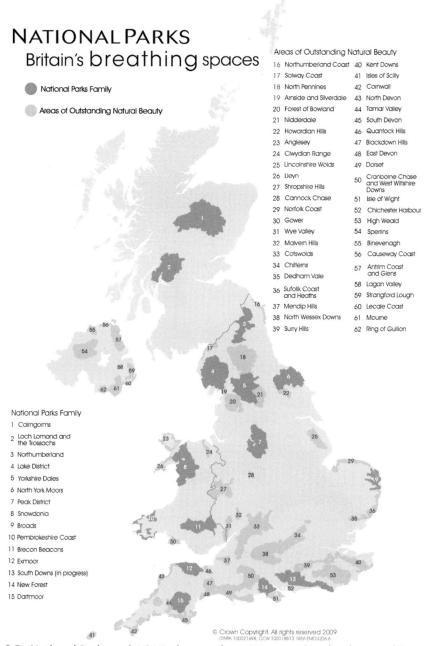

NATIONAL PARKS
Britain's breathing spaces

- National Parks Family
- Areas of Outstanding Natural Beauty

Areas of Outstanding Natural Beauty

16	Northumberland Coast	40	Kent Downs
17	Solway Coast	41	Isles of Scilly
18	North Pennines	42	Cornwall
19	Arnside and Silverdale	43	North Devon
20	Forest of Bowland	44	Tamar Valley
21	Nidderdale	45	South Devon
22	Howardian Hills	46	Quantock Hills
23	Anglesey	47	Blackdown Hills
24	Clwydian Range	48	East Devon
25	Lincolnshire Wolds	49	Dorset
26	Lleyn	50	Cranborne Chase and West Wiltshire Downs
27	Shropshire Hills	51	Isle of Wight
28	Cannock Chase	52	Chichester Harbour
29	Norfolk Coast	53	High Weald
30	Gower	54	Sperrins
31	Wye Valley	55	Binevenagh
32	Malvern Hills	56	Causeway Coast
33	Cotswolds	57	Antrim Coast and Glens
34	Chilterns	58	Lagan Valley
35	Dedham Vale	59	Strangford Lough
36	Suffolk Coast and Heaths	60	Lecale Coast
37	Mendip Hills	61	Mourne
38	North Wessex Downs	62	Ring of Gullion
39	Surry Hills		

National Parks Family

1. Cairngorms
2. Loch Lomond and the Trossachs
3. Northumberland
4. Lake District
5. Yorkshire Dales
6. North York Moors
7. Peak District
8. Snowdonia
9. Broads
10. Pembrokeshire Coast
11. Brecon Beacons
12. Exmoor
13. South Downs (in progress)
14. New Forest
15. Dartmoor

3.5 National Parks and AONBs (source: http://www.nationalparks.gov.uk/ visiting/maps.htm)

3.6 Traditional Cotswolds village (source: Natural England)

Bill Bryson the American humorist, and other leading figures come from across the party political spectrum. Originally the Council for the Preservation of Rural England, it has changed its name twice whilst retaining the same mnemonic: in 1969 to the Council for the Protection of Rural England and in 2003 to its current name. Thus the organisation modernised its image whilst retaining its objectives and beliefs. Its early membership included prominent architects and planners and it gained cross-party support during the 1920s in opposing urban expansion, especially ribbon development. Under the heading of 'what we've achieved' the CPRE website reports lobbying successfully in the 1930s and 1940s for the post-war planning system with its green belts to 'contain' city expansion and a system of protected national parks (http://www.cpre.org.uk). It is an independent organisation firmly within a long British tradition of anti-urbanism recorded by many historians and sociologists, notably Raymond Williams in *The Country and the City* (1973). Ruth Glass (1968) traced English antipathy to city life back to Roman times, culminating in the triumph of ruling class residence in 'the country house' rather than in cities. She also remarked that many of the founders of British planning, including Robert Owen and Ebenezer Howard, 'had all felt the menace of the towns' (Glass, 1968: 70). The continuing tradition of living in the countryside but maintaining a base in London helps to explain the many pieds-à-terre in the city and why affluent city dwellers opt for second homes in the countryside that is so well protected by the British planning system. The CPRE also encouraged the Urban Task Force, chaired by Lord Rogers, to propose an 'urban renaissance' to protect the countryside. Further, in 2000, 'After years of

CPRE campaigning, new official planning policies on housing mark a radical shift away from low density sprawl and towards using previously developed "brownfield" land for new homes before greenfield sites are built over' (http://www.cpre.org.uk/about/achievements/2000s).

Some of the first reported conflicts over second homes in Britain from the 1960s and 1970s concerned the purchase and rehabilitation of abandoned or dilapidated dwellings in areas of depopulation (Coppock, 1977c). By 2009, however, such debates were anachronistic: few cheap abandoned dwellings remained to be converted as most already were renovated and gentrified or are priced on the basis of inflated expectations. As the supply of abandoned dwellings dried up, people wanting second homes had to purchase existing dwellings coming on the market, especially in National Parks and AONBs (Gallent and Tewdwr-Jones, 2001; Gallent *et al.*, 2005). Such demand spilled over into areas outside designated areas as second home owners purchased dwellings from lower income owner–occupiers or from landlords seeking to capitalise on increasing property values. Many coastal and country villages are now gentrified leisure sites with fancy restaurants and wine bars. Padstow in Cornwall is ironically referred to as 'Padstein' to reflect the influence of the celebrity TV chef and restaurateur, Rick Stein, on the local economy (Figure 3.7). More recently there has been growth of commercially developed new accommodation aimed at second home buyers, often just outside zones of severe constraint on development. These include top-end expensive developments and other mixtures of property types and prices oriented towards mass consumption, with various combinations of resorts, marinas and residential development. Some are marketed in terms of environmental and socio-economic quality, including affluent gated developments in countryside and seaside areas. British 'hot spots' of coastal village gentrification or new marina and other leisure-related development contrast sharply with former working class resorts, especially Margate and Southend, often described as the 'Costa del Dole' and where 'No, we do not like to be beside the seaside' (Girling, 2006).

Affluence and poverty are often found side by side at the seaside. Civic leaders in many seaside resorts seek to reinvent their towns through regeneration projects. Halifax Estate Agents (2005b) claimed that 'We *do* like to be beside the seaside' (emphasis added) as their research showed house prices rising strongly in seaside towns in South East and South West England, including Margate and Southend. Many examples of recent upmarket developments around the British coast combine a range of facilities including residential complexes with hotels, shopping, leisure facilities, health and beauty complexes, marinas and golf courses. Many are within existing built-up areas and thus obtain planning permission, with local authorities eager for prestigious new development. Some are on the edge of established areas and some developers manage to get permission on greenfield sites. In other instances, developers are able to obtain planning permission on the basis of existing use rights or replacement of like for like.

3.7 Padstow, Cornwall (source: Natural England)

One development being advertised in August 2009, Oceanpoint at Saunton Sands in North Devon, comprised 16 two- and three-bedroom apartments near to Saunton Golf Club and overlooking extensive sandy beaches (Figure 3.8). A show apartment was available for inspection and four apartments remained on sale at prices between £535,000 and £695,000. Planning permission had been granted for this development only because it replaced a former hotel and on condition that the development 'shall be occupied for the purposes of holiday accommodation only'. Some apartments have been purchased for use as second homes and others by investors to let them as holiday homes. This project highlights shifting patterns of leisure and tourism overlapping with housing markets: a hotel was replaced by apartments as in the other cases in Northern Ireland and the Irish Republic.

Many other developments are advertised each week in attractive high amenity British coastal areas, though there are conflicting reports of property markets in Cornwall. There were some reports of developers facing ruin and widespread price cutting, but many projects were selling well even during the recession. One report in June 2009 described hundreds of finished but unsold apartments in Newquay, Cornwall, with many more under construction and for sale, and one developer in administration; many old hotels and large stores were 'boarded up, awaiting demolition and redevelopment – and could be so for years' (Norwood and Collinson, 2009). Falling prices in some developments, however, also meant that 'the coast is clear for bargains' (Aslet, 2009), and 'the revival at the top-end has not faltered' with the volume of sales in a 'bumper summer' reportedly better in 2009 than in 2007 (Maciejowska, 2009).

Actual view from terrace of garden duplex

3.8 Ocean Point and terrace view (source: Coastal Partnerships, with permission of John Goodman)

Overall, there are complex overlaps between regional housing markets, with demand for commuting, retirement homes and second homes by the sea, as well as pockets of deprivation and decay. Some areas have faced busts and booms, or both simultaneously in places near each other. A study by English Heritage chronicled the history of English seaside resorts and argued that 'instead of seeing the seaside resort as being in decline, it may be more accurate to consider it as being in transition' (Brodie and Winter, 2007: 183). It concluded that 'whatever challenges face the seaside resort in the future, it will always retain a special place in this island nation's affection' (op. cit.: 186). This is an unfolding story with many twists and turns yet to come.

Many coastal and country areas represent extreme cases of gentrification with planning having constituted a tool of social exclusion. Gallent *et al.* (2005: 130–1) argued that the 'classic' British second homes problem has arisen from a combination of factors. Strathspey in the Scottish Highlands was a 'classic example of the British second home problem' with high-earning incomers including retirees buying properties, plus other dwellings purchased to let to holidaymakers plus growing numbers of dwellings used as second homes (loc. cit.). Their comment that second homes were 'the manifestation of a problem created fundamentally by the planning system' (loc. cit.) echoed Newby's (1979) view that second homes were particularly resented even though they are rarely the only or prime cause of house prices increasing beyond the reach of local working people.

Case study: 'Fishermen take on townies' – the dispute over a new jetty in Helford, Cornwall

In some cases, second home owners in rural areas use the planning system to protect their investment and define their chosen rural or seaside retreat as scenery to be left untouched by others, for example the proposal to construct a small jetty to accommodate the needs of the local artisanal fishing industry at the village of Helford in Cornwall. Cornwall was described as the 'second homes capital' of Britain in a BBC press release, which noted that they comprise 25 per cent of the properties in some parishes (BBC Press Office, 2009). The council area where this dispute occurred, Kerrier District Council, contained around 1,400 second homes overall in 2007 but they only represented around 3 per cent of all dwellings in the district.

The proposal to construct an access road and jetty for fishermen generated intense controversy locally and was reported nationally as 'Fishermen take on townies' (Alderson and Fleet, 2003). Helford had figured in the Daphne Du Maurier novel *Fishermen's Creek*. It is within the designated Cornwall AONB, beside Helford Creek on the southern side of the Helford River (which is actually a 'ria' or drowned river valley). The fishermen claimed they needed a jetty to launch their boats and bring in their catches. The proposal was accepted by the local parish council, despite strong opposition by the Helford Village Society (HVS). Kerrier District Council granted planning permission in January 2008 for an access road leading to a new jetty, despite continuing opposition from the HVS and Cornwall CPRE. But the HVS initiated a judicial review that resulted in the planning permission being quashed in the High Court in March 2009 (*Plymouth Herald*, 2009a).

About 40 per cent of the houses in the village were occupied permanently, with the remainder evenly split between second homes and holiday lets. Some reports depicted this dispute as 'outsiders' versus 'locals', or rich second home owners from London versus downtrodden hard-working Cornish residents. But some facts were unclear or in dispute. The HVS was frequently claimed to be dominated by second home owners, driven by a few dominant activists, but some permanent residents also opposed the proposal and many second home owners had long family associations with the village.

An objective observer has difficulty establishing the facts of the jetty debate, let alone judging the merits of the alternative cases. But feelings were strongly articulated. One celebrity with connections to the area, Roger Knight, drummer of the rock band Queen, sided with the fishermen and a Facebook site supporting the fishermen's proposal gathered over 8,000 supporters. Attitudes and interests often were painted in black and white and a typical comment expressed outrage 'that the people who do not live in the area can have such a profoundly damaging effect on local industry' (*Plymouth Herald*, 2009b). By way of contrast, Cornwall CPRE received many comments supporting HVS and CPRE opposition to the proposal. The CPRE posted an HVS press release after the court decision in March 2009, claiming that 'the dominant industry in the area is tourism', that a 'tragic mistake' had been avoided and that an alternative arrangement could be made to meet the fishermen's needs. The chairman of the HVS claimed 'Everybody who knows Helford and this part of Cornwall and who cares about the future of this wonderful part of the World will be very pleased that his Honour Judge Michael Kay QC has quashed the Helford Jetty planning permission.' However, the local MP, Andrew George, was quoted as regretting the court decision to overturn the planning consent and stated his continuing support of the fishermen (*Plymouth Herald*, 2009a).

This dispute may develop further, with more legal action and argument. Kerrier District Council was abolished in April 2009 when Cornwall County Council became a unitary authority, so new players will become involved. The point of this case study is to illustrate the kinds of issues affecting places in Britain where the planning system can be used to stop development proposed by local primary producers or permanent residents, to maintain environments and scenery valued by second home owners and others investing in and consuming the post-productivist countryside. I was also struck by the unseen actors who passed almost unmentioned: the owners of rental holiday homes in the village. There were about as many holiday homes as second homes in Helford, yet holiday homes owners did not receive the criticism directed at second home owners, nor were they reported to be active participants in this dispute.

Whereas this dispute had been fought out in peaceful ways, the growth of second home ownership has been violently opposed at times by self-proclaimed nationalist groups. Second home owners in rural Wales were vilified by militant locals and supposedly English-owned second homes were fire-bombed by the Welsh nationalist movement Meibion Glyndŵr between 1979 and the early 1990s, though a Plaid Cymru MP reportedly claimed that the fire bombings were orchestrated by security forces to discredit nationalists (http://news.bbc.co.uk/1/hi/wales/4084013.stm). More recently UK newspapers reported that a self-styled Cornish National Liberation Army had defined celebrity chefs Rick Stein and Jamie Oliver as 'legitimate targets' (Morris, 2007). At the time of writing, however, no attacks have been reported.

Diversification of second home ownership in Britain

There has been substantial diversification of second home ownership in Britain during the last 30 years resulting in a varied array of second homes, ranging from the humblest old caravan through to luxurious new mansions. Caravans changed from minority items to mass consumption for rent and ownership. New forms of mobile and static prefabricated dwellings have become widespread, often carefully packaged and marketed for different market segments, with many complex overlaps between housing and leisure markets. New planned developments cater for upmarket second home ownership within high quality landscaped settings based on principles of ecological sustainability with stunning architect-designed houses and apartments. All of these developments have been influenced by the British planning and land-use classification system as well as the usual factors of growing affluence and mobility.

Planning has influenced the location of many developments, especially through prioritising the reuse of 'brownfield' sites and replacement of former buildings with similar types of building. In many instances, planning policies relating to the extraction of sand and gravel in river valleys produced sites that combine two desirable characteristics: they have 'brownfield' status as former 'industrial' areas, and are likely to obtain planning permission for development, and their physical characteristics and locations provide opportunities for regeneration as attractive settings of mixed woodland and lakes. Growing affluence has enabled a wider range of households to acquire second homes and the increased mobility of household members enables them routinely to enjoy the pleasures of weekends and holidays by the coast or in the countryside.

Most studies of second homes have little to say about caravans or camping, though Hall and Müller (2004b) defined them as 'semi-mobile' second homes. Fully mobile forms of camping or the use of caravans towed behind vehicles do not overlap with housing markets. Likewise, caravan parks owned by individuals or companies, where caravans or cabins are let to holidaymakers on a short-term basis, are part of leisure and tourist provision, rather than housing. One distinctive, popular British invention, beach 'chalets' or 'huts' (see Figure 3.9), of which there are around 25,000, are widely distributed in seaside areas but local authorities typically prohibit overnight use so these are day shelters, not second homes (Ferrey, 2008, 2009). Due to their relative scarcity and desirable locations, however, some fetch handsome prices. For example, one on Mudeford beach in Dorset was reported to have sold for £145,000 in 2004 (Lewis, 2004). *The Independent* reported on 1 April 2009 that a beach hut in West Bexington, Dorset, had been sold for £345,000. This may have been an April fool's joke, but in August 2009 huts definitely were on

3.9 Beach huts and caravans by the Norfolk coast (source: Natural England)

sale at Beach Hut World for prices ranging from £3,700 (sold) to £130,000 (http://www.beachhutworld.com/searchHuts.asp).

Many distinctions between dwelling types and their use are not at all clear-cut in practice. For example, Irish Travellers use caravans permanently as their homes albeit often moving them to different sites. People in many countries live on a long-term basis in caravan parks, some by choice and preference, and others for want of any other option: in these cases the caravans are their homes. There is no difference in law between mobile homes and caravans in Britain. Mobile homes are the permanent residences of many thousands of people, especially in substantial 'parks' designed for use by retired or semi-retired people, though these are not classified as 'permanent dwellings' or listed in national building statistics.

The term 'park homes' is defined as 'mobile homes used for residential purposes'; the DCLG describes park homes as 'a unique type of tenure' with specific legislation determining relations between park owners and users. The legislation applies only to 'protected sites' and excludes sites where planning permission or site licences are granted for holiday use only. Park home residents own their dwellings but pay a monthly pitch fee; they have security of tenure subject to continuing to meet the terms and conditions of their agreements with the park owners. Park homes vary enormously; some are virtually indistinguishable from traditionally built bungalows but others are more like caravans (http://www.communities.gov.uk/housing/buyingselling/parkmobile). Some park owners provide specialist permanent accommodation for retired and semi-retired people. Berkeleyparks 'the UK's largest park operator' has parks in all southern English coastal counties from Suffolk to Gloucestershire, and many other locations in England and Wales (http://www.berkeleyparks.co.uk). Homes in these parks come under the park home legislation and are often priced well over £100,000. Although primarily retirement parks, properties could be and probably are used as second homes by older people wanting hassle-free holiday homes in relatively secure environments; this possibility opens up future research opportunities.

Caravans were rare and expensive luxury items in the 1930s and caravan parks were unknown (Brodie and Winter, 2007). Caravan ownership grew rapidly after 1945, extending to all social classes, associated with widening car ownership and affluence. Only 2,500 caravans had been produced in 1939 compared to 65,000 a year in the mid-1960s (op. cit.). Caravan parks also grew with hundreds of thousands of vans available to rent. The Camping and Caravanning Club grew from 51,000 members in 1960 to over 300,000 in 1999 (op. cit.), with over 4,000 diverse places to camp in 2009 as well as self-catering facilities for rent (http://www.campingandcaravanningclub.co.uk). The growth of caravan ownership and parks became regulated in 1960 by the Caravan Sites and Control of Development Act. Large caravan parks were widespread by the 1960s, though their image was more of working class holidays than upmarket second homes. Brodie and Winter (2007) noted that caravans and chalets comprised 90 per cent of the 120,000 holiday bed spaces available on the Lincolnshire coast in the late 1980s. In 2009, hundreds of thousands of caravans, cabins and other mobile and semi-mobile structures provide holiday homes for mass consumption from the most basic old vans to new, expensive luxurious forms of accommodation

Caravan and mobile home parks are substantial land users in many British coastal areas. These sites are part of land markets, albeit subject to planning regulation, if conceptually not part of 'housing' markets as they are a different class of planning land use than residential land. Some caravan park owners seek to have their sites reclassified as residential sites: if successful this could increase the site value significantly. Many caravan parks provide both rental caravans for holidaymakers and 'pitches' where caravans towed behind powered vehicles can be based for varying periods of time. There has been rapid growth in the use of motorised vehicles as mobile homes, typically called 'motorhomes' or 'camper vans' in the UK and RVs in the USA. Many RVs have all of the conveniences of a modern American home and carry a small car or other form of transport for use when the RV is settled onto a pitch for an extended period of time. Some RVs serve as permanent but travelling homes for affluent households with no fixed locational ties (McHugh, 2006).

Caravan parks have become big business. Some large companies control much of the industry, offering holiday rentals and purchase of a diverse range of units in many locations across Britain and overseas. Hundreds of other caravan parks are small businesses run by individual proprietors. There is much overlapping ownership of leisure-related and housing businesses with complex relationships between owners of rental holiday accommodation and developers and sellers of caravans and lodges. Some companies have extensive ownership of parks whereas other industry organisations are purely letting agents. It might need a forensic accountant to identify all of the overlaps! One large company, Parkdean Holidays, has 24 parks across Britain, especially in South West England (http://www.parkdeanholidays. co.uk). Such proprietors provide a diverse range of options, from relatively cheap second-hand static caravans through to luxurious 'lodges' costing over £200,000. Purchasers of caravans and lodges can avail of property management services to generate rental income from their investments.

Product marketing is oriented to different income groups and market niches: caravans tend to be called 'holiday homes' with more upmarket 'lodges' listed separately (http://www.lodges.co.uk). The lodges are situated in attractive 'locations' usually within woodland settings, in or near high amenity areas: the terms 'parks' or 'sites' are not used, perhaps to distinguish 'locations' from caravan parks. Most lodges are finished to a high standard and look just like permanent dwellings. The 'locations' offer many features including 24-hour security systems, gated entrances and a range of leisure facilities, including swimming pools, clubs and restaurants. The advertisement for 'Trehawks', emphasising ownership of lodges, is typical of developments in many locations across Britain:

Fall in love with life again when you buy your very own holiday lodge at Trehawks, Cornwall. This exclusive new development provides the ultimate retreat, designed for luxury living and making memories… Indulge in yourself with your own stunning lodge at Trehawks.

(http://www.lodges.co.uk/our-locations.htm#trehawks)

Lodges in Trehawks were for sale in 2009 from £170,000 for the two-bedroom 'Heritage Glade' models to £195,000 for a two-bedroom 'Wessex Colonial' lodge. This is clearly a form of second home ownership, with tenure reportedly guaranteed for the 40-year lease period, but the dwellings are not available for use all year, and the land remains in the ownership of the park proprietors.

Hoseasons, a large leisure company, provides a variety of self-catering holidays in the UK and overseas in parks, lodges, cottages and boats (http://www.hoseasons.co.uk). Hoseasons does not sell caravans and lodges, but one development where it markets holiday lodges for rental is Kenwick Park in Lincolnshire. Holiday lodges for sale at 'The Woods' in Kenwick Park are marketed through another business, Kenwick Park Estate, which has its own website showing Scandinavian-style wooden lodges in a woodland setting. The development is associated with a 'first class family run country park hotel' with a restaurant and health and leisure club available to lodge purchasers. Holiday lodges at Kenwick Woods are also available for rental from various holiday rental providers, including Hoseasons (http://www.hoseasons.co.uk/lodges/), whose website also features the golf course and leisure facilities and emphasises the location within the Lincolnshire Wolds AONB.

Hawkins (2008) reported that the growing holiday lodge industry had an annual spend of £375 million in 2008; most customers were 'over-50s who have low debt ands and want a hassle-free holiday property within easy reach of home' (op. cit.). Prefabrication of parts and whole lodges is a routine part of this business, with on-site assembly rather than construction using traditional building methods. Many lodges are much larger than recent urban housing developments. At the Repton Lodge development near Harrogate in Yorkshire, 21 lodges in a gated park included 1,100 square foot two-bedroom, two-bathroom dwellings 'bigger than many a London flat' (op. cit.). One lodge type cost £275,000, including site fees for the first year and membership of a golf club and spa and heath club (op. cit.).

The development of luxury holiday home 'lodges' has been part of the diversification of second home provision in Britain, with their status as leisure/tourism developments often being the key to obtaining planning permission. They are rarely in national parks but are often in AONBs or areas adjacent to protected areas. Many developments are on 'brownfield' sites that previously had been used for the extraction of sand and gravel, usually in river valleys where mining below the water table had resulted in the creation of lakes known as 'gravel pits'. The reuse of these former mining sites by leisure industries is considered beneficial by local authorities and planners as potential eyesores and hazardous areas are turned into attractive landscaped leisure facilities.

Some developments are specifically oriented to particular leisure pursuits. For example, *Angling Times* of 4 August 2009 contained a number of advertisements around the theme of owning your own holiday home by fishing lakes. Cosgrove Park in Milton Keynes, Buckinghamshire, and 7 Lakes Country Park in North Lincolnshire both offered lakeside holiday homes from 'only £9,995'. Waveney Valley Lakes advertised caravans and lodges with photographs of large carp and catfish, both highly prized by British anglers who return their catches live to the water rather than eating them (to the mystification of many European visitors). White Acres Country Park in Cornwall, part of the Parkdean group, offered '13 lakes in your back garden' and brand new 'luxury holiday homes' from £17,495.

From industrial wastelands to luxury second homes in the Cotswolds Water Park

Some second home developments in areas of disused gravel pits have been much more upmarket, especially in the Cotswolds Water Park (http://www.waterpark.org). This is not a designated national park or AONB, but was formed by local authorities to manage and coordinate development within the upper Thames catchment area that had been extensively changed as a result of sand and gravel mining.

Lower Mill Estate (LME) is a prestigious development of luxurious second homes in a private estate with abundant wildlife (Pearman, 2007). The LME chairman was reported to suggest 'It's not a property development, it's an art project' (op. cit.). Standards of construction are very high and environmental considerations underpin the whole development. European beavers were reintroduced into the Thames tributary running through the estate, followed by the birth of Britain's first beaver kits for over 500 years (http://www.lowermillestate.com/video/video_beaver.html).

LME is marketed in major national newspapers under the slogan 'Less than 2 hours from London. But a million miles away.' The houses have been designed by a team of architects led by 'RIBA award-winning master-planner, Richard Reid'. In July 2009 the website emphasised the synthesis of modern and traditional materials, a 'fusion of steel, glass, Cotswold stone, and ancient English oaks' (http://www.lowermillestate.com/property-sales.html). In August 2009 new architect-designed homes were advertised in *The Sunday Times* (Lower Mill Estate, 2009): 'With prices from £395,000 to £1.5 million you are sure to find the second home of your dreams.' These are delightful buildings in an attractive setting with high environmental standards, but the idea of spending £395,000 on a second home, let alone £1.5 million, is beyond the dreams of most people! Resale properties ranged from £235,000 for a 'three-bedroom detached cottage' to £735,000 for an exclusive barn-style property beside one of the lakes evocatively named called 'Howells Mere'. Like some holiday lodge developments, properties on LME are owned on a leasehold basis, but as leases are for 999 years this may just be to ensure consistency of design and use.

Pearman (2007) noted that the planning permission had been granted on the condition that these second homes may not be used all year round as permanent residences, and that LME closes for the whole of January. But the distinction between 'permanent residences' and 'second homes' barely applies where affluent households own multiple dwellings in various places, and there does not appear to be any reason why owners should not use these dwellings most of the rest of the year, and retreat in January, for example, to a pied-à-terre in Bristol or ski lodge in Switzerland. House prices at LME are such that it is almost inconceivable that purchasers are unable to organise themselves or their time in ways to get round planning regulations relating to residential periods. It is also inconceivable that any would ever want to remain at LME year after year without ever venturing away for a few weeks here or a couple of months there. Recent purchases included an 'innovative eco-friendly home' for £7.2 million; 'the cost works out at £3,000 per square foot – double that of homes in Beverly Hills and Manhattan' (Pierce, 2008). There even were reports of a £250,000 architect-designed house commissioned for two dogs, adjoining the house being built for their mistress, reportedly a surgeon who wished to remain anonymous (Salkeld, 2008).

One journalist described LME as an emerging segment of the second home market: 'the new weekenders' who formed a new kind of 'community' in this purpose-built environment (Margolis, 2008). He described residents as 'sophisticated but nice middle Englanders, bankers, lawyers, senior corporate types and their families' who appreciated the exclusivity of the development and the fact that everybody was a second home owner, unlike in existing villages 'where your neighbours hate you' (Margolis, 2008: 33) (Figure 10). A sense of the kind of 'community' that may be created in some developments was given by one resident in a holiday village located between Blackpool and the Lake District: 'with the prices here you know you're not going to get rubbish moving in next door' (Margolis, 2008: 36).

Margolis reported other developments near to LME 'each seemingly targeting a distinct segment of the urban middle class and each selling community as a major part of its offering' (Margolis, 2008: 35). The company Watermark claimed to be 'the most established second home developer in the Cotswolds' with a wide range of dwellings and lifestyle features (http://www.watermarkclub.co.uk). The Lakes, being developed by Yoo Design Studio, featured interior designs by Jade Jagger, daughter of rock legend Mick Jagger. Prices started from £775,000 in August 2009 (http://www.thelakesbyyoo.com). This 650-acre private estate is marketed with an emphasis on nature: 'Nature is always perfect and the way yoo [sic] spend time in it should be too.' Its website emphasised how sailing, fishing and riding are allocated their own part of the landscape where 'treehouses, river meadows and woodland walks are all natural scenery'. (What on earth is a 'natural' tree house?!)

3.10 The 'new weekenders' at Lower Mill Estate (source: Muir Vidler, with permission)

The surrounding locality is also sold as part of the package, with an emphasis on organic producers, old pubs and traditional artisanal industries including glass blowing and saddle makers.

The area now known as the Cotswold Water Park had been developed for mineral extraction and so it was literally a disused mining site. Such developments, therefore, have not involved gentrification of existing housing, nor have they displaced local residents. However, the Cotswolds is listed in the Halifax Rural House Price index as one of the most expensive housing areas of England, with very high house price to income ratios. LME and The Lakes are examples of further diversification of second homes development within the changing British countryside. They depend partly on the detailed rules and regulations of the planning system but crucially on high levels of affluence and mobility of households whose incomes are generated far away. They are unambiguously post-productivist parts of the countryside where concepts of 'nature', 'community' and 'the Cotswolds' are commodified selling points for second homes in managed and landscaped environments, combining world-class design, building and management skills to create private, gated enclaves for leisure and tourist consumption: uniquely British manifestations of the urge for hyper-consumption.

Planning and British second homes

The British land-use planning system permeates the diversification of second home ownership, interacting with conscious and clever actors in many private sector businesses, including manufacturers and developers, to affect dwellings types, tenure categories and locations. Restrictions on new development in attractive areas have been a major driver of the gentrification of coastal and country villages; restrictions on additional development encourage gentrification and maintain monopoly pricing effects in desirable areas.

In places where new forms of diverse second homes development have occurred, many legal categories and definitions of 'holiday' or other restrictions on use of dwellings are unrelated to the capacities of affluent households to organise and manage their use of dwellings, space and time. Some planning conditions appear virtually unenforceable in theory, let alone in practice. Do local planners really have the capacity for continuous monitoring and surveillance of how people use their houses and apartments? Would councils actually take enforcement action against affluent people who decide to retire to an apartment that they have owned for many years but which has a planning condition saying it should only be used for holidays? The answers are obvious, except to planners who appear to believe in blueprint planning for an unchanging world occupied by people who are incapable of finding ways round absurd bureaucratic social engineering!

In theory purchasers of lodges or caravans on many developments should use them only as holiday homes, and they are asked to provide evidence of another residential address at the time of purchase. But in practice there is little or nothing to stop people from using them as their 'primary' home and spending a few weeks away on holiday or visiting relatives during the time the park is closed. Indeed, a household could own one of these lodges as well as an apartment in Spain and use them alternately depending on the season; in such cases, neither would fit neatly into a 'primary' and 'second' home classification, thus marking perfectly how leisure and housing markets can overlap and morph one into each other.

Northern Ireland: second homes and a housing boom in 'a place apart'

Home ownership had grown steadily in Northern Ireland since the 1960s, boosted by the sale of public housing after 1980, but house prices remained low in the early 1990s. The growth of home ownership continued during the 1990s, accompanied by extensive suburbanisation with a large proportion of new dwellings comprising

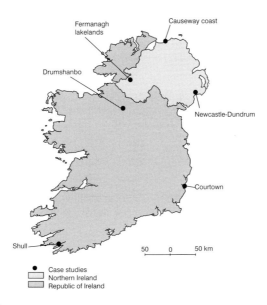

3.11 Second homes case study areas in Ireland (source Michelle Norris, with permission)

single detached homes in the countryside: a pattern of growth unlike anywhere else in the UK.

Second home ownership also grew strongly in Northern Ireland after the early 1990s as rising incomes and buoyant housing markets led to increased demand for second homes used as holiday homes, weekend cottages or as investments. But there was also growing community action by residents groups opposing further developments, especially in the Causeway Coast area, named after the iconic Giant's Causeway (Paris, 2007b, 2008b). Residents groups campaigning against second homes development were joined by environmental organisations and local politicians. Some people objected to the visual impacts of second homes but residents groups argued that escalating house and land values were forcing young locals to leave the area to find more affordable housing. The groups claimed that second home owners bought most new housing in some areas as well as most second-hand houses coming on the market in other areas. They were also concerned about developers buying existing dwellings and replacing them with higher density expensive new houses or apartments aimed at the second home market. They argued that the falling number of permanent residents had resulted in the closure of shops, schools and services, turning coastal settlements into 'ghost towns' for much of the year.

These concerns became sufficiently politicised that the NIHE contracted a study of the growth, impact and policy implications of second homes (Paris, 2007b, 2008b). The research ran from early 2006 to the end of 2007 involving a range of

79

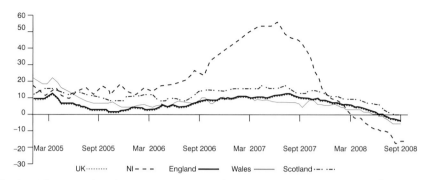

3.12 UK house price changes, 2005–2009 (source: NIHE *Housing Resarch Bulletin*, adapted from original DCLG data)

research methods: literature review; analysis of secondary data; surveys of second home ownership overall within Northern Ireland and of second home owners and residents in 'hot spot' areas of high second home ownership (see Figure 3.11); and semi-structured interviews with actors involved in the issue (estate agents, government, planning and housing officials, local government officials and elected representatives).

Second home ownership in Northern Ireland grew within a distinctive context, with a pattern of housing development unique within the UK, both generally and specifically with second homes. Northern Ireland has been 'a place apart' socially and politically from the rest of the UK and from the Republic of Ireland since partition in 1921 (Murphy, 1978). Planning in Northern Ireland evolved separately from developments in Britain and the Republic, in effect very similar to the Republic up to the 1990s, with urban and regional development much less tightly regulated than in Britain. That changed significantly from the late 1990s as the planning regime became increasingly similar to the British model. There was also a housing boom from the mid-1990s, similar in many ways to Britain, culminating in a house and land price 'spike' between 2005 and 2007, followed by rapid falls in house and land prices, shown clearly in Figure 3.12. Although this sequence was similar to the British experience, it was the first housing boom in Northern Ireland and the first dramatic post-boom retrenchment.

The housing market recession in Northern Ireland after mid-2007 was due partly to the credit crunch, as in Britain, and has clear parallels with the Republic of Ireland, where large stocks of new homes remained unsold in 2009 and house prices have fallen by over 20 per cent. But it also reflected a local housing market that had spiralled out of any relationship between incomes, demographics and prices, with an investment surge pushing prices out of the reach of first time buyers as investors anticipated large capital gains and growing demand from migrant workers and others dependent on rental housing.

Second homes on the Causeway Coast: background and context

The Causeway Coast AONB is one of many protected areas in the UK, but the Giant's Causeway and Causeway Coast is also a UNESCO World Heritage Site. The spectacular cliffs and bays, the Giant's Causeway itself, and many attractive beaches remain central to the area's appeal to permanent residents, visitors and second home buyers. Other attractions include golf courses and historic and cultural sites. Our study focused on four coastal settlements within Coleraine Borough Council, Castlerock, Portstewart, Portrush and Portballintrae, plus nearby Bushmills (Figures 3.13–3.15). Coleraine Borough Council coordinated a forum known as the Balanced Communities Review Group, involving representatives of residents groups, local and central government agency officials, councillors and other interested parties; members of the research team attended and participated in its meetings for over two years.

There have been many changes in the socio-economic and demographic character of the Causeway Coast over the last 150 years. Small farming and fishing settlements in Portrush and Portstewart changed in the nineteenth century with growing seaside leisure and tourism. The tourist industry declined from the 1950s in common with other fading seaside resorts in the UK and Ireland, with a modest revival occurring since the mid-1990s partly due to the more relaxed post-Troubles environment (Boyd, 2000). However, many hotels and guest houses have closed in the coastal

3.13 The Giants Causeway, Co. Antrim (source: NIHE)

3.14 Portrush from White Rocks (source: NIHE)

3.15 Portstewart Harbour (source: NIHE)

settlements to be been replaced mainly with new houses or apartments marketed to second home buyers. Bushmills was an industrial village with tourist trade in the nineteenth century; most of the industry has long gone, though Bushmills Irish whiskey and distillery continue to enjoy a global reputation. The smaller coastal settlements, Castlerock and Portballintrae, barely grew until the 1960s.

The population of the Causeway Coast was boosted from the 1960s by the establishment of a new university at Coleraine, with many staff buying homes locally, and also retiree migration. In the 1990s, however, the populations of Portballintrae and Bushmills were falling. There is a strong ethno-religious dimension in the Causeway Coast, with very high proportions of Protestants recorded in the 2001 census: especially in Portballintrae and Bushmills (97 per cent), though Portstewart is generally considered to be a 'mixed' settlement.

Early second home ownership in the area from the 1930s comprised vernacular building with 'small ramshackle holiday homes often converted from coach bodies', though many were removed in the 1950s (Carter, 1982). There was rapid growth in officially approved caravan sites and in the number of caravans after the Caravan Act 1963 (op. cit). Growing concern was expressed in the 1980s as existing buildings were purchased for use as second homes and the first apartment blocks were developed. In its review of coastal second homes the Town and Country Planning Service (1991) noted that 'public opposition was strongest when apartments were proposed with an anticipated end use as second homes'. The review aimed to resist conversion of hotels and guest houses but appreciated that planners had no powers to stop dwellings being used as second homes or to require that only local permanent residents may acquire dwellings. The number of second homes in the area had doubled during the 1980s to nearly 1,000 in 1989, growing to over 1,400 in 2001 (Planning Service, 2003). Despite the growth of second homes, the number of dwellings occupied permanently increased by 30 per cent between 1984 and 2001 (op. cit.).

The Planning Service (2003) considered that planning controls should relate to 'demonstrable physical considerations', aim to deter developments that were out of character in their proposed settings and indicate areas where there would be 'a strong presumption against approval for apartments'. The Draft Northern Area Plan indicated separate zones where redevelopment for apartments was likely to be approved. The plan also indicated proposed new housing numbers for the settlements, together with tight development limits for expansion. By the time of our fieldwork in 2006, however, new building levels had been much higher than anticipated and there was strong continuing demand from developers for greenfield sites as well as redevelopment opportunities for apartments and houses.

University of Ulster academic Stephen Boyd had conducted a survey in the area in 2005 that included questions about permanent residents' attitudes towards second home ownership. Boyd's respondents tended to be largely older homeowners and retirees, compared to the census age and tenure profile of the area, so their attitudes may reflect the characteristics of this group more than the population as a whole. Even so, a very large majority (72 per cent) thought that the level of second homes development was a bad thing and were against further development of second homes. Around two thirds of respondents had moved into the area from outside; many before second homes were seen as a local issue and others moved in while second home ownership also was increasing. Thus in-migration by 'permanent residents' was itself a major factor in changing the area.

Local house price changes could not be explored perfectly as no data were available at that scale. The University of Ulster/Bank of Ireland House Price Index is disaggregated into 14 regional areas, with the Causeway Coast area included within the 'Coleraine/Limavady/North Coast' (CLNC). Average house prices in the CLNC were around the Northern Ireland average between 1994 and 2002 but increased to 10 per cent above the average in 2006, partly because many new dwellings in the CLNC area were large and highly specified. The CLNC had the second highest regional house prices at the end of 2007. The recorded pattern of change in house prices in the CLNC area was consistent with comments from participants in the semi-structured interviews who saw a step change in the rate of increases after 2001 (see below). But rapid growth in house prices was widespread across Northern Ireland, thus local developments in 2006 and 2007 were also consistent with overall trends.

There has been substantial growth in the number and proportion of second homes but there was also an increase in the number of dwellings occupied on a permanent basis during the 1990s (Planning Service, 2003), so the evidence did not support the residents groups' contention that the settlements were becoming ghost towns. They were certainly changing, but only partly through the effects of growing second home ownership; other changes included growth of the working residential population, many of whom commute to Coleraine, in situ retirement of previous in-migrants, in-migration by other retirees and gradually falling average household size. Changes since 2001, therefore, occurred within an area that already had been changing rather than impacting on a stable and unchanging set of local communities.

Second home owners and the local housing market

The survey of second home owners on the Causeway Coast in 2006 achieved its quota of 100 completed interviews (see Paris, 2007b). Sampling was based on local knowledge of areas of high incidence of second home ownership and investigation of homes in those areas in order to identify and interview second home owners. The questionnaire identified household characteristics of second home owners, how and why they acquired the property, when they purchased and how much they paid, their use of local services, local social networks, the likelihood of acquiring additional leisure residences, and details of their other or primary home. The researchers also interviewed residents groups, local authority officers, local officials from the Housing Executive and Planning Service, and local estate agents; a version of the interview schedule was also sent to developers and their responses were included in the overall analysis (Paris, 2007b, 2008a). These interviews enabled in-depth exploration of many issues indicated in quantitative data sources.

The survey showed that second home owners were an affluent group, with substantial housing assets and high incomes. Their primary homes were estimated to be worth well above the Northern Ireland average of £170,000 in mid-2006: 60 per cent estimated their main homes to be worth over £250,000. They considered that their second homes had increased in value considerably since purchase, especially after 2001. Over half of the stated household incomes were more than twice the Northern Ireland average. Very few had used equity from their main homes to purchase second homes. Sixty per cent owned their second homes outright. Sixteen per cent had more than one 'second' home and a third were contemplating buying more, especially overseas.

Many second home owners were strongly attached to the area. They made regular use of their second homes and had local networks of friends and relatives who had second homes or lived permanently nearby. They shopped locally and used local services, especially bars and restaurants, as well as golf and other leisure facilities. These findings correspond with the literature on place attachment and suggest that these second home owners could be seen as 'occasional locals' more than outsiders. Most had purchased second homes to use for weekends and holidays, with other main reasons being as an investment and for future retirement.

The survey revealed clear evidence of displacement of permanent residents. One third of these second homes previously had been owner-occupied or rented; half had been purchased new, often following redevelopment of dwellings that had been occupied on a permanent basis. The demographic characteristics of households in second homes contrasted strongly with the permanent residents in Boyd's survey. Most second home owners were family or couple households of working age. Overall they were significantly younger, there were more of working age and the household size was significantly larger than permanent residents. Second home owners were also predominantly Protestants (88 per cent) or 'mixed' religion households.

Responses to the semi-structured interviews identified a 'step change' in the local housing market around 2001–2002. Respondents said that most new dwellings were bought by investors or second home owners. Older dwellings coming onto the market typically were purchased by second home owners or developers, with developers especially active near seafront locations. Many respondents referred to the local plan showing where permission would be likely for apartment development; the residents group called it a 'developer's charter'. The only strong opposition to second homes was voiced by the residents groups; other respondents saw a more nuanced picture with second home owners contributing to the local economy, and with little that could be done to limit further second home ownership.

The research findings sharpened an image of the area that had been formed from the literature review and secondary data analysis: growing second home ownership was not affecting a static market, but was one factor interacting with other changes, including the impact of the university, retirement migration and growth of commuting. There were certainly signs of a feeding frenzy among developers during 2006, with escalating land and house prices, but the Causeway Coast was not alone in that regard.

Other 'hot-spots': Newcastle, Co. Down and the Fermanagh Lakelands

The second phase of research in 2007 involved desk research and fieldwork in two other second homes 'hot spots': Newcastle (see Figures 3.16 and 3.17) and Dundrum, in Co. Down and the area around Enniskillen known as the Fermanagh Lakelands (Paris, 2008b). It was impossible to achieve the target of 100 interviews with second home owners in these cases, so responses were indicative rather than representative of a wider population. The views of permanent residents about second homes were explored through local surveys, with an achieved quota of 100 in Newcastle–Dundrum but only 53 in Fermanagh.

3.16 Newcastle, Co. Down, by the Mourne Mountains (source: NIHE)

3.17 Seafront, Newcastle, Co. Down (source: NIHE)

Like the Causeway Coast, Newcastle–Dundrum had a tradition of leisure and tourism, with caravan parks, guest houses and some hotels. Growing concerns had been expressed locally about increased second home ownership, though not as strongly as on the Causeway Coast. Newcastle had experienced significant inward migration by retirees, and strong demand for commuter housing, as it is relatively near the main Belfast labour market. There are strong planning constraints in Newcastle, partly because of natural physical features, but like the Causeway settlements any expansion had become limited by the new planning emphasis on reusing brownfield land and containing settlements within their 'urban footprint'. Newcastle was experiencing its first wave of pressure for private redevelopment both for the general market and second homes. Some local complaints concerned the redevelopment of seafront property with a large apartment block that appeared to be owned by people who visited rarely, if at all. During the fieldwork, moreover, a caravan park was being redeveloped for housing, signifying the changing relations between housing and leisure markets.

The context and geography was very different in Co. Fermanagh, with low housing densities and a high proportion of detached dwellings scattered across the countryside, including second homes (Figures 3.18 and 3.19) . This partly reflects the agricultural base of the local economy and the relatively permissive planning system that operated into the late 1990s. There has been very little redevelopment apart from small schemes in Enniskillen, as well as infill including Portara Wharf development marketed to second home owners (Figure 3.20). Virtually all respondents in semi-

3.18 A second home in Ballinamallard, Co. Fermanagh (source: NIHE)

3.19 Second homes on Inishkeeragh, Co. Fermanagh Lakelands (source: Gardiner Mitchell)

3.20 Portara Wharf, Enniskillen, Co. Fermanagh (source: NIHE)

structured interviews were in favour of second home ownership and there was no sign of groups opposing the growth of second home ownership, though some permanent residents thought second home ownership boosted local house prices. Council officials and estate agents wanted more second home ownership as an antidote to the loss of jobs in traditional industries. One council official remarked 'it's better to have some people living in rural areas some of the time than to have no people living there all the time'. One estate agent went further: 'There aren't enough second homes! They haven't had an impact on the local market as yet. More would be good for the local economy.' Despite reporting strong investor activity in the local market, estate agents also noted in July 2007 that they were seeing the first signs of market slowdown.

The socio-economic characteristics of second home owners interviewed in these case studies were similar to those in the Causeway Coast: affluent homeowners with high incomes, mainly with families and still of working age rather than retirees, with many owning both their primary residences and their second homes outright, as well as further evidence of multiple ownership of 'second' homes and expectation of the purchase of more, again often overseas. As on the Causeway Coast, most second homes had been acquired after 2000 and owners reported high use of local shops and services. But there was little evidence of local social networks and less frequent use of second homes in these case studies than on the Causeway Coast.

Second home ownership more widely in Northern Ireland

The case studies of 'hot spots' provided valuable insights into changing second home ownership in Northern Ireland, but could not say anything about developments outside of those areas. The research therefore sought data comparable to the SEH material on second home ownership in England by placing a 'module' of questions into an omnibus survey carried out by the Northern Ireland Statistics and Research Agency (NISRA). Use of omnibus surveys has advantages and disadvantages. Positives include cost-effective access to large samples and cross-tabulations with other variables that are collected anyway. However, there is limited space available for specialist topics, it is impossible to change sampling methods and sample size means that there may be few respondents regarding minority issues.

The findings from the omnibus survey indicated a higher level of second home ownership than had been shown in earlier estimates (Paris, 2008b). We estimated that around 18,000 households owned second homes within Northern Ireland, and that another 10,000 or so were owned outside Northern Ireland. This estimate was considerably higher than the NIHE estimate of around 8,000 second homes based on the 2006 House Condition Survey; the difference may be due partly to sample error, but is consistent with the widely reported tendency for official studies to record unoccupied dwellings as 'vacant' when in fact they are used as second homes. There was a high level of expectation of future purchase of second homes both among households that already had at least one and from other households, including purchasing overseas. Existing second home owners matched the socio-economic profile of second home owners in the case studies: high incomes, a high level of outright ownership of second homes, with 20 per cent owning more than one 'second' home. Unlike the Causeway Coast, with its characteristic ethno-religious pattern, second home owners across Northern Ireland tended more to match the overall balance between Protestants and Catholics.

The reasons for acquiring second homes also matched those given in the case studies, though investment was emphasised more heavily. Overall use of second homes corresponded more with that reported in Newcastle–Dundrum and Fermanagh than the high usage on the Causeway Coast. This may reflect the number of second homes that were owned overseas, as these are less easy to use as regularly as places easily accessed by car. Small numbers of respondents also noted buying second homes as a base for commuting or for use by family members studying away from home. The study of second homes in Northern Ireland suggested that the rapid increase in outright ownership of main residences helped to explain the growth of second home ownership. This finding initially stimulated exploration of the significance of outright home ownership discussed in Chapter 1.

Second homes in Northern Ireland: growth, impact and policy implications

The research evidence showed that second home owners were much more affluent than the population as a whole, with substantial housing assets, and a high proportion of outright ownership of valuable primary and second homes. There was evidence of the ownership of multiple homes within Northern Ireland and, increasingly, overseas. The second homes have been purchased for the usual reasons identified elsewhere in the literature: to use for weekends and holidays, as investments and for future retirement. The omnibus survey data indicated a strong likelihood that official statistics had undercounted the number of second homes.

A number of variations emerged between the case studies, some in terms of the physical geography and natural limits such as flood-prone rivers; others resulted from the sizes of the areas selected and affected by increasingly tight planning restrictions on settlement growth and one-off housing in the countryside. The impact of planning also varied: in the Causeway Coast and Newcastle–Dundrum cases any settlement growth was restricted by the new planning regime, thus additional demand for second home homes increasingly had to be met by purchases within the existing stock or through redevelopment at higher densities. These constraints were absent in Fermanagh and abundant sites were available for development. In all three cases, though, second home owners appeared to be more like 'occasional locals' than 'outsiders'.

There were strong contrasts in terms of resident action groups: active and vocal on the Causeway Coast where residents groups saw the local plan as a 'developers' charter', growing in Newcastle–Dundrum, but absent in Fermanagh. The ethno-religious concentration and local social networks among second home owners were only significant on the Causeway Coast. The second home owners appeared to be more like 'occasional locals' than 'outsiders' in the case study areas. There was clear evidence of displacement of permanent residents on the Causeway Coast; it was emerging in Newcastle–Dundrum but again absent in Fermanagh, though there was evidence of in situ replacement of older, often abandoned dwellings with substantial modern new homes. Growing demand from second home owners and developers, however, meant that people moving out of the Causeway Coast often benefited from rising house and land prices and sold at a higher price than would otherwise have been the case. There was very little local industry and these were always leisure/pleasure, retirement and commuting settlements, so it hardly seems appropriate to conceptualise these developments as gentrification. Much of the opposition to second home ownership came from retirees, many of whom themselves had moved into the area, either some years early as commuters or just to retire.

Overall it was impossible to separate out the impact of growing second home ownership on local housing markets, as tighter planning restrictions on settlement growth had resulted in intensification of land use across Northern Ireland more

Table 3.3 Regional house prices 2003–2007, Northern Ireland case studies and comparators

	Average regional house prices[1] (£000)			Change during period Price change (%)	
	Q4 2003	Q2 2007	Q1 2009	2003–2007	2007–2009
Coleraine/Limavady/ North. Coast[2]	83.5	277.2	170.2	232	−39
Enniskillen/ Fermanagh/South Tyrone[3]	94.1	244.1	159.6	159	−35
Mid & South Down[4]	106.4	242.2	170.1	128	−30
Belfast	103.6	239.8	155.5	131	−35
Londonderry/Strabane	78.0	189.5	150.0	149	−30
Northern Ireland – all	99.8	240.4	156.9	141	−35

Source: *Northern Ireland Quarterly House Price Index*, various editions, University of Ulster/Bank of Ireland.
Notes:
1. House prices are in money terms not at constant prices.
2. Includes the Causeway Coast case study area.
3. Includes the Fermanagh Lakelands case study area.
4. Includes the Newcastle–Dundrum case study area.

generally and especially in high demand areas. The Regional Development Strategy had been almost wilfully blind to the demand implications of growing second home ownership; land allocation on the Causeway Coast and in the Newcastle–Dundrum areas did not even attempt to take this factor into account.

These findings were consistent with much of the wider literature on second homes. Growing second home ownership was not the only factor affecting the area's three case studies, but combined with other processes of change including retirement migration, leisure investment, counter-urbanisation and the general boom in house and land prices between 2003 and 2007. Table 3.3 shows that the overall growth in house prices from the end of 2003 to the peak of the boom in mid-2007 averaged 240 per cent across Northern Ireland and the subsequent fall over two years was around 35 per cent. The case studies were in the three regions with the highest growth in house prices between late 2003 and mid-2007 but the overall average was held down by lower increases in the North West (Londonderry and Strabane) and North Belfast: most other regions increased above the overall average. The area with the highest increase, which included the Causeway Coast, also recorded the largest fall between 2007 and 2009.

Unlike Britain, there had been strong growth in house building in Northern Ireland since the late 1990s. Completions grew from around 8,500 a year between

1997/98 and 1999/2000 to peak at almost 18,000 in 2006/07. This came to a shuddering halt in 2007: completions fell to 13,000 in 2007/08 and commencements tumbled from round 15,000 a year between 2005 and 2007 to 6,400 in 2008/09. The turbulent environment resulted in a dramatic fall in the volume of house sales and widespread price cutting. Some large building companies have gone bankrupt and NIHE research estimated that over 2,000 new homes remained unsold in July 2009 (Frey, 2009). The research on second homes had identified widespread expectations of further second home purchase, both among those with second homes and more generally in the population. If such growth should occur, given recent developments, it is likely to be in the longer rather than shorter term.

The Republic of Ireland: if we build them, they will come

> The demands of Ireland's upwardly mobile in their choice of holiday home is … soaring, along with the sums they are willing to spend on their get-a-way properties. 'If they're coming from Dalkey and they're living in some fabulous big house they will not slum it in a two-bed cottage', said Catherine O'Reilly of Sherry FitzGerald O'Reilly in Wicklow town.
>
> (O'Toole and Callen, 2008: 8)

> West Cork, Kerry, Donegal, Galway, Wicklow, Waterford and Wexford have long been favourites of Dublin's holidaymakers, with many of them snapping up property in areas such as Brittas Bay, Glengarriff, Dingle and Roundstone. In some cases, the second homes of these city dwellers are larger than their main properties – three or four-bedroom detached houses on at least an acre of land in a coastal location are quite typical holiday homes for many of Dublin's elite, who buy properties as second homes which locals would buy as their family homes.
>
> (Devane, 2008)

The Celtic Tiger boom brought enormous affluence to Ireland and its consequences are spread out across countryside and coast. The quotations above typify the ebullient Irish second homes scene at the height of the boom, though both were published shortly after the Tiger had begun to run out of steam. Around 300,000 second homes had been developed in the Republic of Ireland since the early 1990s. Some particularly large and luxurious examples were enjoyed by 'upwardly mobile' households; others were purchased from the open market, often constructed by small local builders. Many were built for people who had acquired a field somewhere and contracted a builder to construct the second home of their dreams.

93

But there was another side to this boom, hence the subtitle to this section – 'if we build them, they will come' – an amended version of a line in the fantasy movie *Field of Dreams* in which Iowa corn farmer Ray Kinsella hears a voice softly saying 'if you build it, he will come'. Ray thinks this means that he should build a baseball stadium to attract the unspecified 'him' – or in this case 'they' – to come. At the end of the movie, after many twists and turns in the plot, it appears that a huge number of people were at last coming to the stadium. The explosive growth of second homes in Ireland has had something of the same quality about it: regardless of how many were built the buyers would come. But 'they' did not continue to come and as the Celtic Tiger boom went bust by the summer of 2009, so hundreds, if not thousands of unsold new dwellings were spread across large tracts of Ireland.

This case study is informed partly by my research, including fieldwork in the border counties of Northern Ireland and the Republic, where we observed rapid increase in the number of second homes during the late 1990s (Paris and Robson, 2001; Paris, 2005a, 2006). The case study also draws on research by colleagues at University College Dublin (Norris and Winston, 2009), which has provided a basis for a comparative perspective on the issue North and South of the border (Norris *et al.*, 2008).

There was little evidence of second home ownership in Ireland before the 1980s. Finnerty *et al.* (2003) and Quinn (2004) related recent growth in second home ownership to the economic boom of the 1990s. New house building increased dramatically with second homes accounting for a significant part of new production. Norris and Winston (2009: 1306) argued that the high proportion of second homes in the recently built stock 'distinguishes the Irish case from that of a number of other countries … where second homes tend to be purchased from the existing rural housing stock'.

Some of the facts about second homes in Ireland are more difficult to establish than in England or Northern Ireland, as there is nothing equivalent to the English SEH or the House Condition Surveys carried out across the UK. Estimates of the number of second homes in Ireland, therefore, use census household data and new house building statistics, but have to make assumptions and estimates about a number of variables, especially the proportion of new dwellings replacing existing dwellings and/or being used as second homes or for holiday lets, as well as vacancy levels in new and existing dwelling stocks. Census enumerators in Ireland have counted vacant dwellings since 1991, categorising them as 'permanently or usually vacant', 'holiday homes' or 'temporarily vacant'. The Irish census category 'holiday homes' applies to second homes and dwellings usually let to holidaymakers. On that basis, McCarthy *et al.* (2003) and Fitz Gerald (2005) suggested that second homes/holiday homes accounted for around a third of the increase in the habitable dwelling stock between 1996 and 2002, with higher proportions along the Atlantic seaboard from Donegal to Kerry. McCarthy *et al.* (2003) estimated that around

100,000 second homes were built between 2000 and 2004. Official statistics show that around 750,000 new private sector houses were completed between 1992 and 2007 (Central Statistics Office, www.cso.ie/quicktables). If about one third were second homes, they would amount to around 260,000. As well, other dwellings that had been used as permanent residences are also likely to have been purchased for use as second homes, so the net increase in second homes probably is nearer 300,000.

McCarthy *et al.* (2003) noted that the highest number of dwellings recorded as vacant in 2002 was in Dublin, suggesting that 'many of these are city apartments maintained by out-of-town permanent residents' (McCarthy *et al.*, 2003: 18). It would be surprising if there had not been an increase in the number of pieds-à-terre for use in the city during the working week, as in London. This possibility is strengthened by 2006 census data in Table 3.4. Although the proportion of dwellings recorded as permanently vacant was lower in Dublin and the other cities than in the state as a whole, it had increased at a faster rate than in the state as a whole between 2002 and 2006: 156 per cent in Dublin and 131 per cent in other cities, compared to 85 per cent overall. However, at least part of the growth in the number of dwellings recorded as permanently vacant in Irish cities was due to a growing stock of unsold dwellings. The actual situation remains uncertain, however, in the continuing absence of a national housing survey or other mechanisms to improve data collection.

There had been some opposition to the growth of second homes in coast and country areas in Ireland for many years, especially concerning their visual impact. The haphazard development of holiday homes in Bunbeg, Co. Donegal, was bemoaned by an Irish architectural historian (Rowan, 1979: 152): 'It enjoys a remarkable situation, but at the time of writing a complete lack of planning control threatens to turn the area into a rural holiday slum.' Concern turned towards social and economic dimensions of second homes during the 1990s. The National Economic and Social Council (2004) argued that second homes represented a growing share of housing construction, fuelling land and housing prices, especially in rural areas where prices previously had been below national averages. Finnerty *et al.* (2003) argued that growing demand for second homes, together with tax breaks for investors, had pushed up house prices in rural areas, creating excess pressure on infrastructure in summer 'boomtowns' that in winter 'become deserted, alienating, ghost towns surrounded but untouched by the trappings of affluence, and incapable of supporting basic community facilities such as schools, public transport and so on' (op. cit.: 137). They warned of a 'risk of inflating local markets out of reach of existing communities, overloading infrastructure, and bifurcating such areas into self-contained communities of affluent peak season visitors and increasingly marginalised permanent residents' (loc. cit.).

We are not aware of any systematic survey or other data on the characteristics of Irish second home owners. Quinn (2004) reported evidence from a survey of 76 second home owners in Co. Wexford but other evidence derives from comments by respondents in Norris and Winston's (2009) case studies or anecdotal evidence in articles in newspapers, television programmes and other media commentary. The sheer scale of growth, however, suggests that second home ownership extends widely across Irish society, especially middle class and more affluent households.

Recent research on Irish second homes

Norris and Winston's (2009) research on rural second homes in Ireland involved a combination of methods: literature search, analysis of official statistics, and in-depth case studies in areas with large proportions of second homes. The case studies included census data analysis, a review of local research and planning documents, and 10 in-depth interviews in each area with estate agents, local government councillors and officers, local business people and community leaders (clergy, teachers, police and community activists).

Table 3.4, based on their data, shows that the national proportion of habitable dwellings classified as holiday homes increased from 1 per cent in 1992 to 3 per cent in 2002 and 5 per cent in 2006. The proportion of dwellings classified as permanently vacant increased much faster, especially after 2002, from 9 per cent of dwellings in 1991 to 15 per cent in 2006. These changes are more striking in light of the rapid growth in the national dwelling stock, from 1.15 million in 1991 to 1.76 million in 2006, or about 50 per cent overall. The number of dwellings classified as permanently vacant increased *three times* as fast, from around 105,000 to 266,000, hence the widespread assumption that much of this increase was due to second homes being recorded as vacant dwellings. There were clear regional concentrations of dwellings recorded as holiday homes or permanently vacant, in the Border, West and Southwest (Table 3.4), and so Norris and Winston (2009) selected their case study areas from these three regions: Courtown in Co. Wexford, Drumshambo in Co. Leitrim (Figure 3.22), and Schull in Co. Cork. Whilst all exhibiting strong growth in second homes and 'vacant' dwellings, the case study areas differed from one another in terms of geography and public policy concerns.

The context for the growth of second homes in Ireland differed significantly from Britain in three ways. Firstly, the planning regime was highly permissive since its formation, allowing massive overall growth of house building between 1990 and 2007 with a high proportion of new dwellings comprising one-off houses in the open countryside, including second homes. Thus there has been much less gentrification of villages in Ireland than in Britain. Secondly, there were no local property taxes for residential dwellings between the late 1970s and 2009, thus local authorities did not record dwelling occupancy for local tax purposes. Recently, however, the Local Government (Charges) Bill 2009 introduced a €200 charge for each non-primary residence. Thirdly, other national policies boosted investment in housing, including assistance to purchasers of council houses, grants for first-time buyers, fiscal incentives for urban regeneration, with no capital gains tax on primary

Table 3.4 Dwellings by occupancy status and region in Ireland, 1991–2006

	1991			2002			2006		
	All dwellings (000)	Permanently vacant (%)	Holiday homes (%)	All dwellings (000)	Permanently vacant (%)	Holiday homes (%)	All dwellings (000)	Permanently vacant (%)	Holiday homes (%)
Regions									
Dublin	336.0	5	*	407.9	5	*	475.1	11	*
Other cities	88.4	7	*	1067.0	7	*	124.3	13	*
Border	131.2	13	2	168.6	15	6	224.4	20	6
Mideast	98.0	7	1	139.2	7	1	162.8	11	1
Midland	63.8	9	*	80.8	10	1	102.8	16	1
Midwest	84.6	12	2	106.9	12	4	127.8	16	4
Southeast	108.4	10	2	140.1	12	5	173.9	17	5
Southwest	137.3	14	3	175.0	14	6	215.0	19	6
West	99.2	14	2	124.4	16	6	152.5	22	5
Case studies counties									
Cork	93.3	12	3	121.2	12	4	149.7	17	4
Leitrim	10.1	18	2	11.8	22	7	15.2	29	8
Wexford	32.4	11	4	45.1	17	9	58.7	22	11
State	1,150.9	9	1	1,449.8	10	3	1,758.6	15	3

Sources: Norris and Winston (2009) based on published and unpublished census data.

* = under 0.4

residences and low CGT on other residences. In addition, tax incentives boosted growth in holiday homes in some seaside locations, as well as second homes and vacant dwellings in rural areas.

The case studies selected by Norris and Winston (2009) share a water orientation: Courtown and Schull are coastal villages and Drumshambo is on the country's major inland waterway, the River Shannon. Drumshambo and Schull were areas of economic and population decline up to the 1990s whereas growth in Courtown had been stimulated by housing developed for Dublin commuters. Drumshambo and Courtown were associated with caravan or chalet holidays before the 1990s but both experienced a surge of investment between 1991 and 2006, due largely to tax incentives: Courtown was one of the places designated under the seaside resorts scheme (SRS) that operated between 1995 and 1999, and Drumshambo lay within the five counties where the rural renewal scheme (RRS) operated between 1998 and 2006 (Figure 3.21). Schull (Figure 3.23) had been an upmarket holiday home centre in the early 1990s but did not experience the same surge in growth – which Norris and Winston attributed largely to the absence of tax incentives.

Norris and Winston (2009) examined the impact of tax incentives as a driver of second homes in rural Ireland. They showed that second homes accounted for a very large proportion of dwellings recorded as vacant with high concentrations in areas where the SRS and RRS had operated (Figure 3.24). The RRS should only

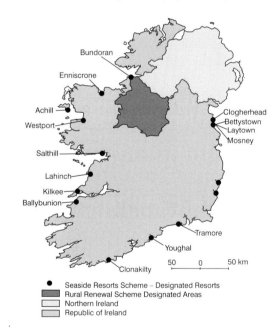

3.21 Areas designated under the seaside resorts scheme and the rural renewal scheme (source Michelle Norris, with permission)

3.22 Drumshambo, Co. Leitrim (source: 'Tower 10', with permission)

3.23 Cola pier and cottages, Schull, Co. Cork (sourcce: Yvon Valdepeñas, with permission)

apply to dwellings that were developed for permanent occupation and so second homes were not eligible for tax relief, but Norris and Winston argued that the scheme resulted in high levels of new construction and refurbishment leading to excess supply, much of which simply remained empty.

Norris and Winston (2009) reviewed the impacts of growing second home ownership along three dimensions: impacts on the local economy, society and

3.24 Bundoran, Co. Leitrim, seaside resort scheme apartments (source: Chris Paris)

environment. Interviewees in all areas thought the economic impact of second homes was beneficial, especially for the local building industry and tourism development. They noted 'a marked reluctance to criticize any potential source of employment' (op. cit.: 1314), though some respondents thought second home owners barely contributed to the local economy. Concerns were raised in Drumshambo about dwellings purchased purely for the tax breaks and then deliberately left empty: locals feared there could be a glut of dwellings coming on to the market at some stage, further depressing local house prices. Around 1,000 dwellings had been developed in Courtown under the SRS, leading to local concerns about overdevelopment. Some additional tourists were using holiday accommodation, but other tourist businesses had suffered with two hotels and the local ballroom closing down.

There was little displacement of existing communities through the growth of second home ownership because most demand for additional second homes was met by new building. The scale of development at Courtown was criticised by local respondents, who were concerned about additional housing developed for commuters. As in the Newcastle and Causeway Coast cases in Northern Ireland, Courtown was affected by many development pressures, not just the growth of second homes and holiday lets. Virtually all respondents thought that second homes development had increased house and land prices locally, but this did not necessarily mean that locals were driven out, for two reasons. Firstly, there has been continuing depopulation due to lack of employment across remoter rural Ireland, so older homes remained abandoned whilst newly built second homes attracted different purchasers to these areas without displacing anybody. Secondly, the permissive planning system and widespread self-building created a separate quasi-market in housing production for local people.

Some environmental impacts of second homes were beneficial, especially where older homes were refurbished or restored. As in other instances, though, concerns were raised about pressures on water supply and sewage treatment, as councils resented having to provide for relatively rare peak demand and having facilities underused for most of the year. Norris and Winston were struck that environmental issues did not figure prominently among their respondents' concerns and suggested that this reflects Irish attitudes generally to the environment. They thought that the environmental consequences of so many new dwellings had been negative, but only one of their respondents mentioned septic tanks 'despite the fact that ineffective and inadequately maintained septic tanks are one of the main polluters of rural waterways in Ireland' (Norris and Winston, 2009: 1318).

Norris and Winston (2009) noted the Irish government suggestion that 'holiday home development can act as a revitalizing force' especially in remote areas (Department of the Environment, Heritage and Local Government, 2005: 5). Our comparison of the development of second homes in the Republic of Ireland and Northern Ireland, however, concluded that the idea of using holiday home development as an element of rural development strategy was extremely problematic (Norris et al., 2008). Some aspects of second home ownership in Ireland were very distinctive: the high incidence of new building in a context of laissez-faire planning, with high concentration in some rural and coastal areas, widespread overdevelopment and growing numbers of long-term vacant dwellings stimulated by generous fiscal incentives in seaside and rural areas. Norris and Winston concluded that over-reliance on housing development left rural areas starkly exposed to the economic downturn and that the growth of second and vacant dwellings in Ireland had 'diverted construction away from population growth centres where housing needs were more pressing' (op. cit.: 1320). Few concerns were raised about the issue of affordability, despite house and land price inflation, as local people were generally able to obtain affordable housing through self-building. The clear evidence of overdevelopment, moreover, suggested a likelihood of substantial falls in house values as 'a flood of empty and second homes to the market may undermine housing markets in those regions' (loc. cit.).

Second homes and Irish housing: overview and prospectus

Second homes and holiday homes were significant elements of the Irish housing boom. Growing second home ownership in Ireland involved new houses, purchased with newly found affluence, so there was little evidence of gentrification, as in Britain. The enduring legacy of depopulation and abandonment of dwellings and a different agricultural history had left no widespread legacy of 'villages' to gentrify. Rather, a different planning regime allowed the development of many thousands of one-off houses across the countryside and coastal areas. Although there were many fine domains and country parks, often owned by the residual heirs of the protestant ascendency in Ireland (Aalen *et al.*, 1997), there was no powerful aristocracy controlling vast acreages of sanctified countryside and able to influence the development of a planning system hostile to growth as in Britain. Norris and Winston's (2009) research highlighted cultural and social factors influencing housing development in rural Ireland. Attitudes expressed were more like those in the Fermanagh case in Northern Ireland, contrasting sharply with the Causeway Coast with its resident group opposition to second homes and developer-led renewal. There was widespread belief in a person's right to build a house on his/her own land and a marked cultural reluctance to criticise any development that created work for local people.

The main focus of scholarly and popular commentary on second homes in Ireland has related to rural and coastal areas. It is likely, however, that a significant element of demand for additional housing in Dublin and other Irish cities also has been for urban second homes but the facts are impossible to pin down with precision, though official data sources provide some clues and likely explanations. The extent and consequences of this phenomenon remain largely unexamined and invisible in official statistics and public commentary in Ireland.

Public policies strongly supported home ownership and housing development generally and tax incentives fuelled developments in seaside and rural areas resulting in widespread underuse of dwellings and long-term dwelling vacancy. Housing production was a large part of the Irish economy as was property development more generally. But the Irish housing market has changed a lot since 2007. House prices and new building rates have tumbled with widespread job losses in construction, especially in rural areas, and even more empty unsold new dwellings. Irish banks have faced major solvency problems. The wider recession caused major problems for public finances, as property-related taxes fell sharply with the end of the building boom and falling dwelling sales. This intensified the problems faced by local authorities, which remain heavily reliant on central government financial support, as the absence of a local property tax meant that second home owners made no contribution to local government revenue. This was particularly vexing in border counties because many second home owners lived in Northern Ireland and did not pay any tax in the Republic, though they used local services. The Local Government (Charges) Bill 2009 introduced a €200 charge for each non-primary residence, including second homes and tenanted rental properties. Owners are required to self-assess for eligibility by contacting local authorities or a website and fines should accrue for non-payment. This measure has been strongly opposed by the Irish Property Owners' Association and it remains to be seen how vigorously it will be applied.

The April 2009 budget announced the establishment of a National Asset Management Agency (NAMA), notionally an independent entity, to take over the land and property development loans of six Irish banks that had been given government guarantees. The aim of transferring debt to NAMA was to enable the banks to resume conventional lending. Many of these loans related to the property market and thus the actual assets may be worth less, if they could be sold, than the notional assets. The Allied Irish Bank Treasury economic research *Housing Market Bulletin* for August 2009 warned that the mortgage market remained depressed and reported an overall fall in house prices of 30 to 40 per cent since the peak in 2007. What the public ownership of property and land assets will mean in practice in a falling market remains to be seen, though many commentators were concerned that NAMA may become a drain on public finances and the economy for a generation or more. The leader of the main opposition party, Fine Gael, pledged his party's opposition to legislation formally establishing NAMA in August 2009, describing it as a 'double or quits' gamble by the government, that would 'shore up a massive spending spree' by developers outside of the state, as it 'transfers the responsibility for dealing with toxic loans from the banks who made them, and the investors who funded them, to the Irish taxpayer' (Michael, 2009).

Any analysis of second homes in Ireland has to utilise data that were not collected with this topic in mind. The census definition of 'holiday homes' lumps together second homes for household leisure use and dwellings purchased for investment purposes and let to holidaymakers. Some professional analysts estimated that second and holiday homes accounted for 30 to 40 per cent of the additional housing stock between 1991 and 2007 (McCarthy *et al.*, 2003; Fitz Gerald, 2005). McCarthy *et al.* (2003) listed a range of improvements that should be made in Irish data sources but nothing appeared to have changed by the end of 2007, so it remains difficult to disentangle the threads of evidence about the impacts of the changing housing market and second home ownership.

3.25 Empty second homes development in Co. Donegal, 2009 (source: Elma Lynn)

3.26 Unsold second homes in Co. Donegal, 2009 (source: Elma Lynn)

With the downturn in the housing market since 2007, moreover, the existence of large numbers of vacant dwellings could mean that many second homes are wrongly recorded and/or there had been growth in the number of vacant unsold dwellings. Any drive through Irish coastal areas leads to the conclusion that there are a lot of unsold new developments as well as many sites having been mothballed, in the hope, perhaps, that demand will return after the recession (Figures 3.25 and 3.26). In the longer term, we suspect, they – being the purchasers of second homes – *will* come. But the wait may be a long and painful one.

Going upmarket: the changing nature of Australian 'shacks'

Once, shacks were built with whatever materials you could scrounge, 'borrow' or steal, and constructed in the quickest way possible, the object being to secure shelter from the elements without having to sacrifice too much fishing time either while physically building the shack or by working flat-out in your day job to pay it off. Today, lake houses everywhere are becoming trophy items where status and investment, or sometimes art and design take precedence over living and affordability.

(French, 2008: 164)

French was writing about shacks in the Central Highlands of Tasmania where there had been a tradition of artisanal self-building since the late nineteenth century.

3.27 Hiccup Hall, by Little Pine Lagoon, Tasmania, 2003 (source: Chris Paris)

Most shacks were constructed by trout anglers and their families for use during the fishing season, especially the summer months around Christmas. Figure 3.27 was taken in 2003, showing 'Hiccup Hall', owned by renowned trout fishing guide Bill Beck; it has been replaced with a more modern structure further from the lake's edge. Similar rudimentary structures were constructed in every state, mainly in coastal areas. Some shacks were developed after squatting on unused land – effectively Crown Land – though many also obtained licences to occupy their sites. Shack development often created places that had not existed (Selwood and Tonts, 2004, 2006), though in many cases state government projects recently have sought to 'regularise' such places.

Similar changes have occurred in many countries as free-and-easy vernacular traditions are replaced by more modern building forms. The Australian case is fascinating in itself, and also serves as an example of 'new world' second home ownership with parallels in New Zealand (Keen and Hall, 2004), Canada (Halseth, 2004) and the USA (Timothy, 2004; Engelhardt, 2006). There was a long tradition of vernacular 'summer cottages' in Canada, though 30 years before French's comments Wolfe (1977: 31–2) noted dramatic changes in Ontario: '... many a summer cottage is no longer such because it has been *winterised* and is now used throughout the year' (emphasis in the original). Inflation in land and house prices made it 'uneconomic to invest in a place which will be used for only a few weeks in the year; as a result, people are more and more likely to travel to their cottages in all seasons, and even to move into them permanently when they retire' (Wolfe, 1977: 31). Wolfe also noted a dramatic increase in the number of second homes that were not purpose built but had been purchased following the abandonment of farms.

Second homes within the Australian housing system

The Australian housing system has changed little since the 1960s 'with an overall rate of home ownership that has remained remarkably stable for over 40 years' (Kryger, 2009: 6). Around 70 per cent of Australian households owned their homes in 2006, though the home ownership rate has been falling among younger age groups since the mid-1990s (Yates, 2003; National Shelter, 2007; Flood and Baker, forthcoming). The level of outright home ownership fluctuated from a peak of around 50 per cent of all households in 1960, to 35 per cent in 2006, around 2.5 million households. The private rental sector has housed around 20 per cent of Australian households since the 1960s, reflecting a high level of rental property ownership among affluent households. A small social housing sector has been heavily residualised since the 1970s. Whereas the balance of household tenures remained relatively stable, the population increased by 96 per cent between 1961 and 2006, mainly through immigration and the number of households increased much faster than population growth, by nearly 160 per cent.

The large numbers of Australian households owning their homes outright have had considerable disposable income with which to buy additional properties, and Robertson (1977: 119) reported 'a dramatic increase in ownership of second homes' during the 1960s. His definition of second homes was similar to ours in Chapter 2: 'dwellings of permanent construction intended primarily for leisure time use on a personal basis' (Robertson, loc. cit). Robertson attributed growing second home ownership to affluence, estimating that around 200,000, or 5.4 per cent, of Australian households owned second homes in 1971. He remained confident in 2009 that his overall estimate had been broadly correct.[5]

Robertson (1977) had anticipated further growth in second home ownership up to the 18–20 per cent of households in France or Sweden in the late 1970s. If that prediction had eventuated, then with over 7 million Australian households in 2006 there would have been over a million second home owners. That seems unlikely, though there are no official data directly informing our analysis because national censuses have not collected data on second homes since 1986. As in Ireland, therefore, it is necessary to introduce assumptions and estimates relating to available data sources: census data on unoccupied dwellings, surveys relating to property ownership and tourism-related studies. Census data are collected midweek in winter so places with a high concentration of second homes have high levels of dwellings recorded as unoccupied (except in alpine resort areas).

The Australian Bureau of Statistics (ABS) provides online census data including a table on dwelling structure by occupied/unoccupied dwellings for 1996, 2001 and 2006 (Cat. No. 2068.0). This shows that 9 to 10 per cent of dwellings were unoccupied at each census, with the total increasing from 679,000 in 1996 to 830,000 in 2006. Frost (2003) had reported that in preparing its tourism data base the ABS included the assumptions that around 25 per cent of unoccupied dwellings were second homes. If that assumption is applied to census data we can derive first cut estimates of about 170,000 second homes in 1996, 180,000 in 2001 and 208,000 in 2006.

Survey data provide other possible bases for estimating the number of second homes. Beer *et al.* (2007) found that 21 per cent of households owned other properties including holiday homes or other houses, apartments or properties in addition to the home in which they lived (excluding businesses or farms, unless the farm was purely residential). The main reasons why households had acquired other properties were as an investment/renting out (15.3 per cent) and for use as a holiday home (2.4 per cent). More recently, Paris *et al.* (2009) placed a module of questions in the 2007 Australian Survey of Social Attitudes (AuSSA) to identify levels of second home ownership and the socio-economic and other characteristics of second home owners. Around 19 per cent of respondents owned additional residential properties; taken together, the main and second main reason for acquiring additional property were as investments (68 per cent), to use as a holiday home (14 per cent), for future retirement (6 per cent) and as pieds-à-terre (4 per cent). These findings were similar to Beer *et al.* (2007) with 2 to 3 per cent saying that the main reason for acquiring additional property was to use as a holiday home. Three per cent of the total number of Australian households in 2006 represented around 214,000 with second homes for leisure use.

The survey-based estimates of the level of second home ownership were similar to the estimate based on 25 per cent of unoccupied dwellings, but lower than Robertson's (1977) prediction. However, it is likely that the survey-based estimates understated the incidence of second home ownership in Australia, for a two main reasons. Firstly, respondents only gave one (Beer *et al.*, 2007) or two main reasons (Paris *et al.*, 2009) for acquiring additional residences, but people purchase second homes for many reasons combining investment, personal use and possible future retirement. Many respondents to Beer *et al.* (2007) who owned investment properties *and* a holiday home would give investment as their main reason; others may have given investment as the main reason for buying a dwelling that is only used as a second home. Secondly, people may not wish to acknowledge that they own additional properties as second homes, mainly due to concerns about CGT. On the basis of doctoral fieldwork, Robertson (1977) concluded that actual second home ownership was well above officially recorded levels.

Overall, therefore, we estimate that second home ownership in Australia in 2006 was 4 to 5 per cent of all households: giving a range of 300,000–350,000 in 2006. Precise estimates are impossible, partly due to the high level of property investment by affluent Australian households and their ability to use residential properties in different ways at different times.

3.28 Beachside shacks at Port Julia, South Australia (source: Clive Forster)

From shacks to mansions

Some Australians have had second homes for well over a century, from the splendid summer houses of affluent Melbournians or Sydneysiders by the coast or in pleasant mountain foothills, to the humble shacks of working class families from the bush or the city (Figure 3.28). Many early second homes have been swallowed up by twentieth century suburban extensions of sprawling metropolitan areas (Selwood and Tonts, 2004, 2006). There was no single pattern; rather diverse developments occurred in all states, often with a high proportion of rural families, with self-building of shacks and later construction of more enduring holiday homes on the coast. Many shack settlements endured as make-and-mend mixtures of dwellings with minimal services but providing a much-loved escape from city life or the enduring hardship of making a living in often harsh farming communities. Canberra business consultant Chris Richards was raised on a large sheep station[6] in the Monaro region in southern New South Wales (NSW), west of the escarpment between the highland region and the coastal plain to the east. His family and many others from the Monaro went to their shacks on the coast for a holiday every summer, taking their local social hierarchies with them, as he describes in Figure 3.29.

Government departments and agencies in most states have sought to regularise shack developments, often on environmental grounds and especially where wastes were considered to have adverse impacts on hydrological systems. Official government documents often refer to shack 'owners' in inverted commas to emphasise that many did *not* own the land on which their shacks are sited but were licensees or sometimes squatters. There was much opposition and resentment from

The long ant-like stream of mainly black cars wound its way bumper-to-bumper down the only two arterial roads to the east, snaking across the mountain range, an annual exodus to the sea. The cars, mainly Holdens and Fords of different vintages, were a testimony to the fortunes of the farmers and graziers[1] whose families crammed into them the week before Christmas to head down to the coastal Meccas of Merimbula, Pambula and Tathra.

The well-to-do grazing families of substance, 'old money', had their enclaves on secluded waterfronts and headlands. Two-story large brick monoliths, never understated, often had a jetty and boat moored out the front. The role model was Jimmy Maslin's architect-designed 100sq balcony-festooned mansion complete with long jetty and huge modern yacht. In all my pilgrimages to the coast I never once saw anyone on the boat, on the jetty or on any of the balconies. I never saw anyone there.

Further back from the water but in walking distance to the beach, with occasional water views and a stumble to the local RSL[2] were the enclaves of the little 'Aussie battler'. These sea side fibro asbestos shanties with their concrete floors and glass shuttered windows were badges of their owners' success. Normally conservative farmers took to painting their pride and joy garish colours, every shade of pink, hues of blue with red contrasting trim, white paling fence with strands of barbed wire to keep the 'roos[3] and bandicoots out. These proud candy boxes had two bedrooms and an enclosed veranda along the length of the house. The kids all slept on the veranda in double decker bunks liberated from shearers' quarters, deemed to be too uncomfortable for the shearers. Ablutions were an outdoor cold shower and a pan toilet in a little shed up the back. The 'night man' came on Thursdays to shoulder his grisly burden and skulk off into the dark with the soil.

The big families of the poorer folk – station hands, shearers, or council road workers – were lined up shoulder to shoulder in their beach front canvas cities. The very poorest set up their shabby tents by the backwater foreshore keeping the camp fire lit to deter the mozzies. Their kids always seemed to have the most fun; they certainly caught the most fish and prawns.

The pilgrimage lasted about four weeks and then as if on a silent cue everyone would pack up and begin the torturous trail up over the mountains and back to the drudgery of grazing, cringing, waiting for the next seasonal disaster or long-awaited drop in wool prices.

Most kids knew one another. Rich ones went away to boarding school: the Protestants to Kings or Shore, the Catholics to St Joeys or Riverview and they only met on the Rugby pitch. The upwardly mobile went to lesser schools. The rest went to the local High School or the Catholic school where they impatiently waited until they were 15 before drifting into the oblivion of the farm. The less fortunate ones became someone else's labourer, shearing shed hand, or workers at the saw mills or abattoir. They procreated and aspired to a little shack by the sea for their annual pilgrimage to the south coast.

Source: Chris Richards

Notes
1   The word 'graziers' is used in Australia to refer to owners of the largest pastoral properties.
2   The 'RSL' is the Returned Service Men's League, which has many clubs throughout Australia; visitors are usually allowed access, especially if they are members of another RSL club.
3   The abbreviation 'roos refers to kangaroos.

3.29 Monaro's modest shacks

3.30 The Wallis shack, Lake Conjola, New South Wales (now demolished) (source: Frank Hicks)

shack owners to these reforms, especially in southern NSW, at 'Chinaman's Island' on Lake Conjola. Shack residents had used the area since the 1920s, with a small summer community of families and friends regularly rebuilding and extending the shacks. Titles are being rescinded on the death of the last member of current licensees' adult families and their shacks are demolished. The local newspaper recorded shack owners' frustration and anger at the demolition of the Wallis Shack, shown in Figure 3.30, originally built by Harold Southwell in the 1940s (Condie, 2006). One shack owner complained bitterly that the demolished shack 'was an artefact that preserved most of the characteristics connecting us to a period whose social and cultural manifestations are rapidly disappearing' and that the 'rush to build new houses and to renovate or transform older houses, especially in our coastal areas, has meant that the visible signs of a dramatically different style of life are rapidly being lost' (op. cit.).

Tasmanian government agencies started work on the Shack Sites Project in 1991, aiming to determine the long-term tenure of around 1,400 shacks on Crown land and remove uncertainty over the future status of shacks. The main programme was run by the Department of Primary Industries, Parks, Water and Environment (PIPWE) over a 10-year period (PIPWE 1999–2009). Shack owners only had annually renewable leasehold tenure, so there was little point in upgrading to more permanent dwellings; they had sought more security but government officials were concerned about a range of issues, including increased pollution risks as people used their shacks more often. The project involved removing some shacks with licensees offered more permanent sites nearby on a secure basis, and regularisation of other sites. With uncertainty

3.31 The 'lawyers' shack' by Little Pine Lagoon, Tasmania, 2007 (source: Chris Paris)

3.32 The 'apple shed' by Little Pine Lagoon, Tasmania, 2009 (source: Chris Paris)

resolved, some shacks have gone upmarket as new owners renovate or replace them with new dwellings; one that had been purchased from the previous owner was known locally for a while as the 'lawyers' shack' (Figure 3.31), but it was replaced by a large modern building, which locals dubbed 'the apple shed' (Figure 3.32), because it resembled farm outhouses where apples were stored!

Elsewhere in Tasmania, along the coast and in the Central Highlands, many 'shacks' had been developed on more conventionally owned sites. Such shacks come in all shapes and sizes, usually conforming to building regulations, often in unconventionally named places such as Flintstone and Wilburville (after *The Flintstones*) by Arthurs Lake, a premium trout fishery. Other recent developments in the Tasmanian Central Highlands include upmarket fishing lodges and complexes combining holiday cottages, hotel and second home purchase opportunities.

Humble shacks are increasingly becoming things of the past, regardless of state government actions, as a result of growing wealth and household preferences. In January 2009 the *Adelaide Advertiser* reviewed the changing nature of holiday homes across South Australia under the heading 'goodbye shacks, hullo luxury'.[7] Quoting real estate agents, Watson (2009) reported a shift away from humble shacks towards luxurious holiday homes with a growing population of full-time, often retired residents. The South Australian president of the Real Estate Association of Australia claimed that the value of coastal properties had doubled over the previous 10 years. One estate agent on the Yorke Peninsula said 'the beach shack is a thing of the past' as 'people are knocking them down and building upmarket homes'. It was a similar story near Port Lincoln, on the Eyre Peninsula, where a local estate agent suggested that 'the shack market has gone' so 'if you want to be near the beach, or near the marina, you have to buy a home post-1990'.

Some new buildings in Australia are marketed as 'shacks', ranging from prefabricated mobile homes to luxurious beachside permanent dwellings costing many hundreds of thousands of dollars. Ray White Real Estate advertised '62 architecturally designed modern beach shacks set against the spectacular Mt Coolum backdrop', designed by 'some of Australia's most renowned coastal architects' including a three-bedroom beach shack with a guide price of $700,000–720,000 (http://www.raywhite.com). These are only 'shacks' for marketing purposes or in the imagination, though the term may retain sentimental significance within Australian culture for a few generations at least. Contemporary Australian second homes range from remaining real shacks in odds and ends of coast and countryside to enormous McMansions-on-sea in huge walled estates or gated upmarket enclaves with full electronic security systems. Entirely unlike the UK, however, there have been no restrictive planning regimes to stop the development of new second homes, so there has been little gentrification. In most cases, of course, there were no villages to gentrify, though some modest fishing settlements have been driven upmarket and a few farming towns in high amenity areas have been reinvented as 'historic villages'. Most Australian second homes are in coastal areas, with some in high amenity inland areas including foothills and high Alpine areas in Victoria and NSW and the Central Highlands region of Tasmania.

An increasing number of Australians have chosen to live in coastal areas and there are many variations between coastal places and regions. There had been a long-term trend of movement out of remote country areas with population concentration in major coastal metropolitan areas. All Australian cities have been developed at low densities compared to European or Asian cities, though there has been some infill at higher densities since the mid-1980s. There was strong evidence of counter-urbanisation from the mid-1960s with extensive suburbanisation and growing ex-urban living (Hugo, 1994; Paris, 1994). New forms of urban development were emerging by the 1980s, related to lifestyle choices, tourism and a preference for living in warmer coastal areas. Drawing parallels with developments in the USA, Australian scholars examined 'sun-belt' migration, especially to Queensland. Mullins (1985, 1991, 1994) explored emergent 'tourist urbanisation' on the Gold Coast in south-east Queensland. Stimson and Minnery (1998) showed that long-distance migration was not just a matter of retirees moving from other parts of Australia but that many factors lead to long-distance migration, with attractors including climate, lifestyle and networks of families and friends (op. cit.). Since the early 1990s, too, there has been extensive regeneration of former docklands areas in Sydney, Melbourne and Adelaide, typically at much higher densities than older suburbs dominated by single storey detached homes.

More recently, changing patterns of population movement tend to be discussed under the term 'sea change'. Initially the title of an Australian Broadcasting Corporation (ABC) series, 'sea change' loosely refers to a range of interrelated processes involving a growing proportion of Australians living in non-metropolitan coastal areas (the term 'tree change' refers to movement to high amenity inland locations). The idea was developed by Burnley and Murphy (2004) in *Sea Change: Movement from Metropolitan to Arcadian Australia* and has been used extensively by other scholars and in the media (Gurran, 2008). Australian urban and regional coastal areas have been changing significantly since at least the 1960s so growing second home ownership only constitutes one element of change. The Gold and Sunshine Coasts in Queensland, for example, contain mixed developments with blends of tourist attractions, hotels, motels, rental houses, apartments, permanent residents including retirees, and second home owners. Many apartments in high density waterside blocks are used as leisure second homes, as in the Gold Coast (Figure 3.33). Also, many such apartments are certain to be used as pieds-à-terre, for example in the Melbourne Docklands (Figure 3.34) or Sydney (Figure 3.35). Gurran (2008: 406) identified instances of gentrification 'as newcomers and tourism developers compete with lower income residents for low cost housing'; caravan parks that had provided cheaper accommodation for retirees were also declining.

Some places stand out as distinctive 'second homes towns'. Noosa in Queensland has a long-established reputation as an upmarket resort with substantial rental properties, hotels and second homes. Further north there has been rapid development of what may be the 'new Noosa' with development of Agnes Water estate at the place named 1770 (in recognition of Captain Cook's landing there in 1770): a modest caravan and campsite has been joined by high quality, upmarket new homes

3.33 Gold Coast apartments, Queensland (source: Clive Forster)

3.34 Melbourne Docklands apartments, Victoria (source: Clive Forster)

3.35 Sydney waterside apartments, New South Wales (source: Clive Forster)

marketed to investors and second home buyers. In both Noosa and 1770 there also are high proportions of holiday rental properties and second homes.

One of the few Australian commentators on second homes, Frost (2003, 2004) discussed the 'second homes belt' between 75 and 110 kilometres from Melbourne. Using 1996 census data, Frost identified places with high levels of unoccupied dwellings, mainly presumed to be second homes or holiday rentals. Over 50 per cent of dwellings in 14 coastal towns were listed as unoccupied in the 1996 census, with Venus Bay topping the list at 81 per cent. Loch Sport, near the popular Gippsland Lakes, was the exception at nearly 300 kilometres. Some inland towns also had high proportions of unoccupied dwellings, mainly tourist areas with a mix of permanent residents, including retirees, holiday rental accommodation and second homes. Frost noted an absence of the social tensions reported in European countries but he suggested there may be tensions between households that have moved to live permanently in these towns and second home owners. People who moved permanently to the towns created 'distinctive social practices and traditions' and characterised second home owners as 'mere tourists' (Frost, 2006: 171). As well, he suggested that second home owners may develop distinctive cultures 'and that some second home owners may see themselves as established (or 'local') in comparison with newcomers or other tourists' (loc. cit.). These suggestions correspond perfectly with attitudes and views articulated in our other case studies: 'permanent residents' who had themselves moved to the Causeway Coast on retirement then complained that the local community was not 'balanced' due to second home ownership; also the HVS activists in Cornwall argued that their families had owned second homes in Helford for many years whereas the local fishermen did not actually live there. Frost's analysis also applies to opposition from permanent residents to changes in seaside towns along the Great Ocean Road in western Victoria, as 'rapid growth in residential and tourism-related development is threatening the unique nature of these towns' (Green, 2004: 73).

We have updated and expanded Frost's analysis by reviewing the situation in Victorian 'second homes towns' at the 2006 census as well as examining rates of unoccupied dwellings in other parts of Australia where we might expect to find relatively high proportions of second homes. Table 3.5 compares changes between 1996 and 2006 in recorded resident populations and unoccupied private dwellings in the top 10 urban centres of coastal Victoria. It shows stronger growth in the total number of dwellings (26 per cent) and resident population (27 per cent) than unoccupied dwellings (23 per cent), with a slight fall in the proportion of all dwellings that were unoccupied. These data suggest that there was a trend towards movement to these towns on a permanent basis, with former second home owners moving in on a more permanent basis as well as new in-migrants. There were notable differences between the top 10 coastal second homes towns: the resident population grew more strongly in Cowes (38 per cent) but less in Anglesea (15 per cent); growth in Venus Bay was stronger than the average for the top 10 in terms of resident population (32 per cent), total dwellings (47 per cent) *and* unoccupied dwellings (48 per cent). Thus the table shows diversity rather than a single motion of change.

For purposes of comparison, Table 3.6 shows 2006 census data on unoccupied dwellings in some other parts of Victoria, as well as NSW, South Australia and Tasmania. Mansfield local government area (LGA) in Victoria had 43 per cent of dwellings recorded unoccupied on census night 2006, compared to the state average of 10 per cent. Mansfield is a high amenity 'tree change' rather than 'sea change' community, including the Mount Buller ski resort and parts of Lake Eildon, a major tourist attraction. Around half its ratepayers live elsewhere, mainly in Melbourne and there is evidence of much recent purchase activity, often with a view to future retirement, as well as growing retirement in the area (McKenzie *et al.*, 2008). The rate of unoccupied dwellings in the Central Highlands LGA of Tasmania (62 per cent) contrasts sharply with state average of 13 per cent; there has been little if any growth of permanent dwellings here. The four LGAs along the southern coast of NSW all have high recorded levels of unoccupied dwellings at the overall level, with much higher proportions in the strip of land adjacent to the coasts. Eurobodalla Shire, where the main road from Canberra brings second home owners and other visitors to the shores of the Pacific Ocean, had the highest recorded level of unoccupied dwellings (32 per cent) (see Table 3.6). Shoalhaven,

Table 3.5 Unoccupied dwellings in urban centres of coastal Victoria, 1996 and 2006

Urban centre or locality	General location	Distance from Melbourne (km)	Private dwellings							
			Population		Total		Unoccupied		Per cent unoccupied	
			1996	2006	1996	2006	1996	2006	1996	2006
Venus Bay	East of Phillip Island	170	385	509	978	1,439	795	1,175	81	82
Loch Sport	East Gippsland	280	791	778	1,319	1,475	933	1,074	71	73
Indented Heads	Bellarine Peninsula	110	453	589	785	846	554	561	71	66
Aireys Inlet–Fairhaven	Great Ocean Road	121	761	1,142	1,035	1,460	719	982	70	67
Cape Paterson	East of Phillip Island	141	593	674	755	885	502	587	67	66
Cowes	Phillip Island	142	3,060	4,215	3,941	5,230	2,665	3,360	67	64
Newhaven	Phillip Island	125	1,091	1,662	1,351	1,779	891	1,093	66	61
Anglesea	Great Ocean Road	111	1,995	2,290	2,340	2,754	1,520	1,801	65	65
Coronet Bay	Near Phillip Island	115	482	644	621	760	386	436	62	57
Flinders	Mornington Peninsula	87	501	573	583	644	354	411	61	64
Total			10,112	13,076	13,718	17,272	9,319	11,480	68	66
Victoria					1,768,720	2,085,113	177,063	215,729	10	10

Table 3.6 Unoccupied dwellings in selected Australian statistical divisions, 2006

Urban centre or locality	General location	Private dwellings		
		Total	Unoccupied	Per cent unoccupied
Carrickalinga	Fleurieu Peninsula	753	542	72
Coffin Bay	Port Lincoln	470	323	69
Beachport	South east coast	410	272	66
Middleton	Fleurieu Peninsula	974	592	61
American River	Kangaroo Island	220	109	50
Port Elliot	Fleurieu Peninsula	1,270	506	40
Goolwa	Fleurieu Peninsula	3,910	1,306	33
Victor Harbour	Fleurieu Peninsula	6,611	2,003	30
Yankalilla	Fleurieu Peninsula	275	53	19
Statistical subdivisions				
Yorke	Yorke	17,391	6,612	38
Kangaroo Island	Kangaroo Island	2,668	854	32
Fleurieu	Fleurieu	22,768	7,277	32
Lincoln	Lincoln	13,593	2,496	18
SOUTH AUSTRALIA		679,662	69,751	10
Local government areas				
Central Highlands	Tasmania	2,609	1,615	62
TASMANIA		216,746	27,680	13
Mansfield	Victoria	5,147	2,205	43
Murrindindi	Victoria	7,331	2,019	28
VICTORIA		2,085,113	215,729	10
Snowy River	New South Wales	4,773	1,093	22
Eurobodella	New South Wales	21,252	6,719	32
Bega Valley	New South Wales	15,514	3,252	21
Shoalhaven	New South Wales	48,514	13,005	27
NEW SOUTH WALES		2,728,721	258,268	9
AUSTRALIA		8,426,559	830,374	10

Source: Census Data Online, mainly ABS Cat No. 2068.0

further north along the coast and nearer Sydney, had three times the proportion of unoccupied dwellings (27 per cent) than the state as a whole. Snowy River Shire in the Alpine region is home to classic ski resorts at Thredbo and Jindabyne, and major recreational lakes Jindabyne and Eucumbene. The census has a perverse effect here because the proportion of unoccupied dwellings is *lower* than in the summer as the census is taken during the ski season.

Most South Australian second homes are south of Adelaide around the Fleurieu Peninsula or to the west on the Yorke and Eyre peninsulas. Some South Australian second homes places are shown in Table 3.6, with the highest numbers of unoccupied dwellings in Victor Harbour and Goolwa, and a particularly high concentration in Yankalilla LGA at Carrickalinga, which is just 30 kilometres from the southern edge of the Adelaide metropolitan area. Carrickalinga has a rather genteel feel, partly due to its association with Adelaide's legal fraternity. Carrickalinga was barely on the map when I first visited South Australia in 1979, though nearby Normanville had a caravan park and chalets. Carrickalinga has grown substantially over the last 30 years to be one of the most expensive second homes developments in the state. There were a few older structures during the 1970s but most have been replaced with much more substantial houses and many additional houses have been developed, especially along the road overlooking the beach frontage. Normanville remains a small seaside town with a range of services for permanent residents and tourists. Carrickalinga is separated from Normanville by mile-long South Beach and a rocky headland; it has no shops or services so it is relatively quiet and little used by day visitors. One interviewee suggested that there is a clear social gradient going south from Carrickalinga to Normanville: 'When you go south the social gradient falls until you reach Normanville with its caravan park, jetty, boat ramp and shops. Roughly, Normanville is the bogan[8] end and Carrickalinga North the lawyers' end' (Anonymous correspondent, January 2009) (Figures 3.36 and 3.37). One of the earliest substantial beachside second homes was owned by the late Dame Roma Mitchell, Australia's first female QC and member of a Supreme Court bench as well as Governor of South Australia from 1991 to 1996.

The growth of second home ownership has not generated significant controversy in Australia, though concerns have been raised about overdevelopment and the environmental impacts of large numbers of new houses in often fragile coastal environments (Selwood and Tonts, 2004, 2006). Local councils are important players in terms of regulating second home development, mainly through land-use planning. Selwood and Tonts (2004) cited Busselton as an example of pro-growth councils that welcomed new subdivisions aimed at catering for the second home market. In contrast, they suggested that some LGAs have sought to limit such developments through planning guidelines aiming to restrict development. Concerns about the impacts of second homes on local housing markets have also been raised

Variations on a theme

3.36 Carrickalinga North Beach, South Australia (source: Clive Forster)

3.37 Carrickalinga, South Australia: second home or holiday rental? (source: Clive Forster

in the Augusta–Margaret River region south of Perth in Western Australia (Kelly and Hosking, 2005) and on the Fleurieu Peninsula in South Australia (Hugo and Rudd, 2004).

State governments have also become concerned about the impact of large seasonal population variations in relation to place-based funding systems used to allocate financial resources from states to LGAs. Funding processes for local infrastructure and services are typically based on the size of recorded *resident* populations. Thus McKenzie *et al.* (2008) questioned whether these systems adequately relate to a society that includes much greater levels of mobility and seasonality (of agricultural workers, incidentally, as well as tourists and second home owners). High intensity use during short periods put heavy strains on councils' budgets that were supported by state grants based on notional 'permanent' residents only.

Second home owners in Australia: evidence from AuSSA 2007

Finally within this case study we examine some of the socio-economic and other characteristics of Australian second home owners and the role of second home ownership in family and household investment and consumption strategies. The overall picture is based on data from a small module of questions in the 2007 AuSSA survey (Paris *et al.*, 2009) with more detailed and nuanced information from a small survey conducted on a snowball basis among 20 of my Australian friends who had second homes.

The module of questions in the 2007 AuSSA survey provides data about second home ownership that can be cross-tabulated with other data collected within the survey to identify a range of socio-economic and demographic characteristics of second home owners and compare these to the population as a whole (Paris *et al.*, 2009). Respondents were asked whether they owned one or more additional residences (ARs) as well as their main home. Around 19 per cent of households owned at least one AR, mainly acquired as investments or for use as second homes (using the term 'holiday homes' on the schedule). One attraction of investment in rental property in Australia is known as 'negative gearing', whereby owners 'gear' their investment by making higher interest payments than rental incomes received and deducting net losses against other taxable income. This tax break is not available unless there is a rental income stream, so it was not surprising to find that outright ownership was less common among households that acquired ARs as investments (38 per cent) than others who stated second home (61 per cent), pieds-à-terre (60 per cent) or for future retirement (52 per cent) (Table 3.7). A high proportion of dwellings purchased for future retirement were also mortgaged and negatively geared, suggesting that these properties were being rented out prior to future retirement. These findings are consistent with the argument that investment in housing for current and future use is a key element of lifetime investment and consumption strategies.

Table 3.7 Ownership status of ARs in Australia, 2007

| | Expressed as % in each category | | | | |
ARs	Own outright	Mortgaged and negatively geared	Mortgaged not negatively geared	Other	Total
Second homes[1]	61	13	21	5	77
Future retirement	52	30	13	6	64
Pieds-à-terre	60	13	23	3	30
Investment properties	38	34	24	4	442
Other	40	22	30	8	105
Total	45	27	23	55	718

Source: Paris et al., 2009, Table 8.
1. Respondents who gave 'holiday home' as main reason for acquiring their only or main additional residence.

Table 3.8 Social class of second homes and other ARs Australia 2007

| | Social class[1] expressed as % in each category | | | | |
ARs	Upper/ upper middle	Lower middle	Working	None/ other	Total
Second homes[2]	57	28	9	6	79
Other ARs[3]	53	25	18	4	422
No ARs	29	31	31	8	2,125
Total	34	30	28	8	
Valid no.	888	794	747	197	2,626

Source: Paris et al., 2009, Table 9
1. Respondents' self-definition
2. Respondents who gave 'holiday home' as main reason for acquiring their only or main additional residence
3. All other owners of ARs not giving holiday home as the main reason

Regardless of the main reasons stated for acquiring them, the average weekly household incomes of those owning additional residences were significantly higher than all other households: between $1,000 and $1,999 compared to between $700 and $999. Paris et al. (2009) tested whether there were any significant differences between those who gave investment as the main reason for acquiring additional residences and those who stated that they were acquired to use as second homes. No significant difference was identified in terms of social class (Table 3.8) as all owners of ARs were much more strongly concentrated in upper/upper middle class (53–7 per cent) than households without additional residences (29 per cent). Likewise, there were no significant differences between holiday home owners and other owners of ARs in terms of educational attainment. The main socio-economic differences were between all owners of ARs and the majority of respondents who did not own ARs. There was no evidence of a significant element of lower income or social class holiday homeowners. This is consistent with the view that the phase of 'vernacular' development of holiday homes in Australia has largely ended and that they are increasingly provided on market terms to higher income households. On the basis of this survey, therefore, owners of second homes and other residential property in Australia are affluent high income households, often with diverse residential property portfolios. Such households have the capacity to mix and match investments to maximise tax advantages and minimise risks of paying capital gains tax.

Second home owners in Australia: my friends' experiences

There is no in-depth survey data on Australian second home ownership, so we conducted a small survey of a group of people known to own second homes for leisure-related purposes. The questionnaire combined elements used in the Northern Ireland case study and NISRA surveys, but with scope for respondents to write at greater length about their own experiences and the history of second homes in the areas where theirs were located. Twenty possible respondents were contacted and a total of 12 replies were received. Despite much prompting it was only possible to achieve a 60 per cent response rate among my own friends, with non-respondents including social scientists who themselves frequently make use of survey data! The point of the survey was to explore the meaning and significance of second home ownership for the people concerned, and to relate the findings to wider debates about second home ownership within housing careers and household investment and consumption strategies. This cameo research exercise highlights diversity, even among a small group of respondents, especially in terms of the age and materials of the dwellings, frequency of visits, length of ownership, and how second homes have related to different households' life course planning (though they all travelled to their second homes by private transport).

The respondents have (or had) primary residences in capital cities: Melbourne (3), Adelaide (4), the ACT (4) and Brisbane (1). In most cases the distance between main and second homes was between 100 and 160 kilometres, though a couple were between 20 and 60 kilometres and one was over 200. Most own or owned one second home apart from one household with two. None was currently considering purchasing additional second homes though a few said that they may do so at some stage. Half had purchased their second homes using normal loans or mortgages and two had obtained loans guaranteed against equity in their primary residences. Three had bought their second homes without loans, using various combinations of savings, inheritance, gifts and pension funds. In most cases buying the second home was considered to have been a good or very good investment, with nine confident that values had risen above or very well above inflation. One who had bought recently, however, thought the value of the second home had *not* kept up with inflation, reflecting the recent downturn in housing markets. The overall pattern of responses regarding investment was similar to responses in the Northern Ireland case studies but also reflected the relatively robust state of Australian coastal and farming property markets.

Two did not know whether or not their second homes had been good investments; one of them, a 'blended' family, emphasised how important it had become in their wider families' lives:

> Our children did not know one another before we formed a couple so this was 'neutral' territory for all of us. We have never seen it as an investment but as a place where we can come together as a family especially in the summer months when all four families come to stay with us. It is not rented out. It has been an important place for us and for our children and grandchildren. It has significantly made it possible for our children and their partners to develop a good set of relationships as they come together and share the holidays playing games and enjoying the surfing and swimming in the lake and beaches.
>
> (Canberra resident)

Other respondents emphasised the central role their second homes had played in their family lives.

> Our home at Pine Point has been a pivotal part of our lives and children's lives. We are all involved in water sports and the house, for a long time, acted as a focus for these activities for our family and friends, spending quality time with the girls, simple pleasures talking, playing at the beach, crabbing, fishing, bonfires, laughing. Now the girls are older they have different interests like taking their friends, jet skies, water boards, but still enjoy fishing and crabbing.
>
> (Adelaide resident)

> It is the greatest environment to get kids to appreciate a lifestyle away from the city. They can catch crabs, go fishing, ride motor bikes and not get influenced by gangs of kids that have little to do. Now that the kids are older they use the shack often without mum/dad there and love it for the same reasons we did.
>
> (Adelaide resident)

3.38 Modernistic second home, Wye River, Victoria (source: anonymous, with permission)

3.39 Older timber-clad beachside second home at Cape Paterson, Victoria (source: Terry Burke)

The second homes are all in the same states as their primary residences, except for Canberra residents' second homes on the southern coast of NSW. Most second homes are detached dwellings of diverse materials and ages, with one attached two-story townhouse of recent construction. One was just a 'large shed with timber panels – a shack in the real sense of the word!' One striking modernistic timber and tin two-storey house sits on a sloping site (Figure 3.38), a large modern brick veneer house replacing a former more vernacular shack, an older timber beachside house (Figure 3.39), and a Federation farmhouse on 216 acres. Nearly all are by the sea, some with beach frontage, though one family has two farms in rural Victoria.

One respondent inherited land and added a shed with wooden panels. Eight purchased existing dwellings; in one case purchasing two separate farm properties in 2003 and 2008. The large brick veneer house built to replace the original shack is also called 'the shack' by the family (Figure 3.40). Two respondents purchased land and built their second homes shortly afterwards. In many cases upgrading work has been carried out at various times over the years. Half of the respondents acquired their second homes in the 1970s and 1980s, one in the 1990s and the rest from 2000. Previous occupants varied considerably: one had been occupied by a private tenant and two were rented to holidaymakers; two had been owner-occupied and two had been used by owners as holiday homes. Four were either purchased as new dwellings or built for the owners. Both of the farms had been occupied by owner–occupier farmers, though one had been subdivided before sale. In none of these instances, therefore, was there evidence of displacement or conflict with 'locals'.

The main reason for respondents having second homes was to use at weekends and holidays, though some cited family-related reasons and investment or business-

3.40 The new 'shack' at Pine Point, South Australia (source: Chris Paris)

related reasons. Other main reasons were for future retirement, local water-related leisure activities and investment. The reasons for getting specific second homes varied, with 'being near the coast' top of most lists, as well as connections with the area and local leisure opportunities; they all knew the areas before buying second homes there. None had relatives of friends living permanently locally but nearly all had friends with second homes in the same area, though in some cases through befriending other second home owners after having acquired their properties. Their use of the second homes varied considerably: two visited under 30 days a year, five others between 30 and 60 days and four between 60 and 100 days. Most visited their second homes for a mix of short and longer visits though two visited mainly just for one to two days. In most cases the pattern of visits had not changed much since acquiring the second home. One respondent had owned the second home for many years but no longer visits it as her second home because she had given it to her son who lives there on a permanent basis. Most respondents made regular use of local shops when at their second homes, though few made much use of other local services and facilities, apart from local council services.

The family with the two farms have a complex pattern and history of visiting their two additional properties. They visited the first at weekends and in summer holidays from 2003 (Figure 3.41) until they bought the second farm in 2008. Subsequently they visit the first only for one day most weeks but are at the second for three days a week and during holidays. Their overall pattern of use has thus

3.41 Brian and Ros Galligan with Ciara and steers at Otway Felix, Victoria, 2007 (source: Chris Paris)

changed with more regular and extended stays overseeing farm renovation and a breeding programme as well as checking their original farm purchase.

Most respondents had stories to tell about the history of second home ownership in the areas where they had second homes as well as the significance of their second homes in family lives and housing careers. They described diverse origins and many changes in second homes areas. One Melbourne-based respondent had owned the second home since 1986 and observed the changed area through the eyes of a part-time resident and as an experienced social scientist:

> This was a small beach development for residents of a nearby regional centre in the 1950s and expanded slowly in the next four decades. Growth accelerated in the 1990s as cashed up Melbournians discovered it. It also now attracts a sizeable retirement population. The balance between permanents and holiday use is about 50:50. It will never be a large community, however, as it has no main road connecting it and it abuts a protected marine parks.
>
> (Melbourne resident)

In two cases the second homes were in areas where previously there had been primary industrial activities: a silica mine by the southern NSW coast and a timber settlement to the west of Geelong, Victoria. One Canberra resident reflected on the changing character of Long Beach, in Eurobodalla Shire, where his family have their second home:

> Coastal shacks have been in the area for decades, and began to grow in the 1950s onwards. It was close to the main coastal centre and was popular with Canberrans. Through time, more blocks have been built on until now 95 per cent of blocks are developed. The size of houses and the cost has increased markedly over time. A new subdivision adjacent to ours is currently doubling the size of Long Beach, attracting many retirees
>
> (Canberra resident)

We stayed in the area in March 2009 amid signs of continuing development and subdivision along the coast and busy estate agency offices urging people to 'buy now' (Figure 3.42).

Some areas where South Australia respondents have second homes also were developed originally with basic shacks but went upmarket, rapidly and boisterously, partly following tighter planning and regulatory control as illustrated by the first of the following quotations. The second quotation illustrates more subtle changes where an area has retained its 'isolated' character:

> The beach front had shacks that had been owned by the same families for years. We bought in a new subdivision as there were no opportunities to buy

3.42 Estate agency sales office, Long Beach, New South Wales, 2009 (source: Chris Paris

in 2000 but by 2004 shacks were going on the market on the beach front and are now selling in the $1million bracket.

(Adelaide resident)

The area was developed with a few shacks in the 1960s and largely remains a shack area as people like to keep it simple and enjoy the fishing in the area. A few have recently built new houses but have maintained the wild scrubland around them hence the area retains its isolated nature.

(Adelaide resident)

One Adelaide resident with a second home in Carrickalinga said that it had been an expensive area since taking off in the 1970s, with a distinctive set of second home owners:

As far as I know it began as subdivision for housing development and it was sort of up market from the start… Many professionals had houses there, especially doctors and lawyers.

(Adelaide resident)

The area that has changed most is in the Sunshine Coast of Queensland. The basic fibro–asbestos and tin house had been built in the 1950s on what was then the outskirts of Caloundra and purchased as a second home in 1976 (Figure 3.43). Caloundra has been transformed since the house was built so it is now in a 'central'

129

3.43 Pen and ink drawing of the Caloundra holiday home in the 1970s, by Noel Ogden (source: Joyce Farr)

location. Thus what was a second homes area is becoming a commercial area and may face further change and redevelopment.

Owning these second homes fitted into well-considered longer term plans for all respondents. Three planned to use their second homes more when they had retired, but they would also keep their primary homes, rather than retiring to live full-time in their second homes. The family with the two farming properties have consciously developed a life strategy to become more involved in farming in future after retirement from their current jobs. Many emphasised how their second homes created an environment for escaping the pressures and stresses of working lives:

> It has been a wonderful outlet from the stress of work. We have used it more than we thought we would and we have made good friends in the complex with whom we socialise.
>
> (Canberra resident)

> It's fantastic! Couldn't cope with my job without it. Brilliant escape.
>
> (Melbourne resident)

Second homes and Australian housing: an overview

As in other case studies, apart from England, this case study was challenged by poor data on levels of second home ownership and use. Various studies, however, showed that an early high level of second home ownership had been sustained and increased since the 1940s, with many changes from pioneer shacks through to contemporary diversity and increasing developer dominance. There is a distinctive Australian geography of second homes, with 'second homes towns' in coastal locations, though second home ownership is not the only driver of change, with many other widespread processes of coastal development.

There are many similarities with the UK and Ireland in terms of socio-economic and demographic characteristics of Australian second home owners. They are typically affluent, middle-aged rather than retired. My friends' experiences highlight the diversity of circumstances but also that many people view second homes as crucial locales for escaping everyday pressures – implying that their primary residences do not provide such opportunities. This again challenges the idea that 'the home' (as primary residence) plays a crucial role in family life. Their evidence also shows diverse planned and actual uses of second homes in retirement – to be used more, but not exclusively, in addition to their primary residences. We can thus see intelligent people actively planning investment in second homes in terms of their ongoing family lives and other investment strategies.

Conclusions

> It is now possible to travel through bucolic parts of Ontario, as one can travel through Sussex in England or the Beauce in France, and pass hundreds of recreational homes that are not recognisable as recreational homes at all, except by the expert.
>
> (Wolfe, 1977: 31)

There are many similarities between the case studies of Britain, Ireland, Northern Ireland and Australia. In all cases it is clear that affluence and mobility have been core drivers of growing second home ownership. In all cases, too, there is evidence of a trend of second homes going upmarket. They are decreasingly vernacular structures and increasingly produced by developers and builders as well as being drawn from what had been the 'normal' housing market (though this trend is not entirely recent, as it was noted by Wolfe over 30 years ago).

Second homes have been a growing sector of both leisure and housing markets, especially in cities. Often the growth of second homes occurs in mixed new developments with hotels, leisure facilities, holiday lettings of houses, cottages and/or apartments. Growing second home ownership in other areas, however, is often accompanied by the loss of other forms of leisure accommodation, with hotels and guest houses closing down. Many caravan park owners want to go upmarket or get their sites re-zoned for housing, including second homes, and/or other commercial development.

In all cases there is blurring between dwelling use and, over time, some are let occasionally but others are not, showing that it only makes sense to think in terms of types of dwelling use rather than trying to classify dwellings by use. This, however, poses a dilemma for planners who wish to specify that dwellings may only be used in certain ways; their usual solution to this dilemma is to ignore it.

Evidence from the case studies also shows that high social/personal values are attached to second home ownership. Second homes are strongly valued as places of escape from everyday pressures, though this suggests that primary homes are not fulfilling that desirable objective. Has work–life interpenetration come to mean that primary homes retain an environment of work pressure, or is this just a rationalisation by affluent second home owners of their high level of residential consumption?

There was strong evidence of similar issues, debates and attitudes across all four case studies. Thus Frost's idea of residential tourism – that is people who have moved to attractive locations to live – and his suggestion that recently arrived 'permanent' residents may invent 'local' traditions, strongly echoed findings from the Northern Ireland case. Second homes were rarely the sole agency of change in any area; rather there were many diverse processes of change in coastal and country areas in all case studies. In some cases though, growing second home ownership has been a major driver of change, as with strong developer involvement in transforming parts of the Causeway Coast settlements in Northern Ireland, with redevelopment aimed at the second homes market. In Australia, unlike the other case studies, there was strong evidence of distinctive 'second home towns' though these appear in some cases also to be changing with growing proportions of permanent residents, including retirees.

There were some significant differences between the case studies, especially the more recent growth of second home ownership in the UK and Ireland contrasting with longer traditions in Australia and many other countries. The case studies show that there has been a continuum of planning contexts from very restrictive planning in Great Britain, through the more permissive albeit changing situation in Northern Ireland, to the highly permissive regime in Ireland. Other distinctive public policies in Ireland favoured property development with tax incentives hugely boosting housing production. Australian planning systems have tended to allow or guide development rather than restrict new initiatives, despite varying between states and territories and with diverse local government attitudes and policies.

These different contexts have created diverse policy and market combinations, with different patterns of opportunities and constraints on second homes. Different planning regimes have influenced what types of dwellings are used as second homes, such as older houses in England's gentrifying villages in countrysides or coasts but new developments elsewhere, such as LME. Second homes are mainly new houses in Ireland, but the stock of dwellings used as second homes is much more mixed in Australia. Such variations also reflect differences between 'new' and 'old' worlds as second home ownership has grown within different patterns of settlements and histories of places. Gentrification as an element of second home ownership has varied enormously, partly due to varying planning constraints affecting new developments but also due to changing demands and preferences elsewhere as areas that had been less popular begin to attract new demand from an increasingly affluent population.

Some differences are harder to identify with any clarity, partly due to poor official data sources in Ireland and Australia. Second homes may be more obvious in small rural settlements but they also have a big impact in urban areas. There may be more urban second homes in England than in the other cases, or this may simply reflect better data sources. It also may be the case that many English people who own two or more homes declare their city home as the 'second' home because local property taxes are higher and the discount is worth more. Even if that is the case, it does not affect the total numbers involved as the same people have at least two residences for their own use. Tax and benefit regimes also have varied considerably between the case studies, from no local property tax at all in Ireland, some reduction of local property tax for second homes in most of England, Wales and Scotland, to full application of local property tax in Australia and Northern Ireland.

The case studies provide many questions for the second homes literature within housing studies but also for the wider literature on second homes. Firstly, it is clear that the impacts of second homes on local housing markets and 'locals' are extremely diverse. In some cases the second home owners *are* the locals. In other cases there is evidence that people who moved to areas popular with second home owners object to the growth of second home ownership in these area. This suggests that it was fine for them to move into the area but that other people should not have the same freedom to decide how to use their homes. Secondly, it is clear that the ownership, use and disposal of second homes constitutes an important element of household investment and consumption strategies, including households' capacities for maximising benefits of tax concessions and investment opportunities over the life course. In all cases it appears that the great majority of second home owners are affluent, mobile, homeowners elsewhere and typically 40–60 years old rather than retirees. In many cases, therefore, second homes are primarily investment items, oriented towards capital appreciation, with the additional benefit of providing a valued leisure resource. Thirdly, the case studies show high levels of place attachment and that many second home owners value their second homes as settings for family life at least as much – and often more – than their primary homes. Thus it may be that 'home' is a conceptual bag of comfort that we can carry from place to place and attach to wherever and whichever dwelling in which we feel most comfortable at the time. Thus we can have numerous 'homes'.

Finally, there are significant differences between the case study countries in terms of the depth, impact and longer-term implications of the recession of 2007–2009 and these differences will influence the future of second home ownership in the various countries. The recession appears to have hit Ireland much harder than the other countries, with large surpluses of unsold dwellings especially in areas of high concentration of second homes. It seems to have had least impact in Australia, where economic growth is fuelled by a minerals boom and the national government confidently predicted substantial inward migration, which will fuel demand for housing for primary residences and for leisure and investment purposes.

4 Transnational second homes

Whether it is a holiday home, a place to retire to, an investment to supplement a pension – or, increasingly, a mixture of all three – some 800,000 of us now own a home abroad. Even concerns about the environmental consequences of air travel look unlikely to put anything more than a small dent in the upward curve.

(Unattributed, 2007)

Savills estimates there are currently 425,000 UK owned overseas properties. This is an increase of 35,000 units in the past 12 months with the total value of UK foreign owned property now stands at £58 billion.

(Savills, 2008)

Introduction

There has been enormous growth of transnational second home ownership, defined as the ownership of residential property in countries other than the owners' primary residences. It was widely expected to continue growing, as in *The Sunday Times* article (Unattributed, 2007). Transnational second home ownership comprises both short distance cross-border ownership, for example Singaporean families with homes in Malaysia, and the complex variety of longer-distance overseas second home ownership. Travel to some overseas second homes only involves a short ferry journey and drive, such as English-owned homes in France; others require long and complex international journeys, for example affluent Irish families buying in Thailand.

The academic study of transnational second home ownership is in its infancy. Most scholarly work on international second home ownership has focused on particular countries or regions, though many scholars have noted non-citizen ownership within these countries and regions (Hall and Müller, 2004a; McIntyre *et al.*, 2006). Very few housing researchers have considered transnational second home ownership.

This topic arouses widespread media interest, partly due to the advertising revenue from estate agents and developers. The property sections of newspapers in many countries are replete with adverts for overseas second homes. In September 2005, the 'Bricks and Mortar' supplement of *The Times* featured sporting personalities extolling the virtues of overseas property investment. Advertisements proclaimed the virtues of opportunities in Cyprus, France, Spain, Italy and South Africa, 'superb value tropical holiday homes' in Thailand, luxury apartments in Dubai and Kuala Lumpur, 'perfect sea views' in Bulgaria, 'superb chalet residences' in Switzerland and 'five star relaxation' in Newfoundland, Canada. Such advertising was still rampant in 2009 irrespective of the credit crunch and recession

Transnational second home ownership is big business, involving considerable assets, as Savills (2008) pointed out. Many reported figures are 'rubbery' and we must wade through marketing hype and glowing journalistic analyses as well as coping with the usual uncertainties caused by lack of solid data and the shifting characteristics of actual dwelling use. But there is some more solid ground: in England the SEH showed ownership of second homes overseas increasing much faster than within Britain: from 91,000 in 1994/5 to 235,000 in 2005/06. Other official data and industry-based estimates indicate growing levels of second home ownership in France and Spain by Dutch and German households. Some other estimates are much less reliable, often based on in-house 'estimates'. It can be hard to distinguish between objective analysis, self-serving journalistic commentary, upbeat sales propaganda and near-bankrupt vendors desperate to convince potential purchasers to buy their properties.

Overseas second homes are promoted through a huge and diverse literature in trade and professional journals plus kaleidoscopic websites. Companies marketing second homes overseas send email 'magazines' to registered users, for example http://www.tailoredhome.net (associated with building company Tailor Woodrow). The promotional activities of international real estate agencies and other 'boosters', including TV programmes and airline magazines, all proclaim the virtues of overseas property investment. The organisation, Overseas Property Expo advertised widely in newspapers and on the internet and ran many exhibitions between 2006 and 2009 (Figure 4.1). The company Homes Overseas holds exhibitions and publishes an electronic magazine (www.homesoverseas.co.uk); issue 36, February 2007, contained stories about homes in Egypt, New Zealand, South Africa and Australia. It also reported the launch of a new TV channel 'Home and Travel' on Sky TV that 'aims to offer viewers the chance to see famous hotspots with their own eyes to help make their buying decisions easier and cheaper'. The channel was claimed to be 'the first to be granted an Ofcom licence as a property shopping channel' (loc. cit).

Some specialist publications, especially Savills' annual reviews of second homes abroad, provide valuable insights into transnational second home ownership. Savills carried out substantial surveys of overseas property owners in association with Holiday-Rentals.co.uk to inform these reviews. Though the methodology is not

4.1 Homes Overseas advertisement, 2008 (photo: Chris Paris)

spelled out in detail, the status of Savills means that these results provide at least a good indicative guide to the topic. The market research company Mintel has also examined the ownership of second homes in the UK and overseas; its reports are too expensive for me but substantial press releases indicate their contents. The rest of this chapter examines the main drivers of transnational second home ownership, considers some of its risks, and examines two illustrative cases: second homes in Spain and the many homes of super-rich households.

Drivers of growing transnational second home ownership

Mintel's (2006) report on home ownership abroad was enthusiastically reported in many newspapers. Under the heading 'homeowners look to profit in the sun', Elliott (2006) reported that 'Thousands of people, inspired by the growth of cheap flights and TV property programmes, are cashing in on the value of their home to buy a bolt hole abroad.' Her report listed a series of reasons to buy abroad and factors influencing property purchase (see Figure 4.2); it did not raise the possibility that anything other than fun and profit could come of such purchases.

Most factors influencing transnational second home ownership are the same as for domestic second home ownership: rising disposable incomes and growing housing and other assets, combined with greater mobility made second home purchase an attractive element within household investment and consumption strategies. The socio-economic characteristics of transnational second home owners are similar to domestic second home buyers: mainly between 45 and 60, with high average household incomes (SEH, 2006/07). Savills' (2007a) survey found a higher proportion of younger buyers with household incomes *twice* the UK average. But other factors come into play regarding transnational second home ownership, mainly relating to differences between opportunities in 'home' and 'overseas' countries: more attractive locations for holidays and/or future retirement, lower house prices in many countries, perceived opportunities for part-time letting opportunities and/or capital growth, as well as new opportunities to access mortgage finance across more liberalised banking systems (Mintel, 2006, 2009; Savills, 2007a, 2008). Whilst lower prices are not always crucial, price differentials reflect different planning regimes, thus people from countries with restrictive planning regimes can acquire desirable second homes in places with more relaxed attitudes to planning and zoning, especially in comparison to Britain, The Netherlands or Germany.

Reasons to buy abroad	Influences when choosing a property
Sunny climate	Plenty of cheap flights
Investment	Good beaches nearby
Somewhere to use in retirement	English understood/other Britons nearby
Somewhere to take the children/family	Low prices
Low cost of living	Easy-to-let property
Sick of this country	Plenty of choice
Somewhere to rent out	Property prices that are likely to rise
Health reasons	Simple buying process
To be close to relatives/friends	Good leisure facilities
To pursue a hobby	Close to an airport
Start a business abroad	Good local tradesmen

Source: Elliott, 2006

4.2 'Getting away': reasons to buy abroad and influences on choosing a property

Transnational second home ownership is not the preserve of the rich, as illustrated by many down-market mobile homes in parks in Spain, Southern France or other popular venues. But the main focus here is on the booming wealth of 'escalator' areas, typically wealthy established global cities (London, New York, Los Angeles and Tokyo), that has enabled their affluent residents to shop globally for second homes and other overseas investments (Forrest, 2008). Savills (2008) reported that the ability to purchase using large cash reserves and equity from primary residences was a key driver of overseas second home ownership.

The huge bonuses being paid in the City of London at the height of the boom resulted in surging demand for luxury second homes overseas:

> Property in France, the United States and Italy is topping the shopping lists of City bankers this bonus season... About 51% of the City's bonus-earning workforce plan to buy property abroad in 2007, a poll by Populus for the property agency Pure International has found... Sean Collins, of Pure, said 'We have sold out a development of 77 units in Switzerland with an average price of £750,000. Many of the buyers were City based ... and reserved speculatively without even visiting.'
>
> (Allen, 2006)

Transnational second home ownership is an aspect of the globalisation of housing and property markets. Affluent families from oil-rich countries in the Middle East buy luxury homes across the globe and wealthy Asian households buy second homes across national borders. Buoyant capitalist super-rich residents of post-communist economic hot spots, especially Moscow, Shanghai and Beijing, shop globally for additional homes (as well as English Premier League football teams). The credit crunch and falling house prices in some countries have made property purchase more attractive for affluent people from other countries. For example, Indian newspapers contained many reports of high net worth Indians buying properties overseas as prices had fallen during the recession of 2008–2009; they were buying in Dubai, across Asia and in top-tier global cities especially London and New York (see, for example, Awasthi and Duttagupta, 2008). They may also take up new opportunities in Australia, where it had been difficult for overseas residents to purchase residential property until restrictions were relaxed during 2009. Australian developers established offices in China to promote off-the-plan developments and real estate agents were actively marketing in China; one Melbourne agency reported at least 40 per cent of recent sales being to overseas Chinese buyers (Dobbin, 2009).

The falling real cost of air travel and the growth of budget airlines serving new locations have enhanced mobility for millions of people, contributing to interest and investment in second homes across Europe and beyond. Savills (2008) noted growing numbers of Britons buying properties outside of Europe, especially in

Dubai, the Far East and the Caribbean, with fly-to-let investors more active in the long-haul market than leisure second home buyers.

Over 120 budget airlines were operating in 2009. Their magazines have routinely contained articles and advertising on second homes and retirement relocation and Ryanair advertised rental properties at many of its destinations, especially at www.RyanairVillas.com. The internet, with its huge search capacity, provides opportunities to advertise and look for second homes across the globe. Linked to this, ironically perhaps, local economic development strategies and advertising campaigns designed to attract tourists also attract second home purchasers. Savills (2007a) identified an average price premium of 37 per cent for local property markets served by budget airlines, with the strongest link between house prices and accessibility in places at a 'medium distance' from the UK, including the Canary Islands and Cyprus. Savills also suggested that the main increase in prices was in places 40–60 miles from airports; this is consistent with scholarly work showing that airport expansion tends to have strong economic multiplier effects (Green, 2007) but pushes prices down immediately around airports (Jud and Winkler, 2006). However, Savills (2007b) warned that destinations served by just one low cost carrier were 'particularly exposed to the withdrawal of that service'.

Growing transnational second home ownership also has been facilitated by restructured international and social relations. Changing relations between countries and the democratisation and development of free markets in former communist countries, especially through EU enlargement, have made it easier for citizens of one country to purchase homes elsewhere. The 2004 EU entrants (Hungary, Poland, Lithuania, Latvia and Slovenia) were marketed as ideal places to purchase second homes. Two more countries joined in 2007 with Bulgaria strongly promoted across the UK and Ireland as the cheapest destination for sun, sand *and* snow.

> Eastern Europeans are here in a big way, we all know, but what is less apparent is that they are part of a two-way traffic: Britons are heading east for holidays and to find holiday homes – and also to work. We hop on a cheap flight to Tallinn, Warsaw or Budapest and scour the emerging property markets, buying homes just about anywhere we can place on a map.
>
> (Adams, 2006)

Around one third of respondents to Savills' (2008) survey of overseas second home owners were 'fly-to-let' investors: people who bought overseas to seek rental income and capital gains, focusing on attractive cities, including Barcelona and Paris, as well as 'increasingly popular city break destinations' in Eastern Europe or further afield in Dubai (Savills, 2008). But the motivation for most overseas buyers was to secure a base for leisure and holidays, though many also planned to let their properties at least part time (Savills, 2007a, 2008). Leisure second home owners were less concerned with rental income and put more emphasis on climate and seaside locations. Most British-owned transnational second homes are in coastal areas of Spain and France, followed by Portugal, the USA and Italy, though the number in other countries has been growing steadily. With the exceptions of the most dangerous, impoverished or reclusive countries, it is a case of 'here, there and everywhere'. Whereas the British seek warmth, sun and sea, residents of very hot countries seek escape in cooler or less humid climates, possibly in the same places that the British visit to find warmth! Saudis take holidays in Malaysia to find relief from the intense heat of their summer within a fellow Islamic country and some rich Saudis buy second homes there.

Household investment and consumption strategies relating to transnational second home ownership involve combinations of factors that come together in various ways for different people including opportunities relating to culture, place, lifestyle, leisure and sporting activities (Mintel, 2006, 2009; Savills, 2007a, 2008). The difference between 'fly-to-let investors' and 'leisure' second home owners may be more a matter of emphasis, changing over time, than a distinctive difference between types of investors. Transnational second home purchasers often buy in localities that combine a range of leisure and commercial functions – resorts, hotels, property investment in holiday lettings (including part-time), second homes (including part-time) and lifestyle migration, often for retirement. In such places, therefore, conceptually separate 'markets' overlap and interweave, including second homes for family use and/or retirement, and/or let to holidaymakers.

The attractions of different cultures and specific places can be important for transnational second home buyers, including lifestyle opportunities less easily available in home countries, such as winter sports, sailing in the tropics, or exotic diving or fishing. Some 300,000 Hong Kong residents, many with middle to low incomes, owned homes across the border in Shenzhen where property was much cheaper and more spacious than at home, for leisure use at weekends, family meetings and/or with a view to future retirement (Chiu, 2006) (See Figure 4.3; these photographs were taken by Professor Chiu specifically for this book).

Many affluent households from overseas choose to have second homes in London and/or other major world cities. Some localities, notably Florida, combine opportunities for marine and city leisure activities and offer the prospect of possible longer-term retirement and/or migration strategies for people from outside the US. Affluent residents of Islamic countries may seek opportunities to enjoy more relaxed attitudes to personal freedom and alcohol in Western countries. Other second home buyers are attracted to wilderness or other exotic urban or rural areas, for example affluent Americans seeking solitude on remote Caribbean islands. Other cultural dimensions of transnational second home ownership include personal or family associations with particular places: second or subsequent generations of the children of migrants seek a base within the country where they feel they have roots. Thus British descendents of post-war Caribbean immigrants have purchased second homes on their ancestors' islands

4.3 Ideal second homes for golfers from Hong Kong – Palm Island golf club in Weizhou, Guangdong Province, China (source: Rebecca Chiu)

and descendents of Irish people who fled the Famine in the nineteenth century have purchased second homes back in the 'auld country'.

Expectations of continued growth in property values were highlighted in Savills' (2007a) report, especially in 'emerging hotspots' in former communist countries. By 2008, however, Savills' commentary noted slower growth, though most buyers remained optimistic regarding the long term. Mintel's earlier report (2006) had been bullish, reporting a claimed 45 per cent increase in British ownership of second homes abroad during just the previous two years. Mintel was still bullish in 2009, claiming that the dream of the 'place in the sun' was unaffected by the recession with around 7 million people in the UK interested in buying overseas – around the same number as in 2007, though people were more concerned about possible risks associated with such investment. It estimated that 425,000 properties were owned overseas by British residents during 2007/08: twice as many as seven years before.

Transnational second home ownership is often an element in longer-term migration and/or retirement strategies (Savills, 2007a, 2008). In some cases this is return migration, as reviewed in Duval's (2004) study of the Caribbean diaspora in the USA and Canada: many bought second homes back on Caribbean islands with a view to retiring there. For many others, buying a second home has constituted a bridge between visiting as holidaymakers and the longer-term commitment to migrate, providing opportunities for 'testing out' the new base (Cuba, 1989). Hundreds of thousands of British citizens have moved more-or-less permanently to France and Spain (Williams *et al.*, 2004). As with counter-urbanisation from UK metropolitan areas there is an element of 'white flight' as minority ethnic groups are under-represented both in the British countryside and enclaves in sunny Spain or France. Retirement migration has grown significantly since the 1980s, also closely linked to growing affluence and mobility, with many permanent migrants retaining some links with their country of origin, often owning a property there that is conceptually their 'second' home.

Risk and transnational second home ownership

For most of those involved, transnational second home ownership has been a pleasant and rewarding experience that has fitted well into household investment and consumption strategies or worked well as a precursor to permanent relocation for lifestyle or retirement reasons. The successful ones may have done their homework better, received better advice and been cautious in their choice of second home and location. Or they may just have been lucky, because whilst there are some risks involved in all property investments, there are distinctive risks involved in buying property in other countries. Many transnational second home buyers were either unaware of potential risks or simply ignored warnings that had been widely available for many years. For example in *The Sunday Times* Robinson (2006) had urged potential purchasers 'Don't be swept away by the thrill of owning abroad. Take a hard look at the market.' Some organisations marketing property warned customers of potential pitfalls involved in buying overseas:

> Releasing equity from a UK home is a great way to enable you to get a second home, however you should make sure that you are not risking your current property... You will need to seek professional advice and speak to a mortgage lender about your finances and whether it will be suitable for you to withdraw equity from your UK property.
> (http://www.asecondhome.co.uk/money-from-uk-home-buy-abroad.html)

Bad experiences of overseas second home ownership often have resulted from ill-informed or unreasonable expectations about legal and/or taxation systems, or cultural practices. Some second home purchasers assumed that other countries had more or less the same legal systems as in their own countries and were then distressed and confused to find that this is not the case. Keenan (2005) listed the 10 'biggest mistakes Irish people make when buying a place abroad'. His list is set out in Figure 4.4 and stands in dramatic contrast to the rosy picture painted by many salespeople and some other journalists (e.g. Elliott, 2006; see Figure 4.2).

With a list like that it may be surprising that anybody gets it right! And there are even more risks because some problems associated with transnational second home ownership result from changing circumstances, possibly due a change of government, whether 'at home' or 'away'. For example, it was suggested that the Leader of the Opposition in the UK 'risks alienating more than 400,000 voters who

1 Picking the wrong location: less reputable neighbourhoods or politically unstable countries.
2 Choosing the wrong sector: e.g. city apartments where prices are falling.
3 Failure to consider Ireland's tax claims: 'when you sell an overseas property you're liable to pay capital gains tax in Ireland'.
4 Failure to secure adequate title or ensuring that homes had proper planning approval and complied with other regulations.
5 Local succession and inheritance rights may be markedly different from at home.
6 Failure to take exchange rates into account, especially outside the Euro zone: 'Buyers can have their profits wiped out by currency fluctuations'.
7 Failure to research local taxation systems; Ireland had no local property taxes but other countries have diverse ways of taxing property. Some also impose income or wealth taxes on second home owners as well as permanent residents.
8 Failure to research an exit strategy: some countries will not allow expatriation of currency and others may charge various levies.
9 Failure to research interstate tax agreements: property sales in some countries would result in tax liabilities both in that country and in Ireland.
10 Failure to recruit local help: 'A local clown is better than no clown at all. There have been cases of buyer purchasing apartments from companies targeting Ireland only to find that they could have bought them far cheaper over there'.

Source: Keenan, 2005

4.4 Mistakes that Irish people make when buying overseas own "a place in the sun" with plans for a tax on air travel' (Fenton *et al.*, 2007). Sometimes overseas governments will change a law or policy with damaging implications for non-citizen home owners. For example, concerns were expressed that the rules concerning foreign ownership in Goa were changed so that hundreds of people were at risk of losing their homes (Smith, 2009):

> Vikram Varma, a local lawyer, said more than 1,000 people could have been caught out by changes in the laws and by builders' scams. More than 400 foreigners, mainly Britons, are being investigated by India's enforcement directorate for alleged violations of property laws and could have homes confiscated. They are allowed to live in the homes but, without deeds, cannot sell the properties. 'Most who come here are as trusting in the efficiency of the system in India as they are in the UK. But here it's entirely different,' said Varma.
>
> (Smith, 2009)

Many agents and developers selling second homes predict high levels of capital gain and relaxed lifestyles within easy-going environments, often 'secure' gated communities. Advertisements stress life-course opportunities and encourage retirement or migration strategies. They never mention that second home owners may be resented by poor locals or that any other risks may attach to such property investment. Issues of equity and choice, however, come into sharper focus as the growth of transnational second home ownerships brings greater differentials of incomes and wealth between 'locals' and second home owners (Smith and Duffy, 2003). 'Hard sell' agencies have often put intense pressure on potential purchasers who fall for stories of easy capital gains and 'guaranteed' rental returns as reported by *The Sunday Times* reporters: 'Home buyers stung for a place in the sun' (Calvert *et al.*, 2006). Irish buyers were reportedly duped into paying a combined amount of more than £10 million by false claims regarding properties in Turkey, though whether they were fooled by an Irish agent or he was fooled by a Turkish villain remained in dispute (Heatley, 2007). Over 500 investors from across Europe were attracted by off-plan seaside apartments to be constructed by a Spanish developer in Brazil. They lost their €30,000 deposits because the development never happened and the developer was sent to prison in Spain (Emmett, 2009). Similar stories abound in Brazil where dreams of 'a paradise and property hotspot' are shattered and 'the coastline of almost continuous beaches, from Bahia to Rio Grande do Norte, is littered with plans for property developments that have never come to fruition' (op. cit.).

Changing exchange rates and interest rate fluctuations present greater risks for people buying overseas rather than in their home country, especially if they take out loans in the local currency. Savills' survey (2008: 4) indicated a dramatic shift in the pattern of indebtedness relating to overseas purchases. Whereas nearly 80 per cent of overseas second homes were purchased without a mortgage or other borrowing in 2000, by 2007 the situation was reversed with 80 per cent of purchasers having mortgages or other loans. Over 60 per cent had borrowed more than half of the cost of their second homes with about half borrowing over 75 per cent. Significant proportions had borrowed against the equity in their primary residences, often in the currency of the country in which they purchased: they are especially vulnerable to exchange rate fluctuations if their incomes fall in real terms against the cost of buying in the foreign currency. Some who purchased in local currency during a period of low interest rates have experienced difficulty in affording the cost of their second homes or simply want to sell it for other personal reasons, only to find that lack of demand combined with falling local property prices and currency values mean that that they have growing negative equity and no realistic prospect of a sale *at all*, let alone at a loss.

Another risk associated with transnational second home ownership comes from volatility in local housing markets containing large proportions of second homes, especially in countries where housing and property development were exceptionally large elements of economic development (Ireland, Spain and Dubai). Dubai fell sensationally from grace during 2009. Firstly, there were reports of construction ceasing on many projects, the departure of many expatriate workers and dramatic falls in property prices (Lewis, 2009). Secondly, news filtered out that major developer Dubai World wanted a delay in debt repayments and that the Dubai government would not bail it out (http://news.bbc.co.uk/1/hi/8385164.stm). Work stopped abruptly on the iconic 'World' project, comprising artificial islands shaped like the countries of the world; it became 'a disjointed and desolate collection of sandy blots – a monumental folly just out of sight of Dubai's shore' (Mclean, 2009). Many celebrities had been reported to have bought into this project, but together with many less affluent investors they may have little prospect of getting their money back, and Mclean (2009) reported that the business person fronting a consortium that bought 'Ireland' had committed suicide.

Ball (2005: 35) warned that 'the longer the second homes markets boom, the greater is the chance that shocks will lead to serious short-term declines'. Media reports highlighted overproduction, excess of supply over demand, creeping interest rate rises and high levels of debt in the Spanish construction industry. Similar news, however, was redefined three years ago as a 'chance to snap up a bargain' (Stucklin, 2006) and more recently falling prices suggested that 'Perhaps the dream holiday home is within our grasp' (Dare Hall, 2009)(!) Much investment in second homes markets in Ireland, Spain and Dubai had been driven by investors hoping to make profits from surging growth in capital values, but demand dried up, confirming Ball's prediction.

> British owners of second homes overseas are facing ruinous losses on their
> investments after plunging price drops in foreign markets wiped as much as

£24bn from the value of UK-owned homes abroad… Dubai and Bulgaria are the worst hit markets, with reported peak-to-trough price falls of 75 per cent on property built for the investment market… The high levels of debt used to engineer transactions have ratcheted up the risk of financial problems for purchasers following the collapse of property markets.

(Barrett, 2009)

Many TV programmes contained seductive stories of luxury and massive capital gains in waiting, but their tone changed dramatically after 2007. The UK's Channel 4 broadcast a programme in January 2006, 'A place in the sun – the 20 best places to make money', suggesting that large capital gains would be made easily by investors in overseas property. In June 2009, however, the same company showed a two-part story of Spain, titled 'Paradise lost', chronicling the devastating impact of collapsing property markets and failed development projects on Britons who had bought dream homes in Spain only to discover that the reality was a living nightmare. *Homes Overseas* advertised a range of discounts on Spanish properties, with 'more than 200 units sold with discounts up to 35%', featuring Mallorca as 'one of the top ten destinations to invest in property' and urging potential customers to 'buy now, while you still have the choice' (August 2009). The advertisements included substantial price cuts, for example a two-bedroom 'modern residential building' in Puerto Pollença was reduced by nearly 50 per cent from €370,000 to €208,400. *Homes Overseas* also announced 'Property alert: Orlando Florida prices slashed a further 50%' but still suggested that this was a good time to buy. Despite price falls and the fact that capital growth can never be guaranteed, some advertisers still promised 'risk-free' investment opportunities in second homes overseas:

Risk Free Investment with Guaranteed Rental Return. Now is the time to Buy! Solid Investment High potential capital gain.

(Advert in easyJet in-flight magazine September 2009 and http://www.castromarimgolfe.com)

It can be hard to untangle the combined effects of changing circumstances, corrupt practices, misleading advertising, salespersons' promises, exaggerations and lies on the one hand, from genuinely unanticipated changes in market conditions on the other. The reported collapse of prices in Bulgaria and Dubai seem almost inevitable with the benefit of hindsight. In both cases there was intensive marketing hype and massive growth from relatively low bases. But the distinctive change in the pattern of indebtedness between 2000 and 2007 resulted in many transnational second home purchasers facing the prospect of substantial losses: 'The extent of price falls across foreign markets means that most of the 35,000 Britons who completed deals in the 2007-08 financial year will already be in negative equity' (Barrett, 2009).

There have been many well-documented cases of compulsory acquisition of second and/or retirement homes with little or minimal compensation as well as corruption scandals involving development in parts of Spain (Diaz and Lourés, 2006). There also has been intense controversy over development of second homes in North Cyprus, mainly for English buyers, where land title has been hotly disputed (Mayer and Baytin, 2006).

> Thousands of Britons with holiday and retirement homes in northern Cyprus face eviction after the Court of Appeal upheld a decision that a British couple must surrender disputed land. David and Linda Orams … have spent six years fighting a legal battle but must now give back the property to the original owners… Around 5000 Britons live on land in northern Cyprus once owned by Greek Cypriots who fled to the south when Turkey invaded in 1974.
>
> (Nugent, 2010)

At a less sensational level, Kerchavel (2008) reported that Irish second home owners had installed online cameras in their overseas homes because they believed that local agents were letting the properties and pocketing the rent themselves rather than paying the owners. This could happen at home, as can a whole host of other criminal risks associated with second homes overseas, but may be harder to detect at greater distances involving international travel. But far worse things can and do happen. In the book *Tourism Mobilities* (Sheller and Urry, 2004: 213), Urry warned: 'Potential death and the fear of death stalk almost all the places that are examined in this book.' Recent examples of deaths include the murder of a former nurse in Jamaica, with police 'hunting for a local man who had been assisting Mrs Scott-Jones with the renovation of her holiday home' (Pavia, 2008). British pensioners murdered near Alicante were feared to be victims of non-Spanish criminal gangs targeting expatriates who were considered easy prey, often living in isolated villages 'and not fully integrated into the Spanish community' (Byers, 2007). Whether there is actually more crime overseas may be in doubt, but people with limited experience of local legal systems or competence in local languages are always more vulnerable.

Other major risk factors relate to the 'low cost' or 'budget' airlines that have stimulated the growth of transnational second home ownership, and to the airports they use. Risks relate to the very existence of individual airlines, the cost of flying, the routes they fly and the frequency of flights. As well, in common with all airlines, they risk losing their massive tax advantage over other forms of travel: aviation fuel has remained untaxed since 1944 and no country wants to put its carriers at risk by breaking ranks and imposing new taxes. But concerns about energy use, atmospheric pollution and sustainability will eventually lead to an international agreement to levy taxes on aviation fuel, thus fundamentally changing the relative cost–income balance of competing modes of transport (Graham and Shaw, 2008).

Some countries with the worst national budget deficits are popular transnational second home destinations: the so-called PIIGS countries (Portugal, Italy, Ireland, Greece and Spain). The viability of regional airports is also at risk because many are subsidised by governments and could face closure if subsidy is withdrawn, and from 2011 tighter EU regulations will reduce state subsidies to non-commercial routes. In the case of Ireland, the combination of fiscal stringency and tighter EU regulations endanger the viability of at least five airports: Donegal, Galway, Sligo, Kerry and Waterford (O'Brien, 2009). Similar considerations will apply in all the PIIGS, especially if road and intercity rail improvements combine with cost pressures to reduce the competitive advantage of regional airports.

The demise of budget airlines had been predicted in 2003 when rising oil prices caused a temporary slowdown in growth, but between 2004 and 2007 there was continued growth in the number of airlines, the routes they flew and the passengers they carried. But even during periods of growth there were many failures, especially long-haul carriers operating out of Hong Kong (Oasis) and Canada (Zoom). Many other budget airlines have come and gone during the last 20 years: over 20 in the USA, around 10 each in Mexico and Canada and 20 in other countries. Second homes in areas covered by just one such airline are particularly at risk of losing easy – or cheap – access. All airlines were affected by the recession of 2007–2009 with falling demand and increasing costs (Robertson and Nugent, 2008). Ryanair announced an 85 per cent fall in profits in 2008 due mainly to increased fuel costs (Pagnamenta, 2008).

> The rampant growth in air traffic is not sustainable and the business model must change. It's not only the incumbent flag-carriers that are threatened but the new low-cost carriers that thrive because of two market miracles – the availability of very cheap fuel and galloping growth in passenger numbers. But these buttresses are crumbling, playing havoc with a business model that has changed the face of aviation over the past decade.
>
> (Mortished, 2008)

Crucially for many transnational second home owners, the number of routes was cut substantially and the frequency of flights was greatly reduced both by 'legacy' airlines like British Airways and by budget carriers. Second home owners who assumed that regular cheap flights would last indefinitely became aware of the harsh realities of commercial aviation; some planned to petition airlines to reinstate routes that had been closed (Swinford, 2008) but Ryanair boss Michael O'Leary clearly stated his view on the subject: 'Please don't ask me to feel sorry for rich people with second homes in France' (Condon, 2008). If recent changes in routes and frequency of flights become permanent, or are followed by more substantial cutbacks, this will have profound implications for transnational second home ownership.

So, with little good news in aviation industry – at least 50 carriers worldwide are thought to be facing bankruptcy this winter, as the price of fuel rockets, passenger demand looks set to fall and fares rise in a worsening economy – our whole attitude to second home ownership abroad may have to undergo a radical shift.

(Wells, 2008)

Spain: the epitome of transnational second home ownership

In Spain, 1m newly built apartments remain unsold, and a further 2m are estimated to be back on the re-sale market as foreign buyers retreat. The newly built properties alone account for five years of supply, based on current sales rates, and local experts believe prices have already fallen by 30 per cent.

(Barrett, 2009)

Spain has the largest number of second homes of any EU state (Ball, 2009), with a high level of indigenous second home ownership as well as transnational second home owners from other EU states and further abroad, especially Russia. It is also the permanent home for thousands of UK and other EU citizens, as well as immigrants from poorer countries (especially Morocco, Ecuador and Colombia). Much of coastal Spain has become highly developed, with resorts and hotels together with concentrations of apartments, villas and other housing: a sprawling mix of commercial vacation homes, holiday lets and second homes as well as longer-term migration for lifestyle or retirement. It was estimated that around a third of Spain's Mediterranean coast was built up by 2006, rising to above 50 per cent in the Costa del Sol and Costa Brava (Burgen, 2006). Spain is also the paradigm case of potentially risky transnational second home ownership within what Ball has described as distinctive and highly volatile local housing markets. Spain had the biggest housing market boom in Europe between 2001 and 2007 followed, perhaps, by the biggest bust (Ball, 2009).

Much of the urbanisation of the Spanish coast and growth of transnational second home ownership is very recent. Spain only emerged from 40 years of military dictatorship in the 1970s. Its first recognisably modern democratic government was formed in 1982 and it joined the EU in 1986. Since the early 1980s, too, there has been significant decentralisation of many state functions to Autonomous Communities within Spain, with 'widely differing urban and territorial policies, based on specific legislation in each Autonomous Community' (Diaz and Lourés, 2006). The Spanish housing system has had more in common with other Southern European countries than other EU members: very high levels of home ownership, small or non-existent social rental sectors and a high level of second home ownership by affluent households (Allen *et al.*, 2004; Leal 2006). Home ownership was boosted to over 80 per cent of households by 2001. Rent controls made investment in rental accommodation unattractive, so wealthier households used disposable income to purchase second homes for personal use rather than invest in rental property (Alberdí and Levenfeld, 1996; Leal, 2006). Their second homes are owned across Spain, often inland within easy access of major cities, and in very different contexts than the Spanish Costas dominated by holiday accommodation and overseas second home ownership, such as Alicante and the Costa del Sol. However, as both Barke (2008) and Ball (2009) have noted, locally owned second homes are part of the overall Spanish housing market rather than constituting spatially separated sub-markets dominated by leisure use. As well, the case of Spanish local second home ownership illustrates how local political and policy contexts can affect patterns of household investment and consumption of housing.

Expert local commentators in the mid-1990s described a stable level of housing construction with an annual average around 250,000 house building starts; they expected a downward trend in new building during the 1990s and towards 2009 (Alberdí and Levenfeld, 1996). Instead, building increased dramatically to a peak of over 700,000 housing starts in 2006 with completions averaging over 500,000 a year between 2000 and 2008. At the height of the boom, in 2005, over 800,000 new housing units were approved in Spain: more than the combined total in Germany, the UK and France (Diaz and Lourés, 2006). House prices rose rapidly across Spain up to 2004, despite the building boom, in response to unprecedented economic growth and demand from a flood of immigrants. Around a third of all new building in Europe was in Spain, with 23 million homes for a population just over 40 million, but nearly two million were officially empty and many more were unoccupied for most of the year (Burgen, 2006).

The boom ended in 2007 and prices fell in nominal and real terms (Ball, 2009; http://www.globalpropertyguide.com/Europe/Spain/Price-History). Much new stock remained unsold in 2009, especially in coastal areas with high concentrations of second homes, many projects were unfinished and many builders had sought refuge in bankruptcy. Other parts of Spain were much less affected by the boom–bust cycle, though most have undergone extensive suburbanisation and comprise complex patterned layers of old and new, with diverse mixtures of renewal, gentrification and regeneration. Barke (2008) emphasised that foreign ownership was widespread throughout Spanish housing markets, both of primary homes (often retirees) and second homes, but suggested that 'relationships between first and second homes within this sub-market may well be different from those in the indigenous sub-market' (Barke, 2008: 262). Thus local families own and use second homes, typically located within relatively short distances from the primary residence, often making many short visits. By way of contrast, foreigners typically use second homes as a stepping stone to longer term migration or for fewer but longer visits. Thus Spanish second home owners tend to be 'circulating' whereas foreign second home users are 'seasonal migrants' (Casado-Diaz, 2004).

British second homes in Spain

Spain has been the most favoured overseas location of British second home owners for many years, as well as a popular location for permanent migration for retirement and lifestyle reasons. The Spanish government requires non-citizens living permanently in Spain to register their status with local authorities, so there are some data on the extent of permanent residence of non-nationals in Spain, but the number of overseas second home owners is more difficult to determine. Stucklin (2004) reported that the 117,000 UK citizens comprised about 27 per cent of the 439,000 European non-nationals registered as living permanently in Spain. Various commentators had suggested that the level of registration was low, and recent legislation has resulted in a higher level of registration, with around 5.6 million foreign nationals registered in January 2009 out of a total population of 46.6 million. This represented a huge increase on previous figures (Barke, 2009, personal correspondence). No data on national origin is available for 2009, but 269,000 UK citizens over 15 years old were registered as living permanently in Spain in 2007 and when the 2009 origin breakdown is available, the figure could be significantly higher again.

The number of transnational second home owners in Spain is hard to establish, as it is impossible to derive accurate estimates based on census or other official data sources (Barke, 2009, personal correspondence). The SEH is the best official statistical source on English second home ownership in Spain but it almost certainly undercounts the number. Strong growth of overseas second home ownership stimulated the SEH to include questions about the location of overseas second homes from 2003/04. This showed Spain as the main location with 57,000 in 2003/04 growing to 81,000 by 2006/07 (see Table 4.1). If there had been a similar proportion in 1996/97, then on the basis of the SEH estimate of the total number of overseas second homes, there would have been around 25,000–30,000 second homes in Spain owned by English households. Overall, therefore, the SEH data suggest that the number of English-owned second homes in Spain doubled between 1996/97 and 2006/07 with the fastest rate of increase between 2003 and 2006. These estimates of the rates of change both overall and specifically with regard to Spain were consistent with other sources including Savills (2007a, 2008) and Mintel (2006).

Other sources, however, suggest that a much larger number of second homes in Spain are owned by UK citizens. Savills (2008) estimated that there were around 425,000 UK-owned properties overseas, including investment properties (though some investors own numerous properties). They suggested that around 34 per cent were in Spain, which would amount to around 145,000. Owen *et al.* (2006) reported in *The Times* that 300,000 properties in the Costa del Sol and 70,000 in the Costa Blanca were owned by British households, though they did not specify their source. Stucklin (2004) cited numerous studies undertaken by consultancies and a leading Spanish business school as the basis for his estimate that around 600,000

Table 4.1 SEH data on English households with second homes abroad

| | SEH year | | | | | | Change 1996/97 to 2006/07 | | Change 2003/04 to 2006/07 | |
| | 1996/97 | | 2003/04 | | 2006/07 | | | | | |
	%	000[1]	%	000	%	000	%	000	%	000[1]
France	n.a.	25–30	24	39	24	60	114	32	54	21
Spain	n.a.	35–40	35	57	33	81	108	42	42	24
Other Europe	n.a.	18–22	18	29	22	55	162	34	90	26
Remainder	n.a.	25–30	23	38	21	52	93	25	37	14
Total	n.a.	115	100	163	100	248	118	135	52	85

Source: SEH 2003/04 (for percentages by country in 2003/04), SEH 2006/07 for percentages by country in 2006/07 and total estimated numbers for all years Paris et al. 2009, Table 9.

1. The totals for 1996/97 are estimates based on a similar proportional distribution as in 2003/04.

n.a. not applicable.

properties in Spain were owned by British residents, including second homes and investment properties. He also claimed that the TV company Channel 4's website had said 'Spain is the number one destination for UK second homebuyers and over two million Britons own a property on its shores.' These numbers vary dramatically, but it can reasonably be concluded that the number of UK-owned second homes, not including properties primarily let to holidaymakers or tenants, was in the order of 300,000 or more. No evidence can be produced at present to disprove this.

Second homes have played an important role in the migration decisions of many Britons moving permanently to Spain though others have made the move on the basis of less experience, such as holidays or simply a quick visit. Many thousands have been and remain very happy with their move, but for others the experience has been anything but happy. The horror stories are legendary: thousands of houses built illegally, without planning permission, or on land that was not legally owned, resulting in demolitions and the loss of homes and savings. More than 200,000 properties may be affected where developers have built and sold properties on land protected by the national Spanish Coastal Law; owners were seeking redress in the European parliament during 2009 but the outcome was uncertain (Stucklin, 2009).

Some eight months before Elliott's gushing (2006) report (above) on homeowners 'cashing in' on second home purchase overseas, fellow *Times* journalists had warned that 'thousands of second homes face bulldozer in Costa scam' (Owen *et al.*, 2006: 12), as 'demand among Britons for second and retirement homes in Spain has helped to fuel an epidemic of illegal construction on the Costas'. Other Murdoch-stable journalists also had reported a 'dark underbelly' of Spanish second homes under the headline 'Pirates of the Mediterranean' (Burgen, 2006). This investigative report claimed that 'the demand for a place in the sun has turned Spain into the money-laundering capital of Europe' and '[v]ast sums amassed through arms-smuggling, drugs and prostitution are being recycled into holiday homes for us British and other north Europeans' (Burgen, 2006: 40). It was reported that money laundering was rife, with 100,000 properties exchanged for cash in 2001. Marbella hit the headlines when the 'mayor, councillors, developers, notaries, lawyers and businessmen' were 'among 23 people arrested for their roles in the alleged racket headed by the chief of urban planning' (Owen *et al.*, 2006: 12). When the deputy mayor of Marbella was arrested, reportedly 'police found €350,000 worth of €500 notes in her house' (Burgen, 2006: 41).

Dreams thus turned into nightmares for many transnational second home and retirement purchasers, with many people unable to offload apartments or villas in unfinished developments, abandoning their properties or enduring the agonies of bank repossessions (Toomey, 2009). The Spanish economic boom was well and truly over with unemployment into double figures across the country and reportedly up to one in three of under-25 year olds (Abend, 2009). Building work had ceased on many projects with some residents of unsellable homes literally having to clean sewage from their gardens during periods of heavy rain. Many retirees, moreover, found that exchange rate changes had reduced the value of their pensions, paid in pounds, when converted to euros. Others, who moved to Spain to work, found difficulty maintaining employment or incomes in an increasingly difficult market. Reports of return migration back to the UK were unable to specify what number of people was involved, partly because many Britons resident in Spain had not notified any authorities, and had chosen 'to remain officially living in Britain for tax or pensions, so to the British authorities they never actually left' (Keeley, 2009).

But falling prices and the ending building boom were not unique to Spain. Prices were also reported to be falling in many other second home markets in Europe, the USA and 'emerging' markets of central and eastern Europe, including 'fly to let' investments, due to 'the surplus of identical blocks along the Mediterranean and Black Sea coasts' and 'the global credit crunch that has driven up mortgage rates across much of the world' (Conradi, 2007). There were some particular parallels with Ireland: both countries had house building booms with high proportions of jobs and new investment in residential construction industries, followed by massive shocks where construction levels and employment declined dramatically leaving a legacy of overproduction, high unemployment, bankruptcies and unfinished projects. One big difference, however, is that in Spain many thousands of transnational second home owners and retirees are affected by these developments whereas in Ireland there has been a much smaller transnational dimension to the second homes boom.

Affluence: the many homes of the global super-rich

> The rapid development of an international property market means that real estate prices at the center of New York City are more connected to prices in central London or Frankfurt than to the overall real estate market in New York's metropolitan areas. In the 1980s powerful institutional investors from Japan, for example, found it profitable to buy and sell property in Manhattan or central London. In the 1990s, this practice multiplied involving a rapidly growing number of cities around the world. German, Dutch, French and U.S. firms invested heavily in properties in central London and in other major cities... And even after the attacks of September 2001, New York City real estate has been bought by a growing number of foreign investors, partly due to the weak dollar, which made these acquisitions profitable [and] force prices up because of the competition between rich investors and buyers.
>
> (Sassen, 2006: 10)

Finally, we come to the ownership of multiple dwellings in many countries by affluent global elites, including business magnates, oil and minerals barons, international financiers and investors, artists and dealers, royalty from many countries, show business and sporting superstars, as well as celebrity politicians like Tony Blair. Global economic actors choose homes in many locations and their purchases can have a dramatic influence on upmarket property prices. Parts of some city-regional and/or national housing markets are 'decoupled' from local and national economic and demographic factors driving housing markets: they are part of a rapidly developing international property market (Sassen, 2006), with new spatial patterns and inequalities including 'quartered' cities (Marcuse, 2006). There are many overlaps between leisure/pleasure, investment and business-related multiple residential ownership at a global rather than merely transnational scale (Hall, 2005; Urry, 2007).

The many homes of the global super-rich include mansions in London's West End, penthouses in Los Angeles, ski lodges in the Alps and exclusive Caribbean island retreats. There has not been any systematic scholarly study of this phenomenon, so this section is based largely on media sources and is illustrative of issues and topics rather than rigorously exhaustive.

One journalist (D. Smith, 2006) wrote about the 'hidden world' of Roman Abramovich:

> Abramovich is part of the rich Russian set that has colonised London's most exclusive neighbourhoods. He has a house in Belgravia worth an estimated £28m as well as an £18m estate in West Sussex. His wife, Irina, a former air stewardess, enjoys the city life and the couple's five children go to English schools. But Abramovich – who also owns a £10m St Tropez villa, two super yachts and a Boeing 767 – does not necessarily regard the British capital as home. 'I live on a plane. I like to visit London. If I had to think where I could live if not Moscow, London would be my first choice and second would be New York. In Moscow I feel most comfortable. I'm used to four different seasons; it's difficult for people in London to understand. People brought up in Russia like my kids want to play in the snow.'
>
> (D. Smith, 2006)

Three years later, having divorced and remarried, Abramovich purchased a 'stunning Caribbean hideaway' for £54 million on the tiny island of St Barts (Todd, 2009).

Some completely new 'communities' have been developed to attract wealthy owners of multiple dwellings to new spaces for hyper-consumption; for example in gated and fortified luxury resorts in the USA or – unsuccessfully – on newly created islands in Dubai. But much transnational multiple home ownership, involving massive amounts of air travel, is found in the world's most expensive residential areas, such as Bishops Avenue in Hampstead or Kensington Palace Gardens in Knightsbridge (Caesar, 2008). Multimillionaires and billionaires with homes in many countries select homes in the most expensive suburbs or ex-urban areas of the most expensive cities, including London.

Britain is 'a haven for the international super-rich. The number of billionaires has surged to 68… About a third are from overseas and only three of the wealthiest 10 billionaires were born here' (Woods, 2007). Thus as Sassen argued (above) the prices of mansions in London or country estates in south-east England reflect the fortunes of global actors rather than the UK economy as a whole. In October 2007, *The Sunday Times* reported that almost half of the country homes in south-east England worth more than £5 million were bought by foreigners as 'Russian oligarchs and tycoons from Asia and the Middle East … emulate the lifestyle of Britain's landed gentry' and that 'up to 75% of country homes worth more than £10m have been snapped up by wealthy investors from abroad' (Gadher and Davies, 2007). Meanwhile, in the UK, the property pages of newspapers such as *The Times*, *The Telegraph* or *The Observer* contain many pages devoted to luxury dwellings for leisure use in dozens of overseas countries. One magazine, *International Homes*, is devoted to this subject. Although it offers free online subscription, it emphasises exclusivity and lifestyle:

> International Homes Luxury Collection has a unique distribution through first and business class in-flight and airport lounge placement with a wide variety of airlines including British Airways, Emirates, American Airlines, Virgin and many more. Complementing this is high street distribution through selected premier outlets. We reach the most desirable high net worth audience with strong spending power and impressive profiles.
>
> (http://www.international-homes.com)

The many homes of the super-rich are ample testimony to Hall's (2005) suggestion that mobility and multiple home ownership make it harder to think in terms of 'home' in the singular. Many London mansions have been purchased by overseas owners who rarely if ever visit them, rather they are investments and possible bolt-holes should political or other problems emerge in their own – typically oil-rich – countries (Caesar, 2008). During the 2008 presidential campaign in the USA, the Republican candidate Senator John McCain was taken by surprise in an interview when asked 'How many houses do you and Mrs McCain have?' He was reported to have answered that he was not sure so 'I'll have my staff get to you. I'll try to tell you about that.' His staff subsequently said that the McCains owned 'at least four (homes)' though a watchdog organisation, PolitiFact.com (2008), claimed that the McCains probably owned eight homes, including a high rise condo in Arlington, Virginia, a six-acre ranch in Arizona as well as various condos in Colorado, Texas and Oklahoma. Some may be rented to tenants, but the diversity of this property portfolio is a splendid illustration of the multiple homes of rich Americans.

Not to be outdone by the Americans, the multimillionaire Secretary of State for Northern Ireland, Shaun Woodward, was reported to have purchased his seventh home, a luxury apartment in an Alpine ski lodge, for £1 million (Henry, 2010). That should nicely complement the villas in the Caribbean and Long Island, Maryland, homes in Oxford and France and a more modest house in his constituency. He also has free use of Hillsborough Castle in his ministerial capacity.

There have been varied reports on how the market for mansions in London and estates in south-east England fared during the 2007–2009 recession but little solid evidence of falling prices. Despite the US sub-prime mortgage debacle 'international estate agents maintain that the market for mansions should be relatively unscathed [because] the high end of the market operated under different rules' (Shearer, 2007) as the 'boom for top London properties seems to go on for ever'. The world's super-rich were 'queuing up to buy in the capital, with billionaires from India and China joining the Russian oligarchs and the oil sheikhs who have overheated the market in the past five years' (Partridge, 2007). Whatever problems the Dubai economy and housing market might have, it was reported in the summer of 2009 that 'Sheik Mohammed bin Rashid al-Maktoum, the ruler of Dubai … is buying a Suffolk estate for £45m – a record price for a British country home' (Conradi, 2009). Dalham Hall estate was once owned by colonial adventurer and mining entrepreneur Cecil Rhodes. Sheik Mohammed bin Rashid al-Maktoum already owned the adjacent 3,000-acre Dalham Hall stud, 'from which he runs his global bloodstock empire and where he spends part of his time' (op. cit.).

It was widely reported in late 2009 that luxury home prices in central London had risen at the fastest rate since early 2008. Many newspapers and websites covered a press notice by upmarket estate agency, Frank Knight, about 'a remarkable revival' in London's residential market (http://www.knightfrank.co.uk/news/London%E2%80%99s-luxury-residential-sector-ends-the-year-on-a-high-084.aspx). Frank Knight's head of research said that the strongest sector was properties selling at between 5 and 10 million pounds, with the London market 'benefitting from substantial inward investment from overseas buyers looking to take advantage of the weak pound and lower overall prices'. Rich buyers from Russia, Italy and the Middle East had been especially active, and 'the revival of the City economy has brought more traditional buyers from the banks, hedge funds and private equity houses back into the market'. Despite the announcement of a new tax aimed at banker's huge bonuses announced in the Pre-Budget Report, in the following week four of Frank Knight's central London offices 'saw contracts exchanged on 22 deals, with aggregate sales prices of over £60m, terms were agreed on a further £45m worth of sales' (loc. cit.).

And so it goes on.

Conclusions

The rapid growth of transnational second home ownership has been driven by the same factors as domestic second home ownership, affluence and mobility, but with some distinctive features. Affluence grew both through incomes and rising housing equity and mobility was especially enhanced by the growth of cheap fares on budget airlines and the routes they served. But whilst offering significant opportunities and advantages for most purchasers, transnational second home ownership has also carried greater risks than domestic second home ownership, as illustrated by the personal tragedies of many people who have lost out through property purchase in Spain, whether for leisure/investment or for retirement.

Overseas property purchases involve both fly-to-let investors and leisure second home buyers, though the two categories frequently overlap and the status of individuals may switch between them over time. We have not tried to incorporate the many complex other forms of purchase, including diverse forms of leasehold arrangements, involved in timeshare and other 'products' in markets where leisure and commercial investment overlap, but this would be a fascinating topic for future work.

The global super-rich are largely unaffected by the vicissitudes of property values. As some individuals and families fall by the wayside so others emerge to take their places in the sun. But the future for mass transnational second home ownership is uncertain. The recession of 2007–2009 has reduced the levels of equity for millions of existing homeowners and the lessons of unwise or unlucky purchases overseas have been widely publicised. More crucially, perhaps, the longer-term viability of air travel may become increasingly undermined on cost and environmental grounds. Growing surveillance and scrutiny within airports due to continuing terrorist activities may make travel an increasingly unpleasant experience. International air travel is also exposed to much greater risks than domestic surface travel, especially regarding possible climatic changes or unpredictable geophysical disturbances, such as increased tropical cyclonic activity or major earthquakes or volcanic disturbances. But doubts about future expansion have been expressed before during downturns in the growth of second home ownership in the 1970s and 1990s, so doubtless Mintel was right to predict strong interest in further purchases overseas. Whether or not it will result in a renewed burst of expansion remains to be seen.

5 Public policy issues and dilemmas

Second homes have become the bane of the countryside. Anywhere remotely picturesque is being overrun by city slickers in retreat from the hell they're helped to create. As the rich become richer and the poor become poorer, the ownership of holiday homes is becoming one of the major causes of deprivation in rural areas all over Britain.

(Monbiot, 1998)

… across rural England as a whole, the impact of second homes is modest. But we acknowledge that the severity of the problem in some parts of the country requires measures aimed at offsetting those detrimental effects and securing a better supply of affordable housing.

(Affordable Rural Housing Commission, 2006: 62)

Introduction

Many commentators in the UK advocate public policy reforms directed at 'problems' associated with second homes, though the quotations above show very different interpretations of the same issue! George Monbiot, in particular, has criticised second home owners for inflating local house prices, creating 'ghost towns' and fuelling excessive travel (Monbiot 1998, 2006, 2009). In other countries, however, there has been little if any debate about public policies specifically relating to second homes. Our review of the international literature showed that many policy concerns and debates relating to second homes are highly country-specific, with great variations in terms of which issues are identified as problems. For practical purposes, therefore, this chapter focuses on policy debates in the countries explored in our case studies within the UK, Ireland, Australia and Spain, and issues relating to transnational second home ownership.

The UK is a very distinctive context for second homes, with its combination of restrictive land-use planning and a dramatically changed housing policy regime within which a 'right to buy'[1] enabled millions of local authority housing tenants to purchase their homes (Jones, 2009). Second home ownership often has been negatively associated with changing rural and coastal areas and recent studies and enquiries have considered the impacts of second homes on housing affordability (Affordable Rural Housing Commission, 2006; House of Commons ODPM Housing Planning, Local Government and the Regions Committee, 2006; Oxley *et al..*, 2008; Taylor, 2008).

By way of contrast, the topic of second homes was never a matter of concern for governments in Ireland, rather public policies encouraged housing development in seaside resorts and rural areas (Norris and Winston, 2009). The absence of any local tax on residential property, plus other policies promoting housing investment, boosted growing domestic housing consumption and was marketed by estate agents to attract second home owners from other jurisdictions, especially Northern Ireland. The topic has not been significant politically in Australia, though the intensification of development along coastal zones, including lifestyle migration, retirement and second homes, has featured strongly in public debate. The issue of seasonality of dwelling use and the likely impact of large numbers of baby boomers retiring to their second homes has been examined by Australian planning authorities and academics (McKenzie *et al..*, 2008). In Spain, as in Ireland, governments encouraged housing development generally and many municipalities were strongly in favour of additional construction for second home owners, though some elected representatives and municipal officials turned blind eyes to irregularities and illegalities and others were themselves involved in illegal and corrupt activities.

Scholarly work on second homes has had little impact on public policies in the UK despite the recent efforts of Gallent *et al..* (2005) who reviewed policy issues and options relating to second homes in rural Britain. They proposed a new framework for policy including reforms to planning, taxation and spending tools. One of the reforms was underway regarding local property taxes ('council tax' in Britain, 'rates' in Northern Ireland). The 50 per cent discount on council tax for second homes in Britain was reduced so that most English and Scottish councils gave a 10 per cent discount in 2009 and some Welsh councils gave none. There had never been a discount for second homes in Northern Ireland and no local property tax was charged in the neighbouring Republic of Ireland. The intricacies of policy minutiae in the UK and its immediate neighbour highlight the impossibility of a comprehensive international analysis of policy issues, so this chapter just aims to assess the policy and political significance of second and multiple homes, rather than to become involved in those debates.

The literature review and case studies showed that many issues associated with second homes apply equally well to *any* housing. This is partly because second homes are a moving target: the term refers to how dwellings are used at a particular time or over time, rather than being inherent characteristics of dwellings or their owners. Concerns about environmental impact, including physical and visual pollution, never apply only to second homes because they relate to the impact of any dwellings, not just their use. Some commentators express particular moral outrage when second homes are considered to cause visual or physical pollution, but the dwellings would have the same effect if occupied on a permanent basis. Indeed, physical pollution can be worse if some dwellings were occupied full-time rather than part-time especially regarding poorly fitted and/or maintained septic tanks as in much of rural Ireland (Crowley, 2006; Price, 2009).

The following list represents one attempt to identify a range of recurring public policy issues that can be distinctively associated with second homes, though they are often matters of degree, applying more in places with high concentrations of second homes. There are many overlaps between policy issues and debates within and across countries:

- the need for better systematic and comparative data about second homes;
- concern about the impact of second homes on local communities and housing markets;
- the basis for intergovernmental transfers to local governments;
- the varied impact of planning systems on the development of second home ownership;
- the role of taxation in housing investment and consumption decisions;
- distinctive dimensions of transnational second homes.

Policy issues relating to data

Data sets relating to second homes are extremely variable. Policy issues include lack of clarity and consistency in defining 'second homes', identifying the incidence of second home ownership, and the widespread likelihood that national censuses and surveys record a significant number of second homes as 'vacant'.

Some governments may seek to obtain better records of second home ownership but this will never be easy due to flexible use of homes and the probability that many second home owners seek anonymity. It is unlikely that better comparative data will be available in the near future. Differences in definition and legal status will persist as there are no international agreements or agencies promoting standardised definitions or methods of data collection. Housing policy remains a matter for individual EU states so there is unlikely to be any systematisation across Europe, let al.one more widely.

This issue is of considerable policy significance because it should better inform us about how households invest and consume housing resources. Patterns of investment and consumption are also influenced by other government policy measures relating to taxation, fiscal policy, residence and citizenship. Countries that allow easy entry and property purchase by non-citizens are more attractive locales for transnational second home ownership that may fuel house price increases and/or building booms, partly depending on local planning regimes. Some governments may encourage such investment whereas others may prefer to discourage it. Unless there is a solid evidence base to identify the magnitude of second home ownership and use it would be impossible to monitor the effects of any changes. The requirement in Spain that non-nationals must register with local authorities should provide evidence on permanent residence but not for non-resident second home ownership.

Domestic surveys can provide useful data on second and multiple home ownership. The SEH is the best data source for England but evidence from Spain suggests that the SEH under-records the level of English home ownership there. Systematic data could be obtained through tax collection systems; indeed, some countries require citizens to declare ownership of primary and other residences. This would still vary considerably between countries but is probably the best way for individual countries to record the ownership of second homes by their citizens. But it would depend on self-certification by people who may not want tax authorities to know about overseas second homes and thus risks non-compliance. The risk of non-compliance may be greater regarding their citizens' ownership of residential property in other jurisdictions. It would be even more difficult for governments to record accurately the ownership of residential property by non-domiciles.

Researchers in our case studies reported that second homes often are recorded as 'vacant' in censuses and surveys. This reflects the priorities of national censuses, which are primarily counts of people, and have cost constraints on acquiring data about properties that are found to be empty. This issue is related to periodicity of dwelling use as censuses are rarely taken at times when second home owners are resident. Future censuses could require all households to state whether they own other residential property for their own use, rather than as rental investments or holiday lettings. This is likely to happen in the UK in 2011 and could provide a useful data base, though again there could be non-compliance by households wishing to obtain untaxed capital gains from their ownership of other properties. Official data collection agencies in Ireland and Australia could also consider asking questions in national surveys or better-designed census questions relating to second home ownership

Methods such as measuring the periodicity of utility use, especially electricity consumption, can be utilised to develop a more reliable picture of the proportions of dwellings that are used periodically rather than lying vacant. The turnover of vacant dwellings, however, is a routine element of housing markets so it would be necessary to make assumptions about 'normal' vacancy, long-term vacancy and second home use. Overall, unfortunately, there are no easy solutions to problems of data uncertainty, diversity and variability regarding second homes, so 'best estimates' are likely to remain all that is possible in many cases.

Policy issues relating to impacts on communities and local housing markets

Two main issues relating to the impact of second home ownership on communities and housing market were discussed in Chapter 2: firstly, that second home buyers fuel house price inflation, thus causing affordability problems for low income locals; and secondly, that seasonality of dwelling use and service demand cause problems in places with high levels of second home ownership, destroying local communities and creating 'ghost towns'. The first is largely a British concern though it has also arisen in Ireland, but the second is much more widespread, albeit taking diverse forms.

Affordability

Second home ownership in Britain has often grown in high amenity areas where local incomes are relatively low and supplies of social housing have been reduced by right-to-buy sales since the early 1980s. Tight planning constraints on development, reduced house building and falling supply of social housing have resulted in widespread gentrification of former agricultural or fishing villages. Some new social housing has been provided under 'rural exceptions' policies, but this only addresses new construction and cannot affect transfers of existing dwellings from 'permanent' to second home use. High need areas in Scotland can be exempted from the right to buy, and the National Assembly for Wales has restricted the right to buy within National Parks and AONBs. Under current policy settings in England and Northern Ireland, however, it is impossible to stop social housing being purchased under the right to buy and subsequently sold into the 'normal' housing market, including second homes. Jones and Murie (2006) noted that restrictions on resale of dwellings bought under the right to buy had been introduced in England for National Parks, AONBs and 35 specifically designated 'rural' areas, but these restrictions were neither monitored nor implemented effectively (Murie, 2008, personal correspondence).

Many studies of second homes and housing affordability were undertaken for devolved authorities in Wales, Scotland and Northern Ireland, and for many local councils. A systematic literature review by Wallace et al.. (2005) assessed how much policies addressed 'the effects of empty or irregularly occupied properties on the sustainability of rural communities' (pvii). This showed that only a minority of local authorities and National Parks in England and Wales had specific policies on second homes, mainly regarding occupancy controls on new dwellings. Wallace et al.. (2005) found little evidence of rigorous evaluation of policies relating to second homes and limited occupancy controls on new dwellings.

Concerns about housing affordability in the countryside were focused on in England by the Affordable Rural Housing Commission (ARHC) and the Liberal

Democrat MP Matthew Taylor. The ARHC was established to enquire into the shortage of affordable rural housing in England and 'to make recommendations to help address unmet need'. Taylor was commissioned by the Prime Minister to review how land use and planning could better support rural business and deliver affordable housing. The ARHC (2006) concluded that a widespread shortage of affordable housing in rural England was due to the combined effect of rapidly rising prices in areas where constraints on additional supply were greater than in urban areas, with strong demand from commuters, retirees and owners of second or holiday homes, with right-to-buy sales exceeding new social construction. Subsequent enquiries into the impact of second homes on rural housing affordability agreed that second homes were only one element among other causal processes affecting housing affordability in the British countryside, including people moving permanently to country and coastal areas (House of Commons ODPM Housing Planning, Local Government and the Regions Committee, 2006; Taylor, 2008). The government-funded National Housing and Planning Advice Unit commissioned yet another review of the topic and it reached the same conclusion: second homes had at most a small impact on overall house prices in rural areas (Oxley *et al..*, 2008).

The ARHC advocated an increased supply of affordable housing for small rural settlements and that government and professional organisations should review approaches to estimating housing need in rural areas. The ARHC report stimulated much media commentary and speculation about possible new taxes to prevent the growth of 'ghost villages' (for example, Elliott and Emmett, 2006) but its recommendations were mild, including: developing 'a robust measure for identifying second homes based on the system of self certification for tax purposes'; that consideration be given to a 'second homes impact tax' in stress areas; and, that local authorities ensure that holiday home owners pay full and proper local property taxes. Other possible measures included restricting right-to-buy sales, ensuring that subsequent sales were restricted to people with demonstrable local connections and need, and varying discount levels. The ARHC also suggested exploring new ways of ensuring that new affordable housing could remain so in perpetuity, for example by Community Land Trusts.

The expert advisory reports all agreed that something should be done about second homes but no strong measures were proposed and no government proposals had been made by the end of 2009. This reflects the absence of any simple and unambiguous 'problem' to solve. Rather the issue lacks clarity of definition, with diverse perspectives on what the 'problem' may be and conflicting interests involved in problem definition. So it is not surprising that little has actually *happened* in terms of policy development and implementation relating to second homes.

Concerns about housing affordability are widespread in many other countries (Paris, 2007a), including Ireland (Norris and Shiels, 2007) and Australia (Beer *et al..*, 2007), but second homes were not identified as a causal factor in these cases and the main affordability problems were found in cities. The issue of expensive rural housing is due to the British housing and planning regimes that have created and reproduce conditions of restricted housing supply in attractive country and coastal areas, rather than simply being due to greedy second home buyers. Chapter 3 showed just how ingenious and inventive market providers have been when operating within the extraordinary constraints of the British land-use planning system, so markets could easily provide a range of new second home opportunities if planning restrictions were relaxed to enable more flexibility in new production.

None of the British commentators on second homes and housing affordability raised the possibility that growing second home ownership may be driving up urban house prices, though the chair of the AHRC and Matthew Taylor MP themselves both reportedly owned second homes in London (Elliott and Emmett, 2006; http://www.matthewtaylor.info/local9036.html). Chapters 3 and 4 revealed a high level of second home ownership in British cites, including affluent overseas buyers of upmarket homes in London and south-east England. Thus booming second home ownership was also a factor fuelling house price inflation in London as well as rural England. This hypothesis at least may be worthy of further exploration in future work.

Concerns about access to affordable housing for low income workers were explored in the USA and Canada by Hettinger (2005) with detailed case studies of four 'tourism communities': ski resorts and upmarket coastal settlements with high proportions of jobs in leisure/tourism. Hettinger's policy analysis and proposals reflected the context of work in countries with small social housing sectors and traditions of charitable and self-help provision of housing. He argued that community organisations should assist local low income workers into affordable home purchase or low cost rental through the establishment of non-profit schemes. Such provision would not be at risk of losing stock through a 'right' to buy as in the UK. These are all tightly zoned, specifically resort localities, so the concern was primarily about lower income workers and their families, rather than displacement of lower income households as in Britain. But similar considerations could apply in Britain, where the biggest challenge is to find a way of providing additional affordable market or social housing that can remain available for low income or other target groups without being lost through right-to-buy sales.

Seasonality and 'ghost towns'

The concern that places are changed by growth of second home ownership recurs in many countries, often regarding the transformation of places from communities involved in primary production to recreational communities used on a seasonal basis (Diamond, 2005; Gallent *et al..*, 2005). The initial growth of second home ownership often occurred in areas that had been losing population due to labour shedding or decline in 'traditional' primary industries, thus involved replacement rather than displacement of 'local' populations. As Chapter 3 showed, however, second home owners often were blamed for decline of local communities in places that had been changing anyway. In some cases, of course, displacement has been more direct but often the vendors of older property were themselves low income 'locals' as in other gentrification cycles in cities (Atkinson and Bridge, 2004).

Concerns about displacement do not apply in places that were created through the development of second homes and other leisure-related construction. The Australian case indicated that seasonality has been shifting in some places to periodicity, with growing use at weekends as well as 'holiday' periods. There was also evidence of growing permanent residence in 'second homes towns' with retirees moving in permanently as well as other lifestyle migrants and service workers attracted by growing labour demand. These are places in transition from second homes towns to more permanent communities, albeit not occupational communities.

Seasonality and periodicity of occupation affect patterns of demand for services, including consumption of power and water, use of roads and parking, demand for shops and leisure facilities including bars and restaurants, and council services especially refuse collection. Government agencies in Australia have explored the extent and impacts of seasonality and periodicity of dwelling use especially in 'sea change' and 'tree change' areas. Planners in the state of Victoria examined population fluctuations in agricultural and high amenity areas because they were concerned that census data could not record seasonal fluctuations that had substantial policy-related impacts and implications (McKenzie *et al..*, 2008). Issues included variable use of infrastructure, seasonal peaking of problems relating to law and order and difficulties for local councils that were inadequately funded to meet peak demand (see next section).

Commentators often conflate concerns about second homes with other factors affecting localities and in every study examined in this book it was noted that many factors affect localities and communities. The case studies in Northern Ireland and the Republic of Ireland noted claims that 'ghost towns' were being created by second home owners, but the evidence indicated that other changes, especially retirement migration and growing commuting, also affected demand for services. Thus the evocative term 'ghost town' may be singularly *in*appropriate because such places are not permanently unoccupied but are used seasonally, and often have a high proportion of permanent residents who are retirees. Many other factors also have affected service use, especially the growth supermarkets and internet shopping reducing the demand for small shops. Emails have replaced letters for much interpersonal communication and electronic money transfers have reduced the use of cheques, local bank branches and post offices. The stronger prohibition of drink-driving and cheap supermarket al.cohol are partly responsible for the loss of many traditional pubs and bars.

167

Policy issues relating to intergovernmental transfers

Concerns about the relationship between the use of second homes and intergovernmental financial transfers have been raised in numerous jurisdictions, especially Australia (McKenzie *et al..*, 2008; Paris *et al..*, 2009). Resource allocation from centres to localities is typically on a per capita basis using census population counts. Central agencies determine support for locally provided services using formulae based on the number of permanent residents, often adjusted for a range of factors such as remoteness, but rarely if ever adjusted for population fluctuations. Second home owners usually are recorded at their 'permanent' residential location so *that* local government receives central funding as if they only used services there. In fact, of course, second home owners also use services in the locality of their second (and/or other homes), but those local authorities do not receive any central funding assistance towards local services for these users. This results in imbalances between local governments in terms of central support for local service demands.

This issue also applies in agricultural areas with high seasonal population fluctuations (McKenzie *et al..*, 2008). The 2001 census population of Robinvale, within Swan Hill Shire in north-western Victoria, was around 4,000 persons, but council representatives were certain that the typical population was much higher when seasonal labourers were in the area. A study undertaken for the council estimated the population to be 6,000–8,000 people, rising to 8,000–10,000 during peak harvest season in February (op. cit.). The 2006 census count for the same area, however, was just under 4,000. Thus McKenzie *et al..* (2008) argued that the census formed an inadequate basis for service planning. Other studies in Victoria highlighted the impact of non-resident property owners on seasonality of use of services in Mansfield Shire, in the foothills of the Victorian alpine region, and two coastal areas, Torquay and Phillip Island (McKenzie *et al..*, 2008). The coastal shires had large population fluctuations during the year, with peaks of water usage in January (summer) over three times as high as in August (winter).

Seasonal and periodic population fluctuations are evidence of the increasingly dynamic nature of contemporary society. Population mobility affects the ability of local governments to cope with dramatic seasonal variations, given that their funding base reflects criteria that do not recognise mobility and costs falling disproportionately on local governments with high levels of non-recorded part-time residents. Strong demand in peak periods may help local businesses generate enough income to cope with leaner periods, but councils have to deal with lumpy demand for infrastructure with insufficient fiscal support from central agencies. These issues have been studied most, perhaps, in Australia but they will be of increasing significance globally as affluent mobile populations require service provision from local authorities with limited financial resources.

These concerns would not arise if local services were provided commercially or on a user-pays basis, or if there were equal flows of seasonally mobile households between different localities. In practice, however, there are major equity issues relating to service provision. Some commentators have suggested that central allocations should reflect such disparities but specific proposals for an equalisation formula are not available. This may be because the issue is ignored, is considered to be too much trouble to implement, or has not been considered important enough to merit action. There would be technical issues and potential political conflicts, especially if additional central funding for local governments affected by seasonal or periodic service use by second home owners were to be funded by reductions in assistance to 'exporting' areas, if it were possible to identify them. The issue, however, probably will become more, rather than less, prominent.

The importance of planning systems

In areas of planning restriction second homes may cause social problems: in areas without such restrictions, their impacts may be more environmental in nature. In the Southern European countries, softer approaches to planning mean that second homes are less of a problem.

(Gallent *et al..*, 2005: 124)

As Gallent *et al..* (2005) pointed out, planning regimes have significant effects on how second home ownership is accomplished and how second homes developments occur. National planning systems and operations vary enormously and there are also numerous intra-national variations especially in federal nations where planning powers are the responsibility of sub-national levels of government (e.g. Australia and the USA).

The role of land-use planning is debated widely in relation to second homes and commentators often seek planning 'solutions' to 'problems' relating to second home ownership. But there are a range of quite different issues involved that need to be unpacked in order to understand the scope and limits of land-use planning in relation to second homes. There are at least four analytically separable areas of concern relating to planning and second homes:

- environmental issues – visual and physical pollution, unsafe or high risk locations (e.g. areas with high risk of flooding or erosion), and overdevelopment in sensitive areas;
- protection from development within specified areas (including greenbelts, high amenity areas such as National Parks and AONBs);
- land-use class or zoning categorisation and changes of use;
- strategic planning relating to housing demand and need.

My response to planning concerns about visual or environmental pollution and overdevelopment in sensitive areas is that there is no good reason for treating second homes differently from other homes, as today's second home may be a permanent residence tomorrow, or vice versa. The same consideration applies to designated areas within which no development is to be permitted, though this issue becomes confused regarding the needs for particular groups to live in such areas, often farmers and farm workers. The use of 'rural exceptions' policy in the UK to allow social housing development in areas that are otherwise protected represents an attempt to provide housing for local low income workers. But such measures are outside the purview of land-use planning and relate to legal titles and contracts relating to the nature of tenure. Unless accompanied by measures to ensure that dwellings are retained for use by similar households in future, housing supposedly for essential workers may be sold to other users, including retirees, commuters and lifestyle in-migrants as well as second home owners. Such developments are to be expected because housing systems are open, dynamic and changing. Dwelling usage can change overnight from permanent to part-time or vice versa. Indeed, transfers are not necessarily from 'permanent' to 'part-time' residence: there are many examples of dwellings that had been used mainly as secondary residences being used increasingly on a more permanent basis, especially as metropolitan growth extends into what once were recreational areas, as in Perth and Melbourne in Australia, or Värmdö in Sweden, gradually being engulfed by the growth of metropolitan Stockholm (http://www.pik-potsdam.de/urbs/projekt).

Can land-use planning protect against high market volatility and possible market collapse in places with high concentrations of second homes? Can it play any meaningful role relating to 'overdevelopment' due to market misreading of demand or rational market response to perverse incentives such as Irish government tax breaks for investment in property in coastal and country areas of low demand? It is difficult to see how the management of land use can play positive roles in these situations, as its core mechanisms are limiting development or imposing specific conditions on built forms. The only planning tool that can stop new dwellings being used as second homes is to stop any new development in high amenity areas. This results in gentrification and deflection of development to nearby areas.

If governments or citizens wish to stop existing dwellings being used as second homes, the role of planning is just as problematic. The key issue is whether it makes sense to designate 'second homes' as a land-use class distinct from other residential development, as many have proposed. This would require dwellings only to be used as primary or second homes but overlooks the simple fact that today's permanent residence may become tomorrow's second home whilst owned by the same household. It also ignores the wide diversity of uses that households have for dwellings, as listed in Chapter 2.

Where planning permission has been given for 'holiday' accommodation this often requires closure of a facility or development, typically for a month. But many primary residences are occupied less than 11 months in any year so households could occupy 'holiday' dwellings for 11 months and take a holiday elsewhere while their 'holiday' home is closed. Madness! There is usually no difference in law regarding the ownership of primary and secondary residences and it is impossible for planners to distinguish between 'permanent' and 'temporary' use of owner-occupied dwellings. Any attempts to do so would require levels of continuous surveillance that would be unimaginably intrusive in democratic societies and very expensive to sustain. Non-approved change of use cannot be monitored and enforced but some planning authorities impose conditions on use that even they must realise are unenforceable, simply because they have no other way of resisting the use of dwellings as second homes. Any attempt to define second homes as a separate use class, moreover, would discriminate against citizens and permanent residents of a country as it would be impossible to determine the status of homes owned by non-domiciles. If non-residents are allowed to have second homes within a jurisdiction, what possible justification can there be for denying citizens this opportunity?

The final planning issue relates to debates about housing numbers within regional strategic planning. Planners typically use projected household formation as the basis for estimating the likely need for additional housing. Demand for housing for other uses in addition to primary residences, including second homes, could be included within such calculations without any technical difficulty. In areas that are more popular for second homes, a larger additional allowance could be made for estimated future housing requirements. In practice, of course, things are not that simple. Widespread opposition to any additional housing construction is routinely articulated in Britain by well-orchestrated anti-development lobbies (Bramley, 2009). Even in countries without powerful anti-housing lobbies, such as Australia, regional planning strategies often struggle to cope with the implications of increasingly mobile populations and growing ownership of multiple residences. When this issue was raised in public consultation relating to a new regional development strategy in Northern Ireland, where there was much more support for additional housing development than in Britain, regional planners tried to ignore it. After a public enquiry, a small additional allocation was made, but it was entirely inadequate for the actual level of demand that eventuated. This topic will remain politically contentious in the UK to the bafflement of commentators in other countries where the development of additional housing is not considered to be an indictable criminal offence.

Although many commentators argue that land-use planning should intervene in the provision of second homes, this typically raises more problems than it resolves; in many cases it is the use of national or local planning systems that cause the 'problems' of scarcity and house price inflation that commentators mistakenly ascribe to second home ownership.

Taxation and second home ownership

Issues relating to taxation are very significant influences on the development of second home ownership in different countries, including local property tax and more general taxation of income, expenditure and wealth. National variations affect the costs and benefits of acquiring and disposing of second homes and whether owners choose to define particular dwellings as second homes or in some other way. The literature review noted that owners of residential property may calculate whether it is most beneficial to define properties as 'primary' or 'second' residences or 'holiday accommodation', because some tax or other advantages may accrue to different definitions.

Tax regimes vary enormously between countries and a full exploration of this topic would require a high level of international accounting or legal expertise, including aspects of international corporate investment. The key issue regarding second homes is that taxation regimes in different countries present different combinations of opportunities and constraints on second home ownership. There are also many sub-national variations especially in federal societies and between local government authorities in societies where they have the opportunity to implement variable local tax systems.

Some of the key considerations that apply are:

* the tax treatment of residential property ownership;
* whether second homes are treated specifically for tax purposes;
* the tax treatment of the sale or inheritance of primary and other residences;
* local property taxes and second homes;
* whether wealth taxes operate and how they may be applied;
* how individuals and households are treated for tax purposes.

Tax regimes treat investment in residential property in many different ways, for example regarding deductibility of costs involved in property purchase. Some tax systems allow mortgage interest deductibility for primary residences but not for other property purchases, unless this is done for business purposes and income from that business is liable for tax. Most countries do not have specific definitions of 'second homes' or equivalent, so the purchase of any residential property would be treated either as primary residence, where applicable, or like any other property investment. Crucially, those countries with tax regimes that prioritise home ownership over renting and treat owner occupation in an advantageous way are especially likely to encourage additional housing consumption, whether in the form of larger primary residences or through purchase and sale of second and further homes. Owners can switch between definitions of their primary and second residences to take most advantage of tax breaks.

There is enormous variation between countries in how the disposal or inheritance of residential property is treated for tax purposes, especially whether or not CGT is payable and if so at what rate. Many countries do not have any CGT, others only tax realised capital gains, and levels of CGT imposed vary considerably between countries. In the UK, if second home owners have not sought tax deductibility in buying or using their properties, then they would have to contact the tax authorities themselves in order for CGT to be levied. Under these circumstances, it would be surprising if many people sought out opportunities to pay tax! Thus second home ownership and sale constitute an attractive mechanism for achieving untaxed capital gains in the knowledge that the likelihood of being caught is near to zero.

Local property taxes vary enormously between and within countries, though most Organisation of Economic Co-operation and Development (OECD) countries have local taxes on residential property. The Republic of Ireland is a notable exception; local residential property taxes were abolished in 1977 but businesses must pay rates. In many countries all residential property is taxed on the same basis. Second homes are charged a lower rate in some countries but a higher rate in others. France has numerous local taxes including property taxes on all residential dwellings, regardless of how they are used. Local property taxes may vary between dwelling use designations within countries, thus properties registered as 'second homes' in England pay council tax (discounted) but properties registered as 'holiday accommodation' pay business rates.

The idea of levying additional local tax charges on British second home owners has been raised by many commentators, including the ARHC, but it had not been explored by government by the end of 2009. Some Australian councils charge non-resident ratepayers additional local property taxes in an attempt to recoup potential funding income denied by the existing system of intergovernmental transfers but this may be avoided by nominating the second home as a primary residence and having mail forwarded to a post office block or one's actual main residence.

There are three potential problems with imposing additional property taxes on second homes. Firstly, they are easily evaded and difficult to enforce, especially where household members split notional 'primary' residences for tax purposes. Secondly, even heavy imposts may have little effect because most second home owners can afford to pay more. Thirdly, it would be difficult if not impossible to apply to non-domiciles unless they declared ownership of more than one home in the jurisdiction.

A few countries impose wealth taxes on all residents with assets above specified levels, especially France, which has surprised some foreign-born residents, including British retirees. Such taxes have never applied in the UK, due to the power of the landed aristocracy, and have been abandoned in some other EU countries. How national tax regimes treat the incomes of various household members can also have an effect on property ownership, especially as declared for tax purposes. This also varies between countries and affects the scope for income splitting and designation of multiple residences in terms of primary residences for tax purposes.

Different mixtures of these factors mean that second home purchasers (and sellers) often require specialist local financial and accounting advice, both buying 'at home' and especially when buying in another country (though many fail to seek advice). Key issues include the clarity of definitions and operation of rules, capacity for enforcement, uncertainties and risks, and the diverse interests of various parties

173

(taxpayers, governments and/or citizens). One British policy change relating to the taxation of second homes was the reduction of discounts on property taxes for dwellings that were only occupied part-time. The *Scotsman* newspaper reported a fall in the number of registered second homes (MacMahon, 2007) and Taylor (2008: 115) noted that the number of registered second homes in Cornwall stopped rising after the discount was reduced, 'but the number of registered holiday lets (which pay less business rates than would be paid as council tax for a second home) rose instead. In many cases holiday lets and second homes are the same thing.' This highlights the capacity for actors to redefine the nature of use of their dwellings to maximise potential profit and minimise tax and other liabilities.

Taxation and subsidy issues relating to second homes can be both straightforward and complex. At a straightforward level, there are no specific subsidies available within the UK relating to the purchase and disposal of second homes. Such purchase and resale typically goes on outside the knowledge of tax authorities but is underwritten by other policies that restrict housing supply thus keeping up the cost of all housing. The purchase and sale of second homes can be an effective form of achieving untaxed capital gains, a tax shelter or even, as some commentators suggest, a form of money laundering (Diaz and Lourés, 2006). Subsidy and taxation issues become even more complex when knowledgeable owners and investors, advised by expert finance and legal professionals, organise their affairs to minimise tax obligations and maximise untaxed income.

Policy issues relating to transnational second homes

The extent to which countries make it more or less difficult for non-domiciles to own residential property affects the scope for transnational second home ownership. Opposition to foreign ownership of second homes crops up widely in the literature, whether Germans in Sweden (Müller, 2004) or English in Wales (Coppock, 1977c) or any foreigners in Goa (Smith, 2009). Before 2009 Australia made it difficult for non-residents to own residential property but this changed dramatically during 2009 as the Australian government welcomed investment by affluent foreigners in domestic residential. Concerns about foreign second home ownership, moreover, often overlap with attitudes towards immigration and multiculturalism. Resentment against 'foreigners' competing in local housing markets may arise as much in relation to their use of dwellings as primary residences as with regard to second homes. This issue is likely to feature in political debates in many countries and local political considerations could result in rapid changes in the rights and opportunities of non-domiciles.

Chapter four reviewed risks associated with transnational second home ownership, including the possibility that there may be significant real increases in the costs of international air travel as well as volatile local housing markets in regions with very high levels of second home ownership. These issues, again, will inevitably figure in political considerations in many countries, with a wide range of possible outcomes.

Conclusions

This brief review of policy debates and issues relating to second home ownership shows that the UK is in many ways an odd case. It has a distinctive policy context and second homes often are demonised for destroying rural communities and fuelling housing affordability crises. As all enquiries have shown, however, changes in the British countryside and coasts are driven by many factors, with second home ownership a relatively minor theme. The issue of affordability should be dealt with separately from issues relating to second homes. The possibility of providing long-term sustainable social and/or affordable private housing in areas of stress affected by second homes, among other processes driving up house prices, would require forms of provision to which the right to buy does not apply or enabling local authorities in England and Northern Ireland to obtain exceptions from right-to-buy legislation, as in Wales and Scotland. However, Chapter 3 raised the possibility that this might be even more necessary in urban areas.

A review of debates in Britain in the printed and electronic media reveals extensive but varied commentary on what should be done. No commentator, however, seems able to resolve competing priorities and rights: the asserted right of people born and raised in an area to find accommodation locally within their means; the right of owners to use their dwellings as they wish within the law; and the legitimacy of free exchange of privately owned dwellings in the market.

This chapter has demonstrated that there are distinctive second homes policy issues, but that these are not just about planning. The main British planning policy affecting second homes is the restriction of new development in high amenity areas, which inevitably increases prices and deflects development proposals to nearby areas. *De facto* policies relating to the creation of new second homes, defined as leisure and/or resort developments, were discussed in Chapter 3, primarily defined as leisure and/or resort housing. Some developments obtain planning permission with the condition that dwellings may not be occupied all year round but such conditions are notoriously difficult to enforce. Planning systems in most countries appear not to share the British obsession with preserving certain places as locales only for the rich so development of housing for use as second homes, among other uses, is allowed as part of normal planning procedures.

More widely, issues relating to data quality could and should be addressed by governments if they are interested in how housing markets actually work, because second home ownership is an element of housing markets, not just leisure markets. Issues relating to intergovernmental transfers, too, may become more urgent in some countries as population mobility, seasonality and periodicity impose costs on local service providers in hot spot areas. It is hard to believe that the Irish government can resist reintroducing residential property taxes in the relatively near future.

Taxation is an important policy area where commentators and governments have given little thought to second home ownership. Taxation regimes that favour home ownership have a built-in tendency to encourage further acquisition of second and other homes as part of household investment and consumption strategies. This outcome may be unintended rather than intended, but is it *desirable*? Transnational second home ownership may well continue to increase, despite recent economic shocks and numerous risks, so policy analysts and governments could give more thought to the issues involved, especially relating to the role of non-domiciles in property ownership and taxation.

6 Conclusions

Introduction

This chapter reviews the findings and arguments from previous chapters and concludes with some thoughts about the future of second home ownership. Diversity has been a recurring theme throughout this book, illustrated by many differences between counties and regions both in the past and in recent development. The theme of globalisation also was explored via international economic processes, including growing mobility and the ICT revolution, which together have created widespread opportunities for second home ownership across the globe.

Affluence, mobility and second home ownership

Chapter 1 argued that increasing affluence and mobility were the key drivers of the growth in second home ownership. Much wealth has taken the form of domestic residential property, with high levels of home ownership and growing proportions and numbers of households owning their primary homes outright. Many commentators noted a strong preference for investment in property rather than other assets, especially after stock market shudders during the late 1990s, though the recession of 2007–2009 and falling house prices raised new fears and doubts about any investment. Growing mobility has involved huge growth of car ownership as well as international air travel, especially involving budget airlines. Mobility is increasingly seen to be a central dynamic in diverse and changing societies, but threats to mobility raise questions about its future, especially in air travel.

Much affluence was 'paper wealth' and many fortunes were reduced during the global financial crisis of 2007–2009. Some of the excesses of development aimed at second home buyers resulted in bankruptcies and a legacy of unfinished developments and unsold properties. But many affluent households had reorganised their asset and investment portfolios before or early in the recession and avoided its worst impacts. We should avoid the widespread tendency to overestimate the length and depth of any misfortune (Taleb, 2008); and Krugman (2008: 181) was right to assert that '[t]he world economy is not in depression; it probably won't fall into depression, despite the magnitude of the current crisis'.

We emphasised the importance of the overall growth in wealth, though relativities remain important. Many rich people have lost their fortunes, but most still have fortunes and falling house prices open up opportunities for affluent households to buy homes in places that take their fancy. We have witnessed a repeat of the relations between home ownership in general and second home ownership during previous housing cycles. Coppock (1977b) and Dower (1977) both attributed a fall in second home ownership in the UK during the 1970s to the impact of recession on the economy and housing markets. More recently, Gallent *et al.* (2005) argued that falling UK house prices in the early 1990s dampened the growth of second home ownership. But growth of second home ownership quickly resumed after both recessions and took off dramatically in Ireland during the 1990s economic boom. Chapter 3 showed that there was no evidence by 2009 of falling second home ownership in the UK between 2007 and 2009, and most commentators in the USA and UK thought the worst of the recession was over by the end of 2009.

Homes, second homes and *many* homes

Chapter 2 reviewed my overall approach, defined as the social relation of housing provision, which is similar to Clapham's 'housing pathways' perspective. Both emphasise social practices, choices within environments of mixed and changing opportunities and constraints, and how the circumstances of individuals and households change over time. Both emphasise the importance of lifestyle choices and strategic decision making about housing investment and consumption, though the outcomes of choice and rational decision making may not work out in the ways that individuals or households had expected.

The literature review indicated that housing scholars largely ignored second home ownership. They have been more interested in 'the home', and many have attached greater significance to 'the' home than it merits. An interest in social and cultural dimensions of the home should not divert attention from the other important dimension of homes: physical structures embedded in market relations. Whatever their social or cultural meaning, dwellings in home-owning societies are investments and their investment potential often attracts people towards owning more than one dwelling for their own use. But second homes are distinctive investment items because they combine pleasurable leisure/family consumption with potential for longer-term strategic financial options: whether to use in retirement or to sell, opportunities to acquire untaxed capital gains, or leave to heirs. Second home owners tend to be affluent 40–65 year old homeowners though rapid increase of outright home ownership among younger households, assisted in many cases by inheritance, may reduce the average age of acquiring a second home.

Some of the criticisms of second home ownership, especially in the UK, concern its impacts on communities and local housing markets. Our review of the literature, however, concluded that growing second home ownerships is rarely the only factor causing changes or conflicts in localities, though it can be a significant driver of change. These are empirical questions that work out in different ways in different places and at different times. The ways in which owners use their homes, especially when they own three or more for personal consumption, also varies substantially as the typology in the second chapter illustrated.

Second home ownership in many countries

Chapter 3 reviewed varieties of second home ownership in different countries and emphasised how the UK and Ireland were late starters in this global game. Many European countries had longer traditions of households owning or having access to second homes, whether Scandinavian summer houses, Mediterranean country homes or Russian dachas. Second home ownership also spread across English-speaking new world countries and was growing among new wealthy élites in former communist and rapidly developing countries in Asia and Eastern Europe.

We explored four case studies in depth: Britain, Northern Ireland, the Republic of Ireland and Australia. In all cases it was clear that affluence and mobility were the core drivers of growing second home ownership. All showed that second homes are going upmarket, with fewer vernacular structures, and production increasingly dominated by developers and builders, with others plucked from what was the 'normal' housing market (though the latter feature was noted by Wolfe over 30 years ago).

Second homes have been a growing sector of leisure and housing markets, especially in cities. The British case showed a high level of second home ownership in urban areas, raising questions about this possibility in other case studies where data sources were less useful. The growth of second home ownership often occurs in mixed new developments with hotels, leisure facilities, holiday lettings of houses, cottages and/or apartments. Growing second home ownership in other areas, however, has been accompanied by the loss of other forms of leisure accommodation, with hotels and guest houses closing down. Many caravan park owners want to go upmarket or get their sites re-zoned for housing, including second homes, and/or other commercial development.

In all cases there was a blurring of the use of dwellings: the same dwellings could be primary residences, second homes, or holiday lettings at different times. This reinforces the argument that it is better to think in terms of types of dwelling use rather than trying to classify dwellings by use. This poses a dilemma for planners who wish to specify that dwellings may only be used in certain ways, though their usual solution to this dilemma is to ignore it. It also poses a dilemma for enumerating second homes and/or holiday accommodation. But dwelling tenure also changes over time and censuses and surveys track such change at points in times, so better data on dwelling use also could be obtained on a snapshot basis.

The case studies showed clearly that high social and personal values are attached to the ownership of second homes and that they are valued as places of escape from everyday pressures. But this suggests that primary homes were not fulfilling this function. Has work–life interpenetration come to mean that primary homes retain an environment of work pressure, or is this a matter of affluent second home owners rationalising their high level of residential consumption?

There was strong evidence of similar issues, debates and attitudes across all four case studies, including evidence that people who moved permanently into areas popular with second home owners, often retirees, objecting to the growth of second home ownership. It was fine for *them* to move into the area but they did not want other people to have the same freedom to decide how to use their homes. Second homes were rarely the sole agency of change in any area; rather there were diverse processes of change in coastal and country areas in all case studies. In some cases though, demand for second home ownership has been a major driver of change, as with strong developer involvement in transforming parts of the Causeway Coast settlements in Northern Ireland with redevelopment aimed at the second homes market.

There were numerous differences between case studies, especially the more recent growth of second home ownership in the UK and Ireland contrasted with a much longer tradition in Australia. The case studies reveal a continuum of planning contexts from very restrictive planning in Great Britain, through the more permissive albeit changing situation in Northern Ireland, to the near free-for-all regime in Ireland. Other distinctive public policies in Ireland favoured property development with many tax and other incentives boosting housing production. In Australia, unlike other case studies, there was strong evidence of distinctive 'second home towns' though some were changing due to growing proportions of permanent residents, including retirees. Australian planning systems have allowed or guided development rather than restricting initiatives, despite varying between states and territories and with diverse local government attitudes and policies.

Different contexts created diverse policy and market combinations, with different patterns of opportunities and constraints on second home ownership. Planning regimes influenced what types of dwellings were used as second homes, such as older houses in England's gentrifying villages but new kinds of development elsewhere, such as the Cotswolds Water Park. Second homes in Ireland are mainly new houses, but the dwellings used as second homes were much more varied in Australia. Such variations also reflect differences between 'new' and 'old' worlds as second home ownership grew within different patterns of settlements and histories of places. Whether gentrification was associated with second home ownership also varied enormously, partly due to planning constraints affecting new development and also due to changing demands and preferences as areas that had been less popular attracted new demand from increasingly affluent populations.

Some differences between countries were harder to explore due to poor official data sources, especially in Ireland and Australia. Second homes are more obvious in small rural settlements but they also have a big impact in urban areas. There may be more urban second homes in England than in other cases, or this may just reflect better data sources. Or it may be that many English people owning two or more homes declare their city home as the 'second' home because local property taxes are higher so the discount is worth more; if that is the case, it would not affect the total as the same people have at least two residences for their own use. This topic cries out for more detailed qualitative research. Tax and benefit regimes also have varied considerably between case studies, from no local property tax in Ireland, some discount of property tax for second homes in England, Wales and Scotland, to full application of property tax in Northern Ireland and Australia.

The case studies generate questions for housing studies and the wider literature on second homes. Firstly, the impacts of second homes on local housing markets and 'locals' are extremely diverse, but we need more empirical exploration of the impact of second home ownership on housing markets. Secondly, the ownership, use and disposal of second homes constitute important elements of household investment and consumption strategies, including; households' capacities for maximising benefits of tax concessions and investment opportunities over the life course, but we have few insights into how this happens. Thirdly, the case studies indicated high levels of place attachment, with many second home owners valuing their second homes as settings for family life at least as much, and often more than their primary homes. Is 'home' just a conceptual bag of comfort that we can carry from place to place and attach to wherever and whichever dwelling in which we feel most comfortable – can we can have numerous 'homes'? Some other specific topics cried out for further study, including: the role of 'park homes' in housing markets and as opportunities for second home ownership.

Finally, significant differences between case study countries in terms of the depth, impact and implications of the recession of 2007–2009 suggest that there will be highly variable effects worldwide in terms of the future of second home ownership. The recession appears to have hit Ireland hardest, with large surpluses of unsold dwellings in areas of high concentration of second homes. It had least impact in Australia, where economic growth is fuelled by a minerals boom and the national government confidently predicted substantial inward migration, which will fuel demand for housing for primary residences and for leisure and investment purposes.

Transnational second home ownership

Rapid growth of transnational second home ownership was driven by the same factors as domestic second home ownership, enhanced affluence and mobility, plus additional features of overseas property markets. Affluence grew through rising incomes and housing equity, and mobility was especially enhanced by cheap airfares and new routes served by budget airlines. Transnational second home ownership has offered significant opportunities and advantages for most purchasers, but it has also carried greater risks than domestic second home ownership. The rapid growth of transnational second home ownership was a significant element in the Spanish housing market boom, albeit not accurately documented and often immersed in scandalous behaviour by some developers and public officials. The risks associated with transnational second home ownership also were illustrated by the personal tragedies of many people who have lost out through property purchase in Spain, whether for leisure/investment or for retirement.

The global super-rich are largely unaffected by the vicissitudes of property values. As some individuals and families fall by the wayside so others emerge to take their places in the sun or on the snowfields. But the future for mass transnational second home ownership is less certain. The recession of 2007–2009 reduced the levels of equity for millions of existing homeowners and the lessons of unwise or unlucky purchases overseas have been widely publicised. More crucially, perhaps, the longer-term viability of air travel may become undermined on cost and environmental grounds. Growing surveillance and scrutiny within airports due to continuing terrorist activities also make travel an increasingly unpleasant experience.

Overseas property purchases involve both fly-to-let investors and leisure second home buyers, though the two categories frequently overlap and the status of individuals may switch between them over time. We did not try to incorporate the many other forms of purchase, including diverse forms of leasehold arrangements, involved in timeshare and other 'products' in markets where leisure and commercial investment overlap, but this would be another fascinating topic for future work.

Public policy debates and second home ownership

The review of policy debates and issues about second home ownership showed the UK to be an odd case. It has a distinctive policy context and second homes often are demonised for destroying rural communities and fuelling housing affordability crises. But all enquiries showed that changes in British countryside and coasts are driven by many factors, with second home ownership a relatively minor theme. The issue of affordability should be dealt with separately from second home ownership. The possibility of providing long-term sustainable social and/or affordable private housing in areas of stress affected by second homes, among other processes driving up house prices, would require forms of provision to which the right to buy does not apply, or enabling local authorities in England and Northern Ireland to obtain exceptions from right-to-buy legislation, as is in Wales and Scotland. However, Chapter 3 raised the possibility that this might be more necessary in urban areas.

We identified some distinctive second homes policy issues, including but not restricted to planning. The main British planning policy affecting second homes is the restriction of new development in high amenity areas, which increases prices and deflects development proposals to nearby areas. Other developments may obtain planning permission with the condition that dwellings may not be occupied all year round but such conditions are notoriously difficult to enforce. Planning regimes in most countries do not share the British obsession with preserving attractive locales only for the rich, so development of housing for use as second homes or permanent residences is allowed as part of normal planning procedures.

More widely, issues relating to data quality should be addressed by governments because second home ownership is an important dimension of housing markets, not just leisure markets. Issues relating to intergovernmental transfers may become more urgent as population mobility, seasonality and periodicity impose costs on local service providers in hot spot areas. It is hard to believe that the Irish government can resist reintroducing residential property taxes in the near future. Taxation is an important policy area where commentators and governments have given little thought to second home ownership. Tax regimes favouring home ownership have a built-in tendency to encourage the acquisition of second and other homes as part of household investment and consumption strategies; this may be unintended rather than intended, but is it desirable? Transnational second home ownership may continue to grow, despite recent economic shocks and numerous risks, so policy analysts and governments could give more thought to the issues involved, especially the role of non-domiciles in property ownership and taxation.

Recent and future developments

The recession was ending by late 2009 and 'normally' operating housing systems soon will re-emerge in all their complexity. Most stocks of unsold housing will clear and builders will increase the volume of new construction. First time buyers will buy their first homes, other households will trade up to bigger or more luxurious dwellings and other households will break apart and move into different accommodations. Affluent households, many of whom already own their primary homes outright, will debate whether or not to buy that nice little place by the seaside or to invest in other assets, like bonds or the stock market.

The recession of 2007–2009 may have convinced many folk that it makes more sense to buy that second home. Even if the next boom ends in tears and the pension is not what they had hoped for, at least they will have a place to live in or use more frequently during their retirement, or possibly sell and turn into a cash sum. In many cases, of course, all will not work out as planned, but then people will weigh up their options and make their own decisions based on experience and judgement, informed by a healthy scepticism of the claims of banks and stockbrokers to help them plan for their old age. In making those decisions, households will consider their capacity to travel between their main home and second homes that they may own or consider buying. Thus the relationships between affluence and mobility will remain central to the future of second home ownership.

The likelihood that transnational second homes ownership will grow may become more problematic due to changing housing market conditions and the wider economic context. There has been much negative media coverage of changes in the Spanish housing market, especially falling prices and unfinished projects in coastal areas with high levels of second home owners, retirees and 'lifestyle' migrants. However, economic recovery will probably result in many attractive dwellings becoming available at reduced prices for prospective second home owners.

Growing fuel costs, especially for air travel, may affect behaviour relating to overseas second home ownership. Any reduction in demand for overseas second home ownership, however, could result in growing demand for local second home ownership. Falling levels of disposable income, moreover, could make cheaper second home options more attractive, including caravans and mobile homes. Thus the overlap between these forms of 'holiday' accommodation and housing markets may become even more worthy of further investigation. More generally, second home ownership will remain a significant part of overall housing systems and an area of overlap between housing and leisure markets

Future prospects vary considerably between countries, depending on how they have been affected by the recession. Australia was the least affected of our case studies so demand for second home ownership remains strong though mainly within Australia. Britain was one of the last major economies to come out of recession but reports from Savills (2008) and Mintel (2009) indicated a strong likelihood of renewed demand for additional second home ownership both domestically and overseas. At the other extreme, house prices continued to fall in Northern Ireland and the Republic of Ireland, and unemployment continued to grow throughout 2009. Large stocks of unsold new dwellings risk remaining unsold or selling at substantially reduced prices, especially in more remote coastal areas.

Recent housing market changes, finally, strengthen the advantageous position of outright owners compared to other housing market participants. Growing outright ownership of primary homes, especially among younger households, has expanded the pool of potential second home owners. They cannot fall into negative equity and they are insulated from any rising costs of purchase except when they choose to buy second homes or investment properties. Falling house prices overall make it easier for them to buy second homes.

Many uncertainties and risks remain: what are the implications of ecological changes, especially climate change, for second home ownership in some places? Will rising sea levels and growing desertification render some second homes hot spots too wet or warm for comfort? How would second home ownership be affected in areas experiencing climactic changes such as increased tropical cyclonic activity or geophysical disturbances such as earthquakes or volcanic activity? Major political and social upheavals, too, could have serious implications for second home ownership in some countries, with Thailand currently highly at risk. What are the implications of the end of peak oil for local markets with high concentrations of second homes? This would largely depend on when oil 'peaks', what effect this has on prices, and whether alternative energy sources have been brought to the market in time to compensate for reduced availability of oil.

Over 30 years ago, Dower (1977: 163) argued that second homes 'though still modest in scale from a national viewpoint, are a phenomenon that grows and will not just quietly go away'. He predicted that demand for second homes would grow again with any economic revival, thus the recession in the 1970s was 'not an excuse to stop thinking about future policy related to second homes. Rather, it provides a breathing space for such thinking' (loc. cit.). We are in a similar situation at present in 2010. Although it appears likely that second home ownership *will* continue to grow, it is impossible to be sure quite how that will happen, where it will happen and what forms this will take.

Notes

1 Introduction

1 The DCLG notes that the total number of households with second homes is lower as some have more than one second home or second homes in more than one location.
2 Source: DCLG Live Tables S355; respondents gave more than one reason for owning a second home.
3 The G7 countries comprise the US, Germany, France, Japan, Canada, Italy and the UK (the G8 includes Russia).
4 The term 'negative equity' refers to the situation where the outstanding debt on a dwelling is greater than its current value.
5 At http://www.communities.gov.uk/publications/corporate/statistics/housingstatistics2008

2 Homes, second homes and *many* homes

1 Although large interior areas of Australia had not been settled, large ecosystems had been influenced by centuries of use by indigenous Australians; many areas have subsequently been affected by irrigation and hydroelectricity schemes, river regime changes, extensive grazing by non-indigenous animals and widespread logging of native forests.

3 Variations on a theme

1 Initially called the Irish Free State, after a referendum in 1937 the name was changed to the Republic of Ireland.
2 A small minority of these are rented, rather than owned.
3 Council tax is the local property tax levied on residential dwellings in England, Wales and Scotland; in Northern Ireland the local property tax is called 'rates'. There is no local property tax in the Republic of Ireland at the time of writing.
4 The Scottish equivalent is a 'National Scenic Area'.
5   Personal correspondence from Professor Bob Robertson, September 2009.
6 The term 'station' is used in Australia to describe a pastoral farming property.
7 I am grateful to Alaric Maude for spotting this article for me.
8 Australian and New Zealand slang for a lower-class person, usually male, often a tradesman.

5 Public policy issues and dilemmas

1 The term 'right to buy' is used here also to include the 'right to acquire', which may apply to tenants of non-state social housing providers, especially housing associations.

References

Aalen, F, Whelan, K and Stout, M (eds) (1997) *Atlas of the Irish Rural Landscape*, Cork: Cork University Press.

Abend, L (2009) 'The broken hopes of a generation', *Time*, 20 July: 32–36.

Adams, L (2006) 'Eastern promise', *The Times*, 15 September 2006: 16.

Affordable Rural Housing Commission (2006) *Final Report*, London: Affordable Rural Housing Commission.

Alberdí, B and Levenfeld, G (1996) 'Spain', in P Balchin (ed) *Housing Policy in Europe*, London: Routledge.

Alderson, A and Fleet, M (2003) 'Fishermen take on townies in battle for Helford's new jetty', Telegraph.co.uk, published 9 March 2003, accessed 3 January 2009 at http://www.telegraph.co.uk/education/3309159/Fishermen-take-on-townies-in-battle-for-Helfords-new-jetty.html

Allen, K (2007) 'Big bonus boom', *The Guardian*, accessed 11 January 2007 at http://business.guardian.co.uk/print/0,,329682131-108725,00.html

Allen, J, Barlow, J, Leal, J, Maloutas, T and Padovani, L (2004) *Housing and Welfare in Southern Europe*, Oxford: Blackwell.

Aslet, C (2009) 'The tide has turned', *The Sunday Times*, Home section, 5 July: 6–7.

Atkinson, R and Bridge, G (eds) (2004) *Gentrification in a Global Context*, London: Routledge.

Awasthi, R and Duttagupta, I (2008) 'Indians buying homes in world's expensive cities', *India Times*, accessed 26 July 2009 at http://economictimes.indiatimes.com/markets/real-estate/realty-trends/Mega-realty-deals-dot-Delhis-Golf-Links/articleshow/articleshow/3110228.cms

Ball, M (2005) *RICS European Housing Review 2005*, accessed 7 May 2007 at http://www.rics.org.

Ball, M (2009) *RICS European Housing Review 2009*, accessed 7 June 2009 at http://www.rics.org.

Bardon, J (1992) *A History of Ulster*, Belfast: Blackstaff Press.

Barke, M (2008) 'Second homes in the Spanish housing market: one market or two?', *Journal of Housing and the Built Environment*, 23: 277–295.

Barker, K (2004) *Review of Housing Supply, Delivering Stability: Securing our Future Housing Needs, Final Report – Recommendations*, London: HMSO

Barnett, R (2007) 'Central and Eastern Europe: real estate development within the second and holiday home markets', *Journal of Retail and Leisure Property*, 6 (2): 137–142.

Barrett, C (2009) 'Britons face big losses on holiday homes in Bulgaria', *Financial Times*, 31 August, accessed 6 September at http://www.ft.com/cms/s/0/a0774768-93f6-11de-9c57-00144feabdc0.html.

Bauman, Z (1995) *Life in Fragments: Essays in Post-modern Morality*, Oxford: Blackwell.

BBC Press Office (2009) 'Second home owners block Cornish fishermen's attempt to build new jetty', BBC Press Office press release on 19 January 2009 accessed 5 May 2009 at http://www.bbc.co.uk/pressoffice/pressreleases/stories/2009/01_january/19/cornish.shtml

References

Beer, A, Faulkner, D and Cutler, C (2007) *The State of Australian Housing – Overview*, Information Paper 1, Melbourne: AHURI.

Belsky, E S, Zhu X D and McCue, D (2006) 'Multiple home ownership and the income elasticity of housing demand' (mimeo), Cambridge, MA: Harvard University Joint Center for Housing Studies.

Birch, J (2006) 'The great second homes swindle', *Roof,* May/June: 22–24.

Bjerke, T, Kaltenborn, P and Vittersø, J (2006) 'Cabin life: restorative and affirmative aspects', in N McIntyre, D Williams and K McHugh (eds) *Multiple Dwelling and Tourism: Negotiating Place, Home and Identity*, Cambridge: CABI.

Bonavalet, C (1995) 'The extended family and housing in France', in R Forrest and A Murie (eds) *Housing and Family Wealth: Comparative International Perspectives*, London: Routledge.

Boyd, S (2000) '"Heritage" tourism in Northern Ireland: opportunity under peace', *Current Issues in Tourism*, 3 (2): 150–174

Bradley, J (1999) 'The history of economic development in Ireland, North and South', in A Heath, R Breen and C Whelan (eds) *Ireland North and South: Perspectives from Social Science*, Oxford: Oxford University Press.

Bramley, G (2009) 'Meeting the demand for new housing', in P Malpass and R Rowlands (eds) *Housing, Markets and Policy*, London: Routledge.

Bramley, G, Munro, M and Pawson, H (2004) *Key Issues in Housing: Policies and Markets in 21st Century Britain*, Basingstoke: Palgrave Macmillan.

Brodie, A and Winter, G (2007) *England's Seaside Resorts*, Swindon: English Heritage.

Brooks, D (2001) *Bobos in Paradise*, New York: Simon and Shuster.

Brooks, D (2005) *On Paradise Drive*, New York: Simon and Shuster.

Burgen, S (2006) 'Pirates of the Mediterranean', *The Sunday Times* magazine, 30 July: 38–44.

Burnley, I and Murphy, P (2004) *Sea Change: Movement from Metropolitan to Arcadian Australia*, Sydney: University of New South Wales Press.

Butler, R (1998) 'Rural recreation and tourism', in B Ilbery (ed) *The Geography of Rural Change*, Harlow: Pearson Education.

Byers, D (2007) 'Murder of expat blamed on robber gangs', *The Times*, 12 November: 5.

Caesar, E (2008) 'A street named desire', *The Sunday Times* magazine, 22 June 2008, accessed 29 January 2009 at http://property.timesonline.co.uk/tol/life_and_style/property/article4164403.ece

Calvert, J, Newell, C, Walsh, G and Kirk, J (2006) 'Home buyers get stung for a place in the sun', *The Sunday Times*, 15 October: 3

Carter, R (1982) 'Coastal caravan sites in Northern Ireland', *Irish Geography,* 15 (1): 107–111.

Casado-Diaz, M A (2004) 'Second homes in Spain', in C M Hall and D Müller (eds) *Tourism, Mobility and Second Homes*, Clevedon Buffalo, NY and Toronto: Channel View Publications.

Champion, T, Coombes, M, Raybould, S and Wymer, C (2005) *Migration and Socioeconomic Change: A 2001 Census Analysis of Britain's Larger Cities*, York: Joseph Rowntree Foundation.

Charles, S (2005) 'Paradoxical individualism: an introduction to the thought of Gilles Lipovetsky', in G Lipovetsky *Hypermodern Times*, 1–28, Cambridge: Polity Press.

Chiu, R (2006) 'Second homes across two political systems within a country', paper presented to the ENHR Conference, Ljubljana, July 2006.

Clapham, D (2002) 'Housing pathways: a post modern analytical framework', *Housing Theory and Society*, 19(2): 57–68.

Clapham, D (2005) *The Meaning of Housing: A Pathways Approach*, Bristol: The Policy Press.

Clinch, P, Convery, F and Walsh, B (2002) *After the Celtic Tiger*, Dublin: O'Brien Press.

Coleman, D (1999) 'Demography and migration in Ireland, North and South', in A Heath, R Breen and C Whelan (eds) *Ireland North and South: Perspectives from Social Science*, Oxford: Oxford University Press.

Condie, K (2006) 'Historic cottage demolished', *Milton Ulladulla Times*, 6 October.

Condon, D (2008) 'Rising airfares to affect home owners abroad', *The Sunday Business Post Online*, article dated 8 June 2008, accessed 19 March 2009 at http://archives.tcm.ie/businesspost/2008/06/08/story33431.asp

Conradi, P (2007) 'Distant thunder: the markets in many countries popular with British buyers look wobbly', *The Sunday Times*, accessed 7 July 2008 at http://property.timesonline.co.uk/tol/life_and_style/property/overseas/article2587982.ece

Conradi, P (2009) 'Racing king buys piece of empire', *The Sunday Times*, 5 July: 6.

Cooke, D and Schneiders, B (2008) 'Household wealth leaps for most Australians', *The Age*, 3 July 2008, accessed 19 March 2009 at http://business.theage.com.au/business/household-wealth-leaps-for-most-australians-20080702-30qh.html

Coppock, J T (ed) (1977a) *Second Homes: Curse or Blessing?*, Oxford: Pergamon Press.

Coppock, J T (ed) (1977b) 'Second homes in perspective', in J T Coppock (ed) *Second Homes: Curse or Blessing?*, Oxford: Pergamon Press.

Coppock, J T (1977c) 'Social implications of second homes in mid- and north Wales', in J T Coppock (ed) *Second Homes: Curse or Blessing?*, Oxford: Pergamon Press.

Coxon, I (ed) (2008) *The Sunday Times Rich List 2008*, supplement to *The Sunday Times* on 27 April 2008.

Cresswell, T (2006) *On the Move: Mobility in the Modern World*, Oxford: Routledge.

Crowley, E (2006) *Land Matters: Power Struggles in Rural Ireland*, Dublin: Lilliput Press.

Cuba, L (1989) 'From visitor to resident: retiring in vacationland', *Generations*, 13: 63–67.

Dare Hall, S (2009) 'A place in the sun', *The Sunday Times* Home section, 6 September: 22.

Davies, J, Sandström, S, Shorrocks, A and Wolff, E (2008) *The World Distribution of Household Wealth*, Helsinki: United Nations University – World Institute for Development Economics Research.

DCLG (Department of Communities and Local Government) (2008) *Housing in England 2006/07*, London: Department of Communities and Local Government.

Department of the Environment for Northern Ireland (1993) *A Planning Strategy for Rural Northern Ireland,* Belfast: HMSO.

Department of the Environment, Heritage and Local Government (2005) *Sustainable Rural Housing: Guidelines for Planning Authorities*, Dublin: Stationery Office.

Devane, M (2008) 'Home for the holidays abroad', *The Sunday Business Post Online*, article dated 9 March 2008, accessed 19 March 2009 at http://archives.tcm.ie/businesspost/2008/03/09/story31024.asp

Diamond, J (2005) *Collapse: How Societies Choose to Fail or Survive*, London: Penguin.

Diaz, F and Lourés, M L (2006) 'Housing, tourism and the real estate sector: the Spanish Mediterranean coast', paper presented to the ENHR Conference, Ljubljana, July 2006.

Direct Line Insurance (2005) *Direct Line Second Homes in the UK,* London: Direct Line.

Dobbin, M (2009) 'Chinese buyers fuel top-end property boom', *The Age*, 19 September, accessed 19 September 2009 at http://www.theage.com.au/business/chinese-buyers-fuel-topend-property-boom-20090918-fvga.html

Dorling, D, Rigby, J, Wheeler, B, Ballas, D, Thomas, B, Fahmy, E, Gordon, D and Lupton, R (2007) *Poverty, Wealth and Place in Britain, 1968–2005*, York: Joseph Rowntree Foundation.

Dower, M (1977) 'Planning aspects of second homes', in J T (ed) Coppock, *Second Homes: Curse or Blessing?*, Oxford: Pergamon Press.

Drudy, P J and Punch, M (2005) *Out of Reach: Inequalities in the Irish Housing System*, Dublin: TASC.

Duval, D T (2004) 'Mobile migrants: travel to second homes', in C M Hall and D Müller (eds) *Tourism, Mobility and Second Homes*, Clevedon Buffalo, NY and Toronto: Channel View Publications.

Easthope, H (2004) 'A place called home', *Housing, Theory and Society*, 21 (3): 128–138.

Elliott, V (2006) 'Homeowners look to profit in the sun', *The Times*, 22 November: 20.

Elliott, V and Emmett, S (2006) 'Second homes may be blocked to end winter ghost towns', *The Times*, 18 May, accessed 10 May 2009 at http://property.timesonline.co.uk/tol/life_and_style/property/buying_and_selling/article720677.ece

References

Emmanuel, D (1995) 'On the structure of housing accumulation and the role of family wealth transfers in the Greek housing system', in R Forrest and A Murie (eds) *Housing and Family Wealth: Comparative International Perspectives*, London: Routledge.

Emmett, S (2009) 'All washed up in Brazil?', *The Times*, Bricks and Mortar section, 14 August: 7.

Engelhardt, G (2006) *Housing Trends Among Baby Boomers*, Washington, DC: Research Institute for Housing America, accessed 6 April 2009 at http://www.housingamerica.org/Publications/StudyonHousingTrendsAmongBabyBoomers.htm.

Evans, A (1988) *No Room! No Room!: The Costs of the British Town and Country Planning System*, London: Institute for Economic Affairs.

Evans, N, Morris, C and Winter, M (2002) 'Conceptualizing agriculture: a critique of post-productivism as the new orthodoxy', *Progress in Human Geography*, 26 (3): 313–332.

Fenton, B, Jones, G and Helm, T (2007) 'Tory "tax on homes abroad" will hit 400,000', accessed 14 December 2007 at http://www.telegraph.co.uk/news/uknews/1545355/Tory-tax-on-homes-abroad-will-hit-400000.html.

Ferrey, K (2008) *Beach Huts and Bathing Machines*, Market Harborough: Shire Press.

Ferrey, K (2009) *Sheds on the Seashore: A Tour Through Beach Hut History*, Market Harborough: Shire Press.

Ferri, L (2004) 'Thirty-something: time to settle down?', in I Stewart and R Vaitilingam (eds) *Seven Ages of Man and Women*, Swindon: ESRC.

Finnerty J, Guerin, D, and O'Connell, C (2003) 'Ireland', in N Gallent, M Shucksmith and M Tewdr-Jones (eds) *Housing in the European Countryside: Rural Pressure and Policy in Western Europe*, London: Routledge.

Fitz Gerald, J (2005) 'The Irish housing stock: growth in the number of vacant dwellings', in *Economic and Social Research Institute, Quarterly Economic Commentary*, 42–63, Dublin: Economic and Social Research Institute.

Flood, J and Baker, E (forthcoming) *Housing Implications of Social, Spatial and Structural Change*, Melbourne: AHURI.

Forrest, R (2008) 'Globalisation and the housing asset rich: geographies, demographies and policy convoys', *Global Social Policy*, 8(2): 167–187.

Forrest, R and Murie, A (eds) (1995a) *Housing and Family Wealth: Comparative International Perspectives*, London: Routledge.

Forrest, R and Murie, A (1995b) 'Housing and family wealth in comparative perspective', in R Forrest and A Murie (eds) *Housing and Family Wealth: Comparative International Perspectives*, London: Routledge

Forrest, R and Murie, A (1995c) 'Accumulating evidence: housing and family wealth in Britain', in R Forrest and A Murie (eds) *Housing and Family Wealth: Comparative International Perspectives*, London: Routledge.

Foster, R (1988) *Modern Ireland 1600–1972*, London: Fontana.

Francis, C (2006a) 'Families with second homes set to double', *The Sunday Times*, 30 April, Money section: 1.

Francis, C (2006b) 'Investors dump shares to buy property', *The Sunday Times*, 4 June, Money section: 1.

Frank, R H (1999) *Luxury Fever: Money and Happiness in an Era of Excess*, Princeton, NJ: Princeton University Press.

Frank, R H (2007) *Falling Behind: How Rising Inequality Harms the Middle Class*, Princeton, NJ: Princeton University Press.

French, G (2008) *Artificial*, Sydney: New Holland Publishers.

Frey, J (2009) 'Early signs of a more stable market', *Northern Ireland Quarterly House Price Index*, Q2 2009: 2.

Frost, W (2003) *Second Homes in Australia: An Exploration of Statistical Sources*, Monash University Faculty of Business and Economics Working Paper 81/03, accessed 5 May 2009 at http://www.buseco.monash.edu.au/mgt/research/working-papers.

Frost, W (2004) 'A hidden giant: second homes and coastal tourism in south-eastern Australia', in C M Hall and D Müller (eds) *Tourism, Mobility and Second Homes*, Clevedon Buffalo, NY and Toronto: Channel View Publications.

Gadher, D and Davies, H (2007) 'Shires fall to foreign land rush', *The Sunday Times*, 28 October.

Gallent, N (2007) 'Second homes, community and a hierarchy of dwelling', *Area*, 39 (1): 97–106.

Gallent, N (2008) 'Rural housing – reaching the parts that other policies cannot reach', *Town & Country Planning*, 76 (3): 122–125.

Gallent, N. and Tewdwr-Jones, M. (2001) 'Second homes and the UK planning system', *Planning Practice and Research*, 16(1): 59–69

Gallent, N, Mace, A and Tewdwr-Jones, M (2005) *Second Homes: European Perspectives and UK Policies*, Aldershot: Ashgate.

Giddens, A (1987) *Social Theory and Modern Sociology*, Cambridge: Polity Press.

Giddens, A (1991) *Modernity and Self-Identity: Self and Society in the Late Modern Age*, Cambridge: Polity Press.

Giddens, A (1998*) The Third Way: The Renewal of Social Democracy*, Cambridge: Policy Press.

Girling, R (2006) 'No, we don't like to be beside the seaside', *The Sunday Times*, 23 April, Magazine section: 14–26, accessed 2 May 2009 at http://www.timesonline.co.uk/tol/life_and_style/article707759.ece.

Gkartzios, M and Scott, M (2005) 'Urban-generated rural housing and evidence of counterurbanisation in the Dublin city-region', in N Moore and M Scott (eds) *Renewing Urban Communities: Environment, Citizenship and Sustainability in Ireland,* Aldershot: Ashgate.

Glass, R (1964) 'Introduction: aspects of change', in Centre for Urban Studies (ed) *London: Aspects of Change*, London: MacGibbon and Kee.

Glass, R (1968) 'Urban sociology in Great Britain', in R Pahl (ed) *Readings in Urban Sociology*, Oxford: Pergamon Press.

Graham, B and Shaw, J (2008) 'Low-cost airlines in Europe: reconciling liberalization and sustainability', *Geoforum*, 39: 1439–1451.

Green, R (2004) 'Sea change on the Great Ocean Road', *Landscape Australia*, 26: 73–77.

Green, R (2007) 'Airports and economic development', *Real Estate Economics*, 35: 91–112.

Gurran, N (2008) 'The turning tide: amenity migration in coastal Australia', *International Planning Studies*, 13 (4): 391–414.

Gustafson, P (2006) 'Place attachment and mobility', in N McIntyre, D, Williams and K McHugh (eds) *Multiple Dwelling and Tourism: Negotiating Place, Home and Identity*, Cambridge: CABI.

Halfacree, K (1997) 'Contrasting roles for the post-productivist countryside', in P Cloke and J Little (eds) *Contested Countryside Cultures*, London: Routledge.

Halifax Estate Agents (2005a) 'Buyers priced out of the countryside', press release 29 July.

Halifax Estate Agents (2005b) 'We do love to be beside the seaside', press release 29 August.

Hall, C M (2005) *Tourism: Rethinking the Social Science of Mobility*, Edinburgh: Pearson.

Hall C M and Müller, D K (eds) (2004a) *Tourism, Mobility and Second Homes*, Clevedon Buffalo, NY and Toronto: Channel View Publications.

Hall C M and Müller, D K (2004b) 'Introduction: Second Homes: Curse or Blessing? Revisited', in C M Hall and D Müller (eds) *Tourism, Mobility and Second Homes*, Clevedon Buffalo, NY and Toronto: Channel View Publications.

Hall, P, Thomas, R, Gracey, H and Drewett, R (1973) *The Containment of Urban England,* 2 volumes, London: Allen and Unwin.

Halseth, G (2004) 'The "cottage" privilege: increasingly elite landscapes of second homes in Canada', in C M Hall and D Müller *Tourism, Mobility and Second Homes*, Clevedon Buffalo and Toronto: Channel View Publications.

Harrison, F (2007) *Boom, Bust: House Prices, Banking and the Depression of 2010* (revised paperback edition, original hardback 2005), London: Shepheard Walwyn.

Hawkins, P (2008) 'Is cabin fever spreading?', *The Times*, 11 July, Bricks and Mortar section: 23.

References

Heatley, C (2007) 'Controversy over Turkish holiday homes', *The Sunday Business Post Online*, 3 June, accessed 19 March 2009 at http://archives.tcm.ie/businesspost/2007/06/03/story24119. asp

Henry, L (2010) 'A magnificent seven homes as Woodward buys £1m ski chalet', *Belfast Telegraph*, 18 January: 10.

Hettinger, W S (2005) *Living and Working in Paradise: Why Housing is Too Expensive and What Communities Can Do About It*, Windham, CT: Thames River Publishing.

Hirayama, Y and Hayakawa, K (1995) 'Home ownership and family wealth in Japan', in R Forrest and A Murie (eds) *Housing and Family Wealth: Comparative International Perspectives*, London: Routledge.

HMRC (2005) *Help Sheet IR283*, London: HMRC.

Hosking, P (2009) 'UK house prices rise for fist time in 16 months', *The Times* 2 April, times on line, accessed 16 August 2009 at http://business.timesonline.co.uk/tol/business/industry_ sectors/construction_and_property/article6019883.ece

Hoskins, W G (1955) *The Making of the English Landscape*, London: Hodder and Stoughton.

House of Commons ODPM Housing Planning, Local Government and the Regions Committee (2006) *Affordability and the Supply of Housing*, London: The Stationery Office.

Hugo, G (1994) 'The turnaround in Australia: some first observations from the 1991 census', *Australian Geographer*, 25: 1–17

Hugo, G and Rudd, D (2004) *Keeping Pace: Southern Fleurieu Study, Adelaide*, Adelaide: University of Adelaide National Centre for Social Applications of GIS.

Ilbery, B (1998) *The Geography of Rural Change,* London: Longman.

Irvin, G (2008) *The Super-Rich: The Rise of Inequality in Britain and the United States*, Cambridge: Polity Press.

Jones, C (2009) *The Right to Buy*, Oxford: Blackwell.

Jones, C and Murie, A (2006) 'The right to buy', in P Malpass and R Rowlands (eds) *Housing, Markets and Policy*, London: Routledge.

Jud, G and Winkler, D (2006) 'The announcement of airport expansion on house prices', *Journal of Real Estate Financial Economics*, 33: 91–103.

Keeley, G (2009) 'Pain in Spain is too much as expats pack their bags', *The Times*, 16 May: 18.

Keen, D and Hall, C M (2004) 'Second homes in New Zealand', in C M Hall and D Müller (eds) *Tourism, Mobility and Second Homes*, Clevedon Buffalo, NY and Toronto: Channel View Publications.

Keenan, M (2005) 'The ten most common pitfalls when buying abroad, and how to avoid them', *The Sunday Times*, 11 December, accessed 30 July 2008 at http://property.timesonline.co.uk/ tol/life_and_style/property/article75.

Kelly, G and Hosking, K. (2005) *Augusta-Margaret River Sustainable Future Project, the 'Missing' Segment of the Population: A Survey of Non-Permanent Residents*, Canberra: CSIRO Sustainable Ecosystems.

Kemeny, J (1992) *Housing and Social Theory*, London: Routledge.

Kemeny, J (1995) 'Informal allocation of housing wealth in Swedish social renting', in R Forrest and A Murie (eds) *Housing and Family Wealth: Comparative International Perspectives*, London: Routledge.

Kemp, P (2009) 'The transformation of private renting', in P Malpass and R Rowlands (eds) *Housing, Markets and Policy*, London: Routledge.

Kendall, O (2006) 'It's an East–West divide as smart money goes on holiday hot spots', *The Times* 14 April: 8–9.

Kerchavel, M (2008) 'Online camera check on holiday homes', *The Sunday Business Post Online*, article dated 25 May 2008, accessed 19 March 2009 at http://archives.tcm.ie/ businesspost/2008/05/25/story33068.asp

Krugman, P (2008) *The Return of Depression Economics and the Crisis of 2008*, London: Penguin.

Kryger, T (2009) *Home Ownership in Australia – Data and Trends*, Research Paper, Parliament of Australia, Canberra: Parliamentary Library, accessed 6 May at http://parlinfo.aph.gov.au/parlInfo/download/library/prspub/TNRS6/upload_binary/tnrs60.pdf%3BfileType%3Dapplication/pdf.

Ladányi, J (1995) 'Market, state and the growth of informal networks in the growth of private housing in Hungary', in R Forrest and A Murie (eds) *Housing and Family Wealth: Comparative International Perspectives*, London: Routledge.

Lambert, J, Paris, C and Blackaby, B (1978) *Housing Policy and the State*, London: Macmillan.

Leal, J (2006) 'Multiple residential practices and second homes in southern Europe: the Spanish case', paper presented to the ENHR Conference, Ljubljana, July 2006.

Lewis, N (2004) 'Huts that are hot on the beach', *Daily Mail*, 30 July, accessed 25 May 2009 at http://www.dailymail.co.uk/travel/holidaytypeshub/article-592495/Huts-hot-beach.html

Lewis, P (2009) 'Dubai's six-year building boom grinds to halt as financial crisis takes hold', *The Guardian*, 13 February, accessed 25 May 2009 at http://www.guardian.co.uk/world/2009/feb/13/dubai-boom-halt

Lipovetsky, G (2005) *Hypermodern Times*, Cambridge: Polity Press.

Lowe, S (2004) *Housing Policy Analysis*, Bristol: Policy Press.

Lower Mill Estate (2009) Advertisement in *The Sunday Times* Homes section, 16 August: 5.

Lund, B (2006) *Understanding Housing Policy*, Bristol: Policy Press.

Mac Sharry, R and White, P (2000) *The Making of the Celtic Tiger*, Dublin: Mercier Press.

McCarthy, C, Hughes, A and Woelger, E (2003) 'Where have all the houses gone?', Dublin: Davy Stockbrokers, available at www.dkm.ie/uploads/pdf/reports/where_houses_gone.pdf

McHugh, K E (2006) 'Nomads of desire', in N McIntyre, D Williams and K McHugh (eds) *Multiple Dwelling and Tourism: Negotiating Place, Home and Identity*, Cambridge: CABI.

McIntyre, N, William, D and McHugh, K (eds) (2006) *Multiple Dwelling and Tourism: Negotiating Place, Home and Identity*, Cambridge: CABI.

McKenzie, F, Martin, J, Paris, C and Reynolds, J (2008) 'Fiscal policy and mobility: the impact of multiple residences on the provision of place-based service funding', *Australasian Journal of Regional Science*, 14 (1): 53–71.

MacLaren, A (2005) 'Suburbanising Dublin: out of an overcrowded frying pan into a fire of unsustainability?', in N Moore and M Scott (eds) *Renewing Urban Communities: Environment, Citizenship and Sustainability in Ireland*, Aldershot: Ashgate.

Mclean, J (2009) 'Credit crunch means the end of The World for Dubai', *The Times*, 12 September: 48.

MacMahon, P (2007) 'Second homes numbers fall by 3,000 after council tax discount change', accessed 4 May 2009 at http://news.scotsman.com/counciltax/Second-home-numbers-fall-by.3358542.jp

Maciejowska, K (2009) 'Cornwall, after the storms', *The Times*, Bricks and Mortar section, 28 August: 7.

Malpass, P (2005) *Housing and the Welfare State*, Basingstoke: Palgrave Macmillan.

Malpass, P and Rowlands R (eds) (2009) *Housing, Markets and Policy*, London: Routledge.

Mandelbrot, B and Hudson, R (2005) *The (mis)Behaviour of Markets: A Fractal View of Risk, Ruin and Reward*, London: Profile Books.

Marcuse, P (2006) 'Space in the globalizing city', in N Brenner and R Keil (eds) *The Global Cities Reader*, Oxford: Routledge.

Margolis, J (2008) 'The new weekenders', *The Times*, Magazine section: 30–36.

Martin, P (2008) 'Household wealth crashes', *The Age*, 19 December, accessed 19 March 2009 at http://business.theage.com.au/business/household-wealth-crashes-20081218-71my.html

Mather, A, Hill, G and Nijnik, M (2006) 'Post-productivism and rural land use: cul de sac or challenge for theorization?', *Journal of Rural Studies*, 22: 441–455.

Mayer, B and Baytin, N (2006) 'Minority versus majority: privileges for homes', paper presented to the ENHR Conference, Ljubljana, July 2006.

References

Michael, J (2009) 'Kenny says Fine Gael will vote against Nama bill', *Irish Times*, 21 August, accessed 22 August at http://www.irishtimes.com/newspaper/breaking/2009/0821/breaking38.html

Mintel (2006) *Home Ownership Abroad and Timeshare*, London: Mintel.

Mintel (2009) *Holiday Property Abroad*, London: Mintel.

Monbiot, G (1998) 'Ghost towns', *The Guardian*, 18 July, accessed 10 June 2009 at http://www.monbiot.com/archives/1998/07/18/ghost-towns/

Monbiot, G (2006) 'Second-home owners are among the most selfish people in Britain', *The Guardian*, accessed 1 May 2007 at http://www.guardian.co.uk/commentisfree/2006/may/23/comment.politics3

Monbiot, G (2009) 'Flying over the cuckoo's nest', *The Guardian*, 13 January, accessed 10 June 2009 at http://www.monbiot.com/archives/1998/07/18/ghost-towns/

Morris, S (2006) 'Bishop bemoans Cornwall's property boom', *The Guardian*, accessed 7 December 2006 at http://www.guardian.co.uk/uk_news/story/0,,1965771,00.html.

Morris, (2007) 'Cornish militants rise again – and this time they're targeting celebrity chefs', *The Guardian*, accessed 1 May 2009 at http://www.guardian.co.uk/uk/2007/jun/14/terrorism.ukcrime

Mortished, C (2008) 'Low-cost airlines flying into turbulence', *The Times*, 2 April: 52.

Müller, D (2004) 'Second homes in Sweden: patterns and issues', in C M Hall and D Müller (eds) *Tourism, Mobility and Second Homes*, Clevedon Buffalo, NY and Toronto: Channel View Publications.

Mullins, P (1985) 'Social issues arising from rapid coastal tourist urbanisation', *Australian Urban Studies*, 13 (September): 13–19.

Mullins, P (1991) 'Tourism urbanisation', *International Journal of Urban and Regional Research*, 15 (3): 326–342.

Mullins, P (1994) 'Class relations and tourism urbanisation: the regeneration of the petite bourgeoisie and the emergence of a new urban form', *International Journal of Urban and Regional Research*, 18 (5): 491–608.

Mullins, D and Murie, A (2006) *Housing Policy in the UK*, Bristol: Policy Press.

Murie, A, Niner, P and Watson, C (1976) *Housing Policy and the Housing System*, London: Allen and Unwin.

Murphy, D (1978) *A Place Apart*, London: Murray.

Murray, M (2005) 'Consultation, new countryside housing and rural planning policy in Northern Ireland', in M McEldowney, M Murray, B Murtagh and K Sterret (eds) *Planning in Ireland and Beyond*, Belfast: School of Environmental Planning, Queen's University.

Murtagh, B (2001) 'Social conflict and housing policy', in C Paris (ed) *Housing in Northern Ireland, and Comparisons with the Republic of Ireland*, Coventry: Chartered Institute of Housing.

Murtagh, B (2002) *The Politics of Territory*, Basingstoke: Palgrave.

National Economic and Social Council (2004) *Housing in Ireland: Performance and Policy*, Dublin: National Economic and Social Council.

National Shelter (2007) *Housing Australia Factsheet*, Adelaide: National Shelter, accessed 6 May 2009 at http://www.shelter.org.au/Housing%20Australia%20Fact%20Sheet.pdf.

Newby, H (1979) *Green and Pleasant Land?* London: Penguin.

Norris, M and Shiels, P (2007) 'Housing inequalities in an enlarged European Union: patterns, drivers and implications, *Journal of European Social Policy*, 17: 59–70.

Norris, M and Winston, N (2009) 'Rising second home numbers in rural Ireland: distribution, drivers and implications', *European Planning Studies*, 17 (9): 1303–1320.

Norris, M, Paris, C and Winston, N (2008) 'Second homes within Irish housing booms and busts: North–South comparisons, contrasts and debates', paper at the European Network for Housing Research Working Group on Comparative Housing Policy, Istanbul, October 2008.

Norwood, G and Collinson, P (2009) 'Newquay: for sun, sea and repossessions', *The Guardian*, Money section, available at http://www.guardian.co.uk/money/2009/jun/20/house-prices-repossessions-newquay/print

Nugent, H (2010) 'Thousands more may lose holiday homes after Cyprus ruling', *The Times*, 16 January: 16.

O'Brien, S (2009) 'Funding cuts give airports "a bleak future"', *The Sunday Times*, 20 December: 5.

O'Dowd, L, Corrigan, J and Moore, T (1995) 'Borders, national sovereignty and European integration: the British–Irish case', *International Journal of Urban and Regional Research*, 19 (2): 272–285.

O'Hearn, D (1998) *Inside the Celtic Tiger*, London: Pluto Press.

ONS (2006) *Social Trends 36*, Basingstoke: Palgrave Macmillan, available at http://www.statistics.gov.uk/socialtrends36/

ONS (2008) *Social Trends 38*, Basingstoke: Palgrave Macmillan, available at http://www.statistics.gov.uk/socialtrends38/

O'Sullivan, P (2007) *The Wealth of the Nation*, Dublin, available at http://www.finfacts.ie/biz10/WealthNationReportJuly07.pdf

O'Toole, R and Callen, G (2008) *The Emerald Isle: The Wealth of Modern Ireland*, available at www.nationalirishbank.ie, accessed on 12 February 2009.

Owen, E, Adams, L and Bale, J (2006) 'Thousands of second homes face bulldozer in Costa scam', *The Times*, 3 April: 12–13.

Oxley, M, Brown, T, Lishman, R and Turkington, R (2008) *Rapid Evidence Assessment of the Research Literature on the Purchase and Use of Second Homes*, Fareham: National Housing and Planning Advice Unit.

Pagnamenta, R (2008) 'Ryanair issues warning as profits plunge 85%', *The Times*, 28 July, accessed 30 July 2008 at http://business.timesonline.co.uk/tol/business/industry_sectors/transport/article4414497.ece.

Pahl, R (1965) *Urbs in Rure*, London: Weidenfeld and Nicolson.

Paris, C (1993) *Housing Australia*, Melbourne: Macmillan.

Paris, C (1994) 'New patterns of urban and regional development in Australia: demographic restructuring and economic change', *International Journal of Urban and Regional Research*, 18 (4): 555–572.

Paris, C (ed) (2001) *Housing in Northern Ireland, and Comparisons with the Republic of Ireland*, Coventry: Chartered Institute of Housing.

Paris, C (2005a) 'From barricades to back gardens: cross-border urban expansion from the City of Derry into Co. Donegal', in M Scott and N Moore (eds) *Renewing Urban Communities: Environment, Citizenship and Sustainability in Ireland*, Aldershot: Ashgate.

Paris, C (2005b) 'Housing and the migration turnaround in Ireland', *Urban Policy and Research*, 23 (3): 287–304.

Paris, C (2006) 'Housing markets and cross-border integration', in J Yarwood (ed) *The Dublin–Belfast Development Corridor: Ireland's Mega-City Region?*, Aldershot: Ashgate.

Paris, C (2007a) *Second Homes in Northern Ireland: Growth, Impact and Policy Implications, First Report*, Belfast: Northern Ireland Housing Executive, available at http://www.nihe.gov.uk.

Paris, C (2007b) 'International perspectives on planning and affordable housing', *Housing Studies*, 22 (1) 1–10.

Paris, C (2008a) 'The changing housing system in Northern Ireland 1998–2007', *Ethnopolitics*, 7 (1): 119–136.

Paris, C (2008b) *Second Homes in Northern Ireland: Growth, Impact and Policy Implications, Final Report*, Belfast: Northern Ireland Housing Executive, available at http://www.nihe.gov.uk.

Paris, C (2008c) 'Re-positioning second homes within housing studies: household investment, gentrification, multiple residence, mobility and hyper-consumption', *Housing, Theory and Society*, 22 (4): 1–19.

References

Paris, C (2010) 'Multiple homes', in S Smith (ed) *The International Encyclopedia of Housing and Home*, Oxford: Elsevier.

Paris, C and Blackaby, B (1979) *Not Much Improvement: Urban Renewal Policy in Birmingham*, London: Heinemann.

Paris, C and Robson, T (2001) *Housing in the Border Counties*, Belfast and Dublin: Northern Ireland Housing Executive and the Department of the Environment and Local Government.

Paris, C, Muir, J and Gray, P (2003) 'Devolving housing policy and practice in Northern Ireland', *Housing Studies* 18 (2): 159–175.

Paris, C, Jorgensen, B and Martin, J (2009) 'The ownership of many homes in Northern Ireland and Australia: issues for states and localities', *Australasian Journal of Regional Studies*, 15 (1): 65–80.

Partridge, C (2007) 'Going large in London', *The Times*, Sept 29, accessed 10 October 2008 at http://property.timesonline.co.uk/tol/life_and_style/property/overseas/article2543181.ece

Pavia, W (2008) 'Hunt for holiday-home murder handyman', *The Times*, 24 March: 15.

Pearman, H (2007) 'Water margin', *Sunday Times*, Homes supplement, 6 May 2007, p.41

Periäinen, K (2006) 'The summer cottage: a dream in the Finnish forest', in N McIntyre, D Williams and K McHugh (eds) *Multiple Dwelling and Tourism: Negotiating Place, Home and Identity*, Cambridge: CABI.

Perkins, H and Thorns, D (2006) 'Home away from home: the primary/second home relationship', in N McIntyre, D Williams and K McHugh (eds) *Multiple Dwelling and Tourism: Negotiating Place, Home and Identity*, Cambridge: CABI.

Phillips, M (1993) 'Rural gentrification and the processes of class colonisation', *Journal of Rural Studies*, 9: 123–140.

Phillips, M (2005) 'Differential production of rural gentrification: illustrations from North and South Norfolk', *Geoforum*, 36: 477–494.

Pierce, A (2008) 'Eco-house in Cotswolds sells for a world record £7.2m', *The Daily Telegraph*, 24 April, accessed 6 May 2009 at http://www.telegraph.co.uk/earth/earthnews/3340659/Eco-home-in-Cotswolds-fetches-record-7.2m.html.

PIPWE (1999–2009) *Shack Sites on Crown Land*, first published on the website of the Tasmanian Department of Primary Industries, Water and Environment on 30 October 1999, and withdrawn from the site on 3 September 2009 following project closure; accessed on 6 May 2009 at www.dpipwe.tas.gov.au.

Planning Service (2003) *Second Homes on the North Coast*, Coleraine: Planning Service.

Plymouth Herald (2009a) 'High court overturns controversial jetty plan', 5 March, accessed 25 May at http://www.thisiscornwall.co.uk/homepagenews/High-Court-overturns-controversial-jetty-plans/article-749112-detail/article.html

Plymouth Herald (2009b) 'Helford local community must move', 11 March, accessed 25 May at http://www.thisisplymouth.co.uk/news/Helford-local-community/article-763448-detail/article.html

PolitiFact.com, (2008) 'Updated: eight houses for John and Cindy McCain', from the *St Petersburg Times*, 20 August, accessed on 25 January 2009 at http://www.politifact.com/truth-o-meter/statements/635

Power, A (1993) *Hovels to High Rise*, London: Routledge.

Price, S (2008) 'Our sordid secret', *The Sunday Business Post Online*, article dated 12 October, accessed 19 March 2009 at http://archives.tcm.ie/businesspost/2008/10/12/story36557.asp

Price, S (2009) 'Losing our seaside legacy', *The Sunday Business Post Online*, article dated 1 February, accessed 19 March 2009 at http://archives.tcm.ie/businesspost/2009/02/01/story39097.asp

Prince, D (2009) 'Villages will die unless wealthy people stop buying holiday homes', *Daily Telegraph*, 25 March, accessed on 26 June 2009 at http://www.telegraph.co.uk/property/5045296/Villages-will-die-unless-wealthy-stop-buying-holiday-homes.html

Quinn, B (2004) 'Dwelling through multiple places: a case study of second home ownership in Ireland', in C M Hall and D Müller, D (eds) *Tourism, Mobility and Second Homes*, Clevedon Buffalo, NY and Toronto: Channel View Publications.

Rackham, O (1986) *The History of the Countryside*, London: Phoenix Press.

Reuschke, D (2006) 'Workplace mobility, living arrangements and housing demand in contemporary Germany', paper presented to the ENHR Conference, Ljubljana, July 2006.

Reynolds, D (2008) 'McCain homes flap is no joke', CBS news 21 August, accessed 25 January 2009 at http://www.cbsnews.com/blogs/2008/08/21/politics/fromtheroad/entry4372200.shtml

Robertson, R W (1977) 'Second-home decisions: the Australian context', in J T Coppock (ed) *Second Homes: Curse or Blessing?*, Oxford: Pergamon Press.

Robertson, D and Nugent, H (2008) 'End of cheap flights boom as airlines raise fares in line with oil prices', *The Times*, 28 July, accessed on 30 July 2008 at http://www.timesonline.co.uk/tol/news/uk/article4412857.

Robinson, G (1990) *Conflict and Change in the Countryside*, London and New York: Belhaven Press.

Robinson, K (2006) 'The buying rules', *The Sunday Times*, 30 July, available at http://property.timesonline.co.uk/tol/life_and_style/property/investment.

Rowan, A (1979) *North West Ulster*, Buildings of Ireland series, Harmondsworth: Penguin.

Salkeld, L (2008) 'World's most expensive kennel: Great Dane owner shells out £250,000 for doghouse complete with spa and plasma TV', *Mail on Sunday*, 26 November, accessed 3 May 2009 at http://www.mailonsunday.co.uk/news/article-1089315/Worlds-expensive-kennel-Great-Dane-owner-shells-250-000-doghouse-spa-plasma-TV.html

Sassen, S (2006) *Cities in a World Economy*, 3rd edition, London: Sage

Satsangi, M and Dunmore, K (2003) 'The planning system and the provision of affordable housing in rural Britain: a comparison of the Scottish and English experience', *Housing Studies* 18 (2): 201–217.

Saunders, P (1990) *A Nation of Home Owners*, London: Unwin Hyman.

Savage, M (2009) 'Labour peer faces enquiry over her "empty" second home', *The Independent*, 4 May: 11.

Savills (2005) *Slow Growth in Second Homes Market as Affordability Issues Push Buyers Overseas*, press release and report 3 May, accessed 25 July 2008 at http://www.savills.co.uk.

Savills (2007a) *Second Homes Numbers Continue to Rise*, press release and report 19 March, accessed 25 July 2008 at http://www.savills.co.uk.

Savills (2007b) *Second Homes Abroad 2007*, accessed January 2008 at http://www.savills.co.uk/research/Report.aspx?nodeID=8522

Savills (2008) *Second Homes Abroad 2008*, available at http://www.savills.co.uk/research/Report.aspx?nodeID=9899

Selwood, J (2006) 'The evolution, characteristics and spatial organization of cottages and cottagers in Manitoba, Canada', in N McIntyre, D, Williams and K McHugh (eds) *Multiple Dwelling and Tourism: Negotiating Place, Home and Identity*, Cambridge: CABI.

Selwood, J and Tonts, M (2004) 'Recreational second homes in the south west of Western Australia', in C M Hall and D Müller (eds) *Tourism, Mobility and Second Homes*, Clevedon Buffalo, NY and Toronto: Channel View Publications.

Selwood, J and Tonts, M (2006) 'Seeking serenity: homes away from home in Western Australia', in N McIntyre, D Williams and K McHugh (eds) *Multiple Dwelling and Tourism: Negotiating Place, Home and Identity*, Cambridge: CABI.

Shearer, P (2007) 'Luxury keeps its cool', *The Times*, September 28, accessed 10 October 2008 at http://property.timesonline.co.uk/tol/life_and_style/property/overseas/article2543181.ece

Sheller, M and Urry, J (eds) (2004) *Tourism Mobilities*, London: Routledge.

Shellito, B (2006) 'Second-home distributions in the USA's Upper Great Lakes States: analysis and implications', in N McIntyre, D, Williams and K McHugh (eds) *Multiple Dwelling and Tourism: Negotiating Place, Home and Identity*, Cambridge: CABI.

References

Shirlow, P and Murtagh, B (2004) *Belfast: Segregation, Violence and the City*, London: Pluto.

Smith, D (2002) 'Extending the temporal and spatial limits of gentrification: a research agenda for population geographers', *International Journal of Population Geography*, 8: 385–394.

Smith, S (2005) 'Banking on housing? Speculating on the role and relevance of housing wealth in Britain', paper for the Joseph Rowntree Foundation Inquiry into Home Ownership 2010 and Beyond, available at www.jrf.org.uk. Full Research Report. ESRC End of Award Report, RES-154-25-0012, Swindon: ESRC

Smith, D (2006) 'Inside the hidden world of Roman's empire', *The Observer*, 24 December, accessed 4 May 2009 at http://www.guardian.co.uk/world/2006/dec/24/sport.football

Smith, S (2006) 'Home ownership: managing a risky business?', in J Doling and M Elsinga (eds) *Home Ownership: Getting in, Getting from, Getting out. Part II*, Amsterdam: IOS.

Smith, S (2007) *Banking on Housing: Spending the Home*, Full Research Report, ESRC End of Award Report, RES-154-25-0012, Swindon: ESRC. Smith, N (2009) 'British expats fear losing homes in Goan land grab', *The Sunday Times*, 20 September, accessed 21 September 2009 at http://www.timesonline.co.uk/tol/news/world/asia/article6841248.ece

Smith, D and Butler, R (2007) 'Conceptualising the sociospatial diversity of gentrification: "to boldly go" into contemporary gentrified spaces, "the final frontier"?', *Environment and Planning A*, 39 (1): 2–9.

Smith, M and Duffy, R (2003) *The Ethics of Tourism Development*, London: Routledge.

Smith, D P and Phillips, D A (2001) 'Socio-cultural representations of greentrified Pennine rurality', *Journal of Rural Studies*, 17: 457–469.

Somerville, P (1997) 'The social constriction of home', *Journal of Architectural and Planning Research*, 14 (3): 226–245.

Sprigings, N (2008) 'Buy-to-let and the wider housing market', *People, Place & Policy Online*, issue 2, accessed 6 January 2009 at http://extra.shu.ac.uk/ppp-online.

Stedman, R C (2006a) 'Places of escape: second home meanings in Northern Wisconsin, USA', in N McIntyre, D Williams and K McHugh (eds) *Multiple Dwelling and Tourism: Negotiating Place, Home and Identity*, Cambridge: CABI.

Stedman, R C (2006b) 'Understanding place attachment among second home owners', *American Behavioural Scientist*, 50 (2): 187–203.

Stimson, R and Minnery, J (1998) 'Why people move to the "Sun-belt": a case study of long distance migration to the Gold Coast, Australia', *Urban Studies,* 35 (2): 193–214

Struyk, R J and Angelici, K (1996) 'The Russian dacha phenomena', *Housing Studies*, 11 (2): 233–251.

Stucklin, M (2004) 'Insight briefing: quantifying British property ownership in Spain', *Spanish Property Insight*, accessed 18 October 2006 at http://www.spanishpropertyinsight.com/market/2004-quantifying-british-owners.htm

Stucklin, M (2006) 'A chance to snap up a bargain', *The Sunday Times*, Homes supplement, 17 September: 34.

Stucklin, M (2009) 'Too close to the edge', *Spanish Property Insight*, accessed 18 October 2009 at http://www.spanishpropertyinsight.com/buff/2009/03/23/22-spd-too-close-to-the-edge-ley-de-costas-or-spanish-coastal-law/

Swinford, S (2008) 'Airline squeeze hits holiday homes', *The Sunday Times*, 10 August: 7.

Taleb, N (2008) *The Black Swan: The Impact of the Highly Improbable*, London: Penguin.

Taylor, M (2008) *Living, Working Countryside: The Taylor Review of Rural Economy and Affordable Housing*, London: Department for Communities and Local Government.

Timothy, D J (2004) 'Recreational second homes in the United States: development issues and contemporary patterns', in C M Hall and D Müller (eds) *Tourism, Mobility and Second Homes*, Clevedon Buffalo, NY and Toronto: Channel View Publications.

Todd, B (2009) 'Roman's £54m retreat', *Daily Mail*, 23 December: 3.

Toomey, C (2009) 'Living in the lap of anxiety', *The Sunday Times Magazine*, 26 April: 22–29.

Town and Country Planning Service (1991) *Second Homes on the North Coast: A Policy for Apartments in the Coastal Settlements of Coleraine District*, Coleraine: Department of the Environment (Northern Ireland).

Tuulentie, S (2006) 'Tourists making themselves at home: second homes as a part of tourist careers', in N McIntyre, D Williams and K McHugh (eds) *Multiple Dwelling and Tourism: Negotiating Place, Home and Identity*, Cambridge: CABI.

Urry, J (1995) *Consuming Places*, London and New York: Routledge.

Urry, J (2000) *Sociology Beyond Societies*, London and New York: Routledge.

Urry, J (2004) 'Death in Venice', in M Sheller, M and J Urry (eds) *Tourism Mobilities*, London and New York: Routledge.

Urry, J (2007) *Mobilities*, Cambridge: Polity Press.

Unattributed (2007) 'Overseas property: where, how and what to buy', article published in *The Sunday Times*, 27 May, accessed on 10 June 2009 at http://property.timesonline.co.uk/tol/life_and_style/property/overseas/article1833888.ece

Unattributed (2008) 'House prices spike in university towns', *thisismoney.co.uk*, 30 August 2008, accessed 10 June 2009 at http://www.thisismoney.co.uk/mortgages-and-homes/house-prices/article.html?in_article_id=451265&in_page_id=57

Unattributed (2009) 'Caught in the downward current, the global housing market goes from bad to worse', *The Economist*, accessed on 23 March 2009 at http://www.economist.com/finance/displaystory.cfm?story_id=13337869

Wallace, A, Bevan M, Croucher, K, Jackson, K, O'Malley, L and Orton, V (2005) *The Impact of Empty, Second and Holiday Homes on the Sustainability of Rural Communities: A Systematic Literature Review*, York: Centre for Housing Policy.

Watson, C (2009) 'Goodbye shacks, hullo luxury', *The Advertiser*, 9 January, accessed 8 May at http://www.news.com.au/adelaidenow/story/0,22606,24867075-5006301,00.html

Webster, P (2009) 'Sorry Chancellor who fumbled his own finances is left dangling', *The Times*, 2 June: 6.

Wells, E (2008) 'No-fly zones', *The Sunday Times*, 10 August: 18.

Wilcox, S (2008) *Housing Finance Review 2008/09*, Coventry and London: Chartered Institute of Housing and Building Societies Association.

Williams, R (1973) *The Country and the City*, London: Chatto and Windus.

Williams, D R and Van Patten, S (2006) 'Home *and* away? Creating identities and sustaining places in a multi-centred world', in N McIntyre, D Williams and K McHugh (eds) *Multiple Dwelling and Tourism: Negotiating Place, Home and Identity*, Cambridge: CABI.

Williams, A M, King, R and Warnes, T (2004) 'British second homes in Southern Europe: shifting nodes in the scapes and flows of migration and tourism', in C M Hall and D Müller (eds) *Tourism, Mobility and Second Homes*, Clevedon Buffalo, NY and Toronto: Channel View Publications.

Winnett, R and Beckford, M (2009) 'Kitty Ussher resigns from Government over £17,000 tax dodge: MPs' expenses', 17 June, Telegraph.co.uk, accessed 17 June 2009 at http://www.telegraph.co.uk/news/newstopics/mps-expenses/5562772/Kitty-Ussher-resigns-from-Government-over-17000-tax-dodge-MPs-expenses.html

Wolfe, R (1977) 'Summer cottages in Ontario: purpose built for an inessential purpose', in J T Coppock (ed) *Second Homes: Curse or Blessing?,* Oxford: Pergamon Press

Woods, R (2007) 'Super-rich treble wealth in last 10 years', *The Sunday Times*, April 29, accessed 10 July 2008 at http://www.timesonline.co.uk/tol/news/uk/article1719880.ece

Yates, J (2003) 'Has home ownership in Australia declined?', *AHURI Research & Policy Bulletin*, Issue 21 May, available at http://www.ahuri.edu.au.

Index

Index